The telephone system of the British post office. A practical handbook - Primary Source Edition

Thomas Ernest Herbert

Nabu Public Domain Reprints:

You are holding a reproduction of an original work published before 1923 that is in the public domain in the United States of America, and possibly other countries. You may freely copy and distribute this work as no entity (individual or corporate) has a copyright on the body of the work. This book may contain prior copyright references, and library stamps (as most of these works were scanned from library copies). These have been scanned and retained as part of the historical artifact.

This book may have occasional imperfections such as missing or blurred pages, poor pictures, errant marks, etc. that were either part of the original artifact, or were introduced by the scanning process. We believe this work is culturally important, and despite the imperfections, have elected to bring it back into print as part of our continuing commitment to the preservation of printed works worldwide. We appreciate your understanding of the imperfections in the preservation process, and hope you enjoy this valuable book.

Electricity, in our Homes, Walker, 6s.
—— Static, Atkinson, 6s. 6d. [6d.
—— Supply, Gay and Yeaman, 10s.
—— Municipal, Gibbings, 15s.
—— and Magnetism, Ashworth, 2s. 6d.
—— —— Bottone, 2s. 6d.
—— —— Gerard, 10s. 6d.
—— —— Houston, 3s. 6d.
—— —— Maycock, 2s. 6d.
Electro-motors, Bottone, 3s.
—— Houston, 5s.
Electro-platers' H. B., Bonney, 3s.
Electrolytic Analysis, Neumann, 6s.
Elliott's Gas and Petroleum Engines, 2s. 6d.
—— Industrial Electricity, 2s. 6d.
Emmet's Alt. Current Wiring, 5s.
Engineer Draughtsmen's Work, 1s. 6d.
—— Fitting, Horner, 5s.
—— Locomotive, McDonnell, 1s.
English and American Lathes, Horner, 21s. net.
Explosives, Guttmann, 2 vols., 2l 2s.

Farman's Auto Cars, 5s.
Farrow, Specifications for Building Works, 3s. 6d
—— Stresses and Strains, 5s.
Field Work and Instruments, Walmisley, 7s. 6d.
Findlay's English Railway, 7s. 6d.
Fitting, Horner, 5s.
—— Electric, Maycock, 6s.
—— Electric Light, Allsop, 5s.
Fitzgerald's Nav. Tactics, 1s.
Fletcher's Architectural Hygiene, 5s.
—— Carpentry and Joinery, 5s.
—— Steam-Jacket, 7s. 6d.
Foden's Mechanical Tables, 1s. 6d.
Forestry, Webster, 3s. 6d.
Forth Bridge, 5s.
Foster's Central Station Bookkeeping, 10s. 6d.

Galvanic Batteries, Bottone.
Garratt's Modern Safety Bicycle, 3s.
Gas and Petroleum Engines, 2s. 6d.
Gaseous Fuel, 1s. 6d.
Gatehouse's Dynamo, 1s.
Gay and Yeaman's C. S. Electricity Supply, 10s. 6d.
Gearing, Helical, 7s. 6d.
Geology, Jukes-Browne, 2s. 6d.
Gerard's Electricity and Magnetism, 10s. 6d.

German Technological Dictionary, 4s. net.
Gibbings' Dynamo Attendants, 1s.
—— Electricity Supply, 15s. net.
Gore's Electro-chemistry, 2s.
—— Metals, 10s. 6d.
Gray's Electrical Influence Machines, 4s 6d.
Griffiths' Manures, 7s. 6d.
Guttmann's Explosives, 2 vols., 2l. 2s.

Hatch's Mineralogy, 2s. 6d.
Hatton's Mathematics, 2s. 6d. and 3s.
Haulbaum's Ventilation, 1s.
Hawkins' and Wallis's Dynamo, 10s. 6d.
Heat Engines, Anderson, 6s.
Helical Gears, 7s. 6d
Herbert's Telegraphy, 3s. 6d.
—— Telephone System of the Post Office, 3s 6d.
Hering, Electric Railways, 5s.
Hertzian Waves, Bottone, 3s.
Hewitt's Organic Chemical Manipulation, 4s 6d.
Hobbs' Electrical Arithmetic, 1s.
Hoblyn's Medical Dictionary, 10s. 6d.
Holtzapffel's Turning, 5 vols., 5l. 9s.
Hopkinson's Dynamo Machinery, 5s.
Horner's Helical Gears, 7s. 6d.
—— Iron-founding, 4s.
—— Metal Turning, 4s.
—— Pattern Making, 3s. 6d.
—— Principles of Fitting, 5s.
—— English and American Lathes, 21s. net.
Hospitalier's Polyphased Alternating Currents, 3s. 6d.
Houston's Electrical Terms, 31s. 6d.
—— Electrical Measurements, 5s.
—— Electricity and Magnetism, 3s. 6d.
—— Transmission of Intelligence, 5s.
Hurter's Alkali Makers' Handbook, 10s. 6d.
Hutton's Mathematical Tables, 12s.
Hydraulic Motors, Bodmer.

Incandescent Lighting, Houston, 5s.
Indicator Handbook, Pickworth, 3s. net.
Induction Coils, Bonney, 3s.
Industrial Electricity, 2s. 6d. [net.
Inventions, How to Patent, 2s. 6d.
Iron Analysis, Arnold, 10s. 6d.
—— Analysis, Blair, 18s. net.

THE
TELEPHONE SYSTEM
OF THE
BRITISH POST OFFICE.

MANUAL OF TELEPHONY, by Preece and Stubbs, 15s.

PRACTICAL TELEPHONE HANDBOOK, by J. Poole, 5s.

TELEGRAPHY, ELECTRICITY IN ITS APPLICATION TO, by T. E. Herbert, 3s. 6d.

TELEPHONE SYSTEM OF THE BRITISH POST OFFICE, by T. E. Herbert, 3s. 6d.

ELECTRIC TELEPHONE, by E. J. Houston & A. E. Kennelly, 5s.

ELECTRIC TELEGRAPHY, by E. J. Houston & A. E. Kennelly, 5s.

ELECTRICAL INSTRUMENT MAKING, by S. R. Bottone, 3s. 6d.

WIRELESS TELEGRAPHY, by S. R. Bottone, 3s

ELECTRICITY AND MAGNETISM, by W. Perren Maycock, 2s. 6d.

PRACTICAL MAGNETISM AND ELECTRICITY, by J. R. Ashworth, 2s. 6d.

WHITTAKER & CO., LONDON, E.C.

THE
TELEPHONE SYSTEM
OF THE
BRITISH POST OFFICE.

A Practical Handbook.

BY

T. E. HERBERT, A.M.I.E.E.,

ENGINEER, POSTAL TELEGRAPHS;
LECTURER, MUNICIPAL TECHNICAL SCHOOL, MANCHESTER,
AUTHOR OF "ELECTRICITY IN ITS APPLICATION TO TELEGRAPHY."

SECOND EDITION, REVISED.
WITH ADDITIONS

WITH ONE HUNDRED AND FORTY-SIX ILLUSTRATIONS.

WHITTAKER AND CO,
2, WHITE HART STREET, PATERNOSTER SQUARE, LONDON;
AND 66, FIFTH AVENUE, NEW YORK.

1901

ENTERED AT STATIONERS' HALL.

PREFACE.

The acquisition of the telephone trunk lines by the State led to the design of a system of working which differs in many particulars from any previous system. Since the transfer many developments have taken place, and as no adequate description of the system existed, a series of articles dealing with it were undertaken by the writer of the present volume. These articles in their crude form proved to have filled a distinct want amongst the employees of the Post Office—so many of whom, in one form or another, were for the first time brought into touch with telephony.

The primary object of the articles was to describe in detail the trunk system; but it was considered desirable to give some account of first principles, and accordingly the transmission of speech, transmitters, receivers, and, in fact, telephone stations generally, were briefly described. The writer is aware that much of this has been described times without number, but his experience as a teacher leads him to believe that the inclusion of this matter will render the book useful to a larger circle of readers.

The first eight chapters may be said to be introductory to the subject of telephony generally. The permanent current systems nextly receive attention, and their various classes of switch sections. After this follow special switches, such as transfer boards, record table switch sections, etc.

A chapter upon inductive disturbances has here been interpolated with the object of rendering the subsequent chapter, dealing with the conditions under which superimposing is practicable, more intelligible. The writer begs to express the opinion that too much attention cannot be paid to the questions arising from a consideration of these chapters, and especially so to any whose lot it is to have anything to do with the testing and fault localisation of telephone circuits.

Test boards, lightning protectors, etc., now receive consideration; and at this point it may be said that the original articles ended.

In order to reduce the large number of batteries incidental to the permanent current system, arrangements will shortly be made to work exchanges from a single set of cells. The complications thereby introduced form the subject of Chapter XXV.

The writer has also considered it desirable that a short description of the Company's local systems should be added to facilitate the comprehension of all the operations involved, and with this object Chapters XXVI. to XXIX. were written.

The Newcastle system is next briefly described. This chapter may at first sight appear somewhat meagre, but it should be recollected that the system is only in force in some half dozen exchanges, of which Newcastle is by far the largest. Apart from that, the system is interesting inasmuch as it presents some very novel features. The most recent arrangements are dealt with.

In Chapter XXXI. is given a description of several special arrangements for which it was somewhat difficult to find places anywhere else, entailing, as some of them did, a more detailed knowledge of the Company's local systems; and the volume closes with a chapter on switch section faults.

A very brief mention of the KR law is included in the appendix. A list of the numbers of the tags and their uses is supplied for purposes of reference, as also is a table of the resistance and capacity of aerial and underground conductors, for which latter the writer begs to acknowledge his indebtedness to Mr. A. Eden, one of the Technical Officers to the Post Office.

It will be observed that the testing of trunk lines has not been dealt with. This differs little from the testing of telegraph lines, and with the aid of the chapter upon inductive disturbances no difficulty should arise. The subject of telegraph testing has been dealt with in so many other works that the writer deemed it advisable to exclude it as beyond the scope of the present volume, the original object of which was merely to describe the trunk line system.

As this little volume was originally designed for the especial use of officers of the Department, the official nomenclature has been rigidly adhered to. The familiar "jack" or "spring-jack" gives place to "switch-spring," and similarly, "plugs," "translators," "listening keys," are replaced by "pegs," "transformers," and "speaking keys." The latter two designations appear to be a distinct improvement.

In its present and somewhat extended form it is hoped that the book will also prove useful to students for the City and Guilds Examinations.

The writer begs to express his thanks to Messrs. Ericsson and Co., Stockholm, the General Electric Co., and the Consolidated Telephone Co., for the illustrations of apparatus manufactured by them; also to the Journals of the Institution of Electrical Engineers for much information.

In conclusion, the writer begs to here place upon record his deep sense of obligation to Mr. G. W. Bannister, Engineers Department, Manchester, who took entire charge of the illustration of both the original articles and of the present volume, and who has also rendered other most valuable aid.

PREFACE TO SECOND EDITION.

In the present edition a chapter entitled "Recent Advances in Switchboard Design" has been added. Its primary object is to briefly state the principle of the central battery system which the Department propose to use for the competitive telephone scheme in London. Since it will probably be some considerable time before the details of this system, adapted to the varying requirements of the trunk and local services, have finally settled down, it has been considered undesirable to include arrangements which can only be regarded as tentative. In the same chapter a brief account of the working of one or two non-multiple or divided board systems has been included in order to indicate the lines upon which opponents of the multiple board are working.

An index has been added, but with these exceptions few changes have been made.

ENGINEERING DEPARTMENT, T. E. H.
    POSTAL TELEGRAPHS,
        MANCHESTER.

CONTENTS.

	PAGE
CHAPTER I.—INTRODUCTORY	1

Principles involved in the transmission of speech—Pitch, volume and *timbre*.

CHAPTER II.—THE BELL TELEPHONE 4

Lines of force—Effects of an electric current—Production of current—Bell telephone, description and theory—Transformations of energy involved—Relative dimensions of parts.

CHAPTER III.—EARLY TRANSMITTERS 10

Edison transmitter—Necessity for induction coil—Principle of induction coil—Resistance of various parts of circuit—Hughes microphones, descriptions and theory—Microphonic joints—Necessity for divided core in induction coil.

CHAPTER IV.—MODERN RECEIVERS 17

Swiss—Phelp's pony crown—Gouloubitzky—Ader—Du Moncel's investigations on design of telephones—Gower—Double pole Bell—Watch.

CHAPTER V.—MODERN TRANSMITTERS 24

Classification of transmitters—Gower—Ader—Mix and Genest—Pendulum—Blake—Hunning's transmitters—Packing difficulties—Deckert—Solid-back—Ericsson transmitters.

CHAPTER VI.—BATTERY TELEPHONE STATIONS 34

Trembler bells—Switches, etc., and their purposes for telephone stations—Connections in skeleton—Switch-arms.

CHAPTER VII.—THE LECLANCHÉ CELL 40

Chemical action of cell—Agglommerate type—Six block type—Shallow circular zincs.

CHAPTER VIII.—MAGNETO TELEPHONE STATIONS 44

Magneto bell—Magneto generator—Theory of instrument—Armature cut-outs—Complete station—Ericsson table telephone.

CHAPTER IX.—POST OFFICE TELEPHONES 53

Gower-Bell—Post Office telephone.

CHAPTER X.—THE LOCAL EXCHANGE SYSTEM 57

History—Requirements for exchange working—Secret systems—Switch-springs—Flat pegs—Polarised indicator No. 2—Telephone relay—Subscriber's instrument—Switch board telephone—Telephone tablet—Polarised indicator relay—Working of system—Circular pegs—Local switch for trunk exchanges,

Contents.

	PAGE
CHAPTER XI.—Principle of Permanent Current System	70

Normal arrangement—Automatic calling—Cross-connection strips—Five and eight-point switch-springs—Actual connections of trunk line.

CHAPTER XII.—Auxiliary Apparatus ... 75

Telephone Exchange galvanometer and self-restoring indicator.

CHAPTER XIII.—Operating Connections ... 79

Ringing key—Skeleton of cord connections—Complete connections of speaking and ringing keys and cords—Mechanical design of speaking key—Switch telephone connector circuit—Operator's telephones—Breast-plate transmitter—Double pegs—Headgear receiver.

CHAPTER XIV.—The "A" Switch Section ... 88

Arrangement of apparatus—Post Office subscribers—Service wire—Junction circuit—Local contacts.

CHAPTER XV.—The "B" Switch Section ... 93

Arrangement of apparatus—Junction clearing—Generator and reed ringers—Transfer circuits—Visual indicator—Principle and connections of transfer circuits.

CHAPTER XVI.—Up and Down Call Wire ... 101

Service circuits—Record table—Up and down call wires—Call key—Record table tablet.

CHAPTER XVII.—The "C" Switch Section ... 103

Disposition of apparatus—Transfer circuits—Local switch junctions and call wire.

CHAPTER XVIII—The Transfer Board ... 107

A and B circuits—Principle and design of board—Combination key—A circuit diagram—B circuit diagram—Cross-connection strips—Fault tracing.

CHAPTER XIX.—The Record Table Switch Section ... 115

Object and design—Method of working—Connections—Night calls

CHAPTER XX.—Direct Junction Circuits ... 118

Arrangements for terminating upon trunk switch sections—Record table transfer section—Junction transfer sections.

CHAPTER XXI.—Call Office Circuits ... 123

Silence cabinets—Counter communication switch for one cabinet; —for five cabinets—Stock Exchange circuits.

CHAPTER XXII—Inductive Disturbances ... 130

Static induction—Effects upon circuits—Dynamic induction—Combined effects of static and dynamic induction—Crossing and symmetrical twist systems—Effects of faults.

CHAPTER XXIII—Superimposed Circuits ... 137

Transformers—Principle of superimposing—Conditions necessary—Signalling—Non-polarised indicator relay—Complete connections—Testing

Contents. xi.

	PAGE
CHAPTER XXIV.—TEST ROOM APPLIANCES	144

Test cases—Test boards—Lightning protectors—Line tablet—Battery tablet—40-circuit tablets—Switch-spring test boards—Small protectors—Cross connections—Manchester arrangements.

CHAPTER XXV.—THE UNIVERSAL BATTERY SYSTEM 152

Object and theory—Secondary cells—Speaking fuse tablet—Charging switches—Overhearing—Permanent current working—Connections and theory—Signalling fuse tablet—Primary battery universal working—Test board arrangements

CHAPTER XXVI.—SMALL LOCAL EXCHANGES 160

Design of switch board—Connections—Junction arrangements.

CHAPTER XXVII.—THE SERIES MULTIPLE 165

Junction and multiple boards—Appearance of multiple board—Engaged test—Connections—Working.

CHAPTER XXVIII.—THE SELF-RESTORING BOARD 171

Principle of parallel multiple—Engaged test—Operating connections—Flat boards.

CHAPTER XXIX.—THE CALL WIRE SYSTEM 175

Principle of system—Single cord working—Engaged test—Operating connections—Night control switch—Service peg—Cross-connection fields—Advantages and disadvantages.

CHAPTER XXX.—THE NEWCASTLE SYSTEM 179

Distinctive features—Subscribers' station—Description of multiple—Operating connections—Method of working—Short circuit wire—Engaged test—Call and detector switch—Trunk working.

CHAPTER XXXI —MISCELLANEOUS SPECIAL ARRANGEMENTS .. 185

Trunk engaged tests at Manchester—Common return—Night arrangements—Intermediate stations on trunk lines—Single wire trunks—Supervisor's switch section—Special keyboard—Cord testing—Auxiliary receiver.

CHAPTER XXXII.—SWITCH SECTION FAULTS 195

Method to be adopted in tracing—Faults in telephone sets—Disconnections in long lines—Trunk circuit apparatus faults—Cords—Keyboards—Earths on junctions—Operator's telephone—Local circuits—Record table switch sections—Transfer circuits.

CHAPTER XXXIII.—RECENT ADVANCES IN SWITCHBOARD DESIGN 200

Central battery system—Kellog system—Chicago express system—Sabin's divided board system—Engaged subscribers—Automatic ringing—Equal distribution of work.

APPENDICES—
 A.—THE KR LAW 206
 B.—RESISTANCE AND CAPACITY OF WIRES 209
 C.—SWITCH SECTION CROSS-CONNECTION STRIP NUMBERS .. 210
INDEX 214

THE TELEPHONE SYSTEM

OF THE

BRITISH POST OFFICE.

CHAPTER I.

INTRODUCTORY.

The invention of the electric telephone dates back to 1854, when M Charles Bourseul published a paper in which the following remarkable passages occur:—"*Suppose that a man speaks near a movable disc sufficiently pliable to lose none of the vibrations of the voice, that this disc alternately makes and breaks the currents from a battery, you may have at a distance another disc which will simultaneously execute the same vibrations.*" "*. . . It is certain that in a more or less distant future speech will be transmitted by electricity I have made experiments in this direction; they are delicate, and demand time and patience, but the approximations obtained promise a favourable result*" This undoubtedly contained the germ of the electric telephone, but to Philip Reis, in 1861, belongs the credit of actually carrying the idea into effect. His telephone took advantage of the fact that an iron bar when magnetised emits an audible "click." If the rate and intensity of these clicks can be controlled, musical notes and other more complex sounds may be reproduced. For instance, a musical note is often produced by a circular saw when cutting through wood. This is caused by the excessive frequency with which the teeth strike the wood. Reis's transmitting instrument consisted of a membrane with a contact arranged in its centre by means of which the current was made and broken by every movement of this diaphragm

The first practical telephone was due to Graham Bell, in 1876, but before describing this remarkable instrument, which is to-day very much as originally invented, a little information upon the subject of sound will prove advantageous, as it is impossible to have a clear idea of the transmission of sound without a knowledge of the essential principles involved. A sound is any disturbance such that, when communicated to the ear *and transmitted by the nervous system to the brain, the sensation which we call sound is experienced* A sound is produced by any action which throws the surrounding air into a state of sufficiently vigorous vibration When a tuning fork is struck the prongs are thrown into a state of rapid vibration Let us for the moment confine our attention to one of these prongs This prong moves backwards and forwards at a great speed, and in so doing alternately condenses and rarefies the air in contact with it. This effect is passed on to the next layer of air, and this on to the next, and so on, the disturbance thus spreading outwards in every direction.

Wave motion consists in *any* regular periodic disturbance. Sound waves are not up and down vibrations, but are propagated in straight lines. The immediate cause of the sound is the vibration of the sounding body, and these vibrations are communicated to the surrounding air, which is carved into a series of waves of alternate condensation and rarefaction. These waves are maintained so long as the sounding body vibrates.

The sound emitted by a tuning fork is greatest just when it is struck, and if it is watched it will be seen that the amplitude of vibration, or the distance through which the prong is moving, gradually grows less and less, consequently the surrounding air will not receive such vigorous pushes, and the sound will not be so loud. In fact, the subsidence of the sound may be seen from the amplitude of vibration of the tuning fork as well as heard. Now a tuning fork is an instrument so designed that when once thrown into a state of vibration it will continue to vibrate at the same rate, but with gradually decreasing amplitude. It can only vibrate at one rate, and to this fact it owes its utility for tuning instruments by

If the surrounding air were thrown into vibration by means of some instrument which vibrates at the same rate as the tuning fork, the fork would be thrown into vibration, emitting its own distinctive note. The annoyance caused by a loose gas-globe when singing is an excellent example of this. It is frequently only one note which will cause this globe to vibrate, and trouble is sometimes experienced in finding the offender. Now nothing of the nature of a tuning fork can be used for receiving the vibrations caused by articulate speech, which vary in loudness, in pitch, and in quality. The tuning fork is what may be termed a persistent vibrator, and as has been already pointed out the amplitude of vibration determines the loudness of the sound The rate at which the fork vibrates backwards and forwards determines the pitch of the note. The reader will doubtless have noticed the great amount of vibration which is actually felt in addition to the sound produced by the very low notes of an organ. These vibrations are much lower even than the deep bass of a man's voice, which latter may cause sixty or seventy sets of waves of alternate rarefaction and condensation to succeed each other in one second. In the case of a woman's voice the vibrations are much quicker, reaching, perhaps, one thousand per second.

There is yet another way in which sounds differ from one another, and this is the difference which exists between a piano and a violin, both of which sound the same note, and that is the characteristic of the sound. This characteristic is called the *timbre* of the sound. *Timbre* is a French word meaning tone, but conveying far more than its English equivalent. The *timbre* of the voice is due, not to the amplitude of the wave or its frequency, but to the shape of the wave. The vibration is seldom, if ever, a simple regular backward and forward vibration, but may make several small excursions before moving bodily over to the other side to execute a similar vibration. Articulate speech causes waves of the most complicated nature. The difference between a spoken word and a note of the same pitch and volume is due to the difference in the shape of the waves.

If these waves are allowed to impinge upon some mobile plate sufficiently flexible to lose none of the vibrations, the plate would be thrown into vibration, executing a series of movements which would be synchronous with the movements of the sounding body. If these movements could subsequently be reproduced in the plate we should have the surrounding air carved into waves which would exactly resemble those produced in the first instance by the sounding body, and these waves would produce the same effect upon our auditory senses. The principle of the transmission of speech to a distance depends upon our ability to cause a plate or disc to vibrate in exactly the same manner as a distant disc which is thrown into a state of vibration by means of the waves produced by the human voice. A certain toy, which the majority of my readers have seen at some time or other, may serve to illustrate the above proposition. The toy consists of a couple of tins with the bottoms knocked out and replaced by paper diaphragms. The centres of the two drums are connected by means of a tightly stretched string. On speaking into one tin the paper diaphragm is alternately slackened (moving inwards) and tightened (moving outwards). The movement alternately slackens and tightens the string, and the distant diaphragm is slackened and stretched—*i.e.*, if the pull on the string is slackened the diaphragm moves inwards, and if tightened outwards. Thus whatever movement is made by one diaphragm is reproduced at the other. The sound waves impinge on the first diaphragm, causing it to execute vibrations in unison with those waves. The distant diaphragm executes vibrations in synchronism with the first one, therefore causing waves precisely similar to the original ones. Its effects upon the auditory senses are also similar.

The electric telephone merely consists of an electro-magnetic mechanism by means of which two diaphragms are made to control each other so that a movement of one causes an exactly similar movement of the other.

CHAPTER II

THE BELL TELEPHONE.

In order that the *modus operandi* of the Bell telephone may be clearly apprehended, it is essential that we should feel perfectly familiar with the theory of the electrical phenomena upon which it depends. As the majority of my readers are familiar with the fundamental principles of magnetism and electricity, it is proposed to pass quickly over them.

In the region around a magnet there is a field of force, since a compass needle will be deflected. To produce this deflection force must be required, since the needle is held in its north and south position by the earth's magnetic field. It is not possible for any thinking person to believe that action at a distance, without any connection between, is possible. The magnet creates some peculiar disturbance in *the ether** which permeates all matter, and this disturbance in the ether may be made to re-act on magnetic bodies, and thus produce an effect. To the practical man these theories are of very small moment, but if, from a consideration of these points, we can deduce a working hypothesis, we shall not have wasted our time. Faraday explained nearly all the magnetic phenomena by means of "*lines of force.*" The amount of magnetic disturbance at any point will depend upon the strength of the magnet originating the disturbance, and upon its proximity. Clerk Maxwell gave to these lines of force definite quantative values, that is to say, the strength of a magnetic field was expressed in lines of force present. A certain magnetic field was chosen, and this was termed a unit magnetic field. Through this unit field we suppose one line of force passes in every unit of area. A field twice as strong would have twice as many lines per unit area, and so on.

Three effects may be produced by an electric current, viz., the magnetic, the thermal, and the chemical effects. The magnetic and thermal effects are always present when there is an electric current, but chemical effects are not produced unless the current is made to pass through a conducting chemical compound. The thermal effect is not noticeable unless special means are taken to render it prominent. A wire conveying an electric current is surrounded by a magnetic field. This magnetic field we represent by lines of force, as shown in Figure 1. If we wish to increase this

---

* Lodge's "Modern Views of Electricity" contains a non-mathematical and thoroughly readable account of these ideas.

magnetic field, we may either increase the strength of the current, or we may wrap the wire round and round into the form of a coil or solenoid, thereby bringing a greater length of current conveying wire together.

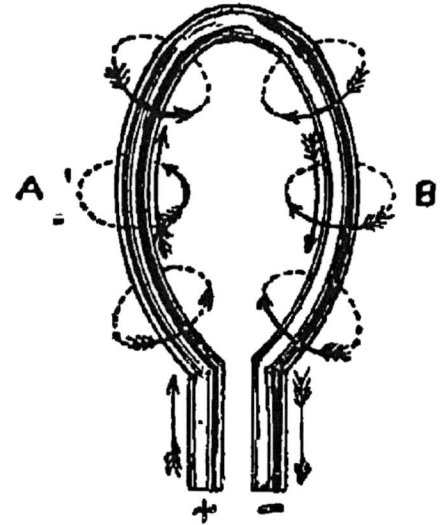

FIGURE 1.

This results in an increased number of lines of force, as every added inch of wire adds its lines to those already there. The necessity for bringing the wire together is merely to concentrate the effect.

There are many ways in which an electric current can be produced. Firstly, there is the chemical method, *i.e.*, by means of a voltaic cell. A voltaic cell is an arrangement which in return for chemical energy will furnish electrical energy Such cells usually consist of two dissimilar metals, immersed in some conducting liquid, which will attack one of the metals, or elements as they are usually called in this connection. Secondly, there is the electro-magnetic method, and this is the method to which it is desired that careful and particular attention be paid Whenever a conductor is cut by a line of force, or whenever a line of force cuts a conductor, an electromotive force is generated in that conductor, and if the ends of the conductor are joined by a wire (while the lines are cutting the conductor) a current will flow through the circuit thus formed during the time that the lines are cutting the conductor. Generally, we may say that whenever any alteration in the number of lines of force embraced by a conducting system is made an E.M.F. is set up. The value of the E.M.F. generated depends upon the strength of the magnetic field, and upon the rate at which the conductor is cut For instance, the absolute unit of E.M.F. is the E.M.F. produced between the ends of a conductor, which cuts a unit magnetic field at unit rate—*i.e.*, that cuts one line of force per second. In a unit magnetic field there is one line of force per unit area. The volt, or practical unit of E M F, is made very much larger than the absolute or C G S unit The direction of the current depends upon the direction in which the lines cut the conductor

The Bell telephone consists of a mobile iron plate placed in a magnetic field with a system of conductors, *e.g*, a coil of wire This iron plate, or diaphragm, usually of ferrotype, is made very thin, so as to be flexible. Sound waves impinging upon this diaphragm result in movement or vibration, and this movement causes an alteration in the distribution of the lines of force in the magnetic field. The coil of wire is so arranged that this disturbance in distribution results in some of the lines cutting through the conductors, and as we have seen that whenever a line of force cuts a circuit, a current is the result.

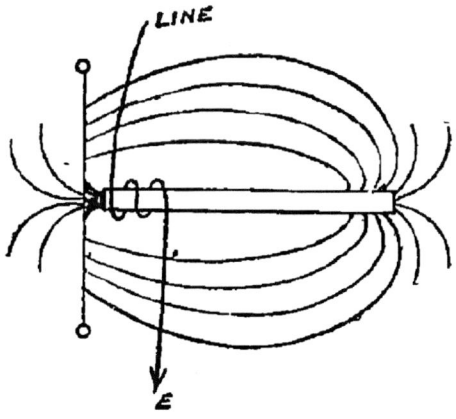

FIGURE 2.

Every movement of the diaphragm causes an electric current The magnetic field will be disturbed to the greatest extent at or near the poles of the magnet . consequently, the coil of wire is made to surround one pole of the magnet (as shown in Figure 2) The lines we may imagine as moving laterally through a small distance. In order that by these movements the lines may cut as many turns of wire as possible, we must make our coil of wire very small ; that is, bring the greatest possible number of conductors into the region where the maximum disturbance takes place. We see then, from these considerations, that very fine wire must be employed, and that if the space taken up by the wire is large, there will be a large number of turns of wire which will remain in a practically constant field, and will therefore merely be useless resistance The coil must have the largest possible number of turns which can be got into the space. Beyond this space additional turns of wire will be worse than useless.

It is now necessary to show clearly how movements of the diaphragm produce currents proportional to those movements, also how these currents again reproduce upon a second diaphragm the movements of the first The

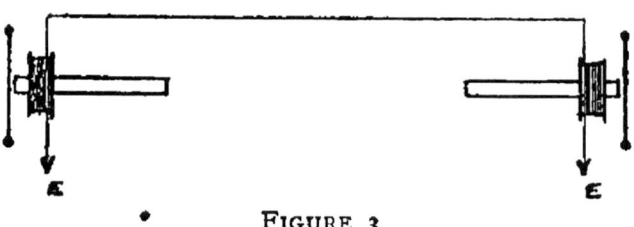

FIGURE 3

magnetic circuit, it will be seen, includes the diaphragm. The lines of force starting from the magnet pass through the air gap between the magnet and the diaphragm into the diaphragm, then out again, and back to the other pole of the magnet. The diaphragm is consequently attracted and is thus strained inwards to the magnet The distance to which the centre of the plate is pulled in depends upon its thickness or stiffness, and upon the strength of the magnet There is a very delicate balance between the two, the diaphragm remaining in such a position that the pull of the magnet inwards is exactly equal to the "fly-back" tendency of the diaphragm, which is tightly clamped round its outer edge. When sound waves impinge upon this delicately-balanced diaphragm, vibrations which are in synchronism with the sound waves are executed by it. Let us suppose that the effect of the first wave is to move the diaphragm further inwards. The nearer approach of the diaphragm causes several lines of force, which formerly entered the coil, to pass straight from the magnet to the diaphragm It will also cause fresh lines at the sides to pass through the coil. These lines in taking up their new positions cut through the conductors of coil, and, as we have seen, an electric current is the result. The strength of this current will depend upon the amount of movement which the diaphragm executes In this instance the lines cut through the coil from the sides to the centre. A rarefaction wave will cause lines which formerly passed through directly from the magnet to the diaphragm to move towards the sides, thus cutting the coil of wire in the opposite direction, and so producing a current in the opposite direction. From a consideration of these points, it is obvious that currents of varying strength and direction, in direct proportion to the strength and direction of the sound waves, are sent out, and thus complex sounds result in complex currents

As we have seen (Figure 3) the transmitting instrument is precisely the same as the receiver, or, in other words, each instrument will, in turn, act as either transmitter or receiver. The undulatory currents which pass through the coil of the receiving instrument alter the distribution of the lines of force in precisely the same manner in which they were altered by the movement of the transmitting diaphragm; hence the receiving diaphragm executes precisely the same movements as the transmitting diaphragm. For instance, a current in one direction tends to reduce the strength of the magnet, causing the diaphragm to move outwards: whereas a current in the opposite direction would act with the magnet, and thus bring about the near approach of the diaphragm. The effects produced are directly proportional to the strength of the currents; therefore the movements executed are in exact synchronism with the movements of the transmitter, and thus the exact sounds will be reproduced—*i.e*, the movements of the receiving diaphragm will carve the air into waves, which are precisely similar to the original waves. It is quite immaterial in which way the two telephones are joined up, since it will only mean that the diaphragm will move inwards to the same extent that it might, if carefully joined up, move outwards. This will not alter the sound produced.

The energy of the sound waves is, in the transmitter, converted into electrical energy in the form of current. A certain proportion of this energy is wasted in overcoming the resistance of the line. The greater proportion of the energy is utilised in moving the diaphragm at the distant end. Here then there are several transformations of energy, hence there is bound to be a proportion lost; that is to say, the reproduced sounds cannot be as loud as the original sounds. They will be precisely similar in all save this one respect. If the line is very long, then the sounds will be almost inaudible. The energy of the voice is used to produce the distant effect in the Bell telephone, and therefore the arrangement is not as efficient as those arrangements in which the received sounds are produced by some secondary set of arrangements in which the energy of the voice is merely used to direct.

The question as to the relative dimensions of the various parts of a telephone is an exceedingly important one. Unfortunately, the explanation of the Bell telephone is by no means satisfactory, and it is not possible to treat the subject with the same certainty that we may treat an action which is thoroughly understood. It is not, at present, possible to use our mathematical knowledge to determine the best possible dimensions. However, the following general rules have been deduced by Mercadier:—

(*a*) The stronger the magnetic field the thicker should the diaphragm be

(*b*) Having ascertained the correct thickness of the diaphragm there is a certain diameter which will give a maximum effect. The stronger the magnetic field, the larger should the diaphragm be.

(*c*) The relative positions of the coils, magnets and diaphragms must then be determined by considering what arrangement will, for the smallest movement of the diaphragm, produce a maximum disturbance of the magnetic field. The coils must then be so arranged as to be cut by as large a number of lines as possible for a given alteration in the magnetic field.

It would at first sight appear that we might indefinitely increase the sensitiveness of our receiver by increasing the strength of the magnet, but this is not so, as the diaphragm loses much of its elasticity under the stronger attraction between it and the magnet. These general remarks as to designing telephones should be borne in mind when considering the various forms of receivers. Mercadier's researches led him to design telephones with exceedingly small diaphragms, whereas the telephones first introduced had diaphragms over three inches in diameter. Present day practice, as we shall see, seems to indicate a medium between these two extremes.

It was previously remarked that the theory of the Bell telephone was by no means satisfactory. It is not conceivable that the exceedingly small currents generated by the transmitting instrument will be sufficiently powerful to cause the distant diaphragm to move bodily backwards and forwards, thus generating the vigorous sound waves which we recognise. It would seem that the slight alterations in the magnetic field at the receiving end were out of all proportion to the magnitude of the effects produced. It is suggested by Du Moncel,* who has made a special study of the theory of the telephone, that there are many causes which act together to reproduce speech. There is firstly the bodily movement of the diaphragm such as has already been described. Secondly, it has been suggested that there are molecular movements taking place in the diaphragm. Thirdly, the molecular vibrations of the magnet consequent upon its alternate magnetisation and demagnetisation by the undulatory currents. In regard to this last effect it should be mentioned that when an iron rod is magnetised or demagnetised it alters very slightly in shape, at the same time emitting a slight "tick." Telephones have been constructed without diaphragms upon this principle It will be obvious that a series of ticks will form a musical note if they succeed each other with sufficient rapidity. The magnitude of the tick produced depends upon the strength of the current producing it. It will thus be seen that the action of the telephone is somewhat obscure.

---

* Du Moncel, "Le Téléphone," 4me édition

CHAPTER III.

Early Transmitters.

In the Bell telephone the energy of the voice is used to produce the distant effect, therefore the effects produced cannot be as strong as the original ones. In order to increase the effects, Edison in 1877 invented his carbon transmitter. This was the first of the carbon transmitters, and opened quite a new vista in telephonic research. The instrument is illustrated in Figure 4. It consists essentially of a piece

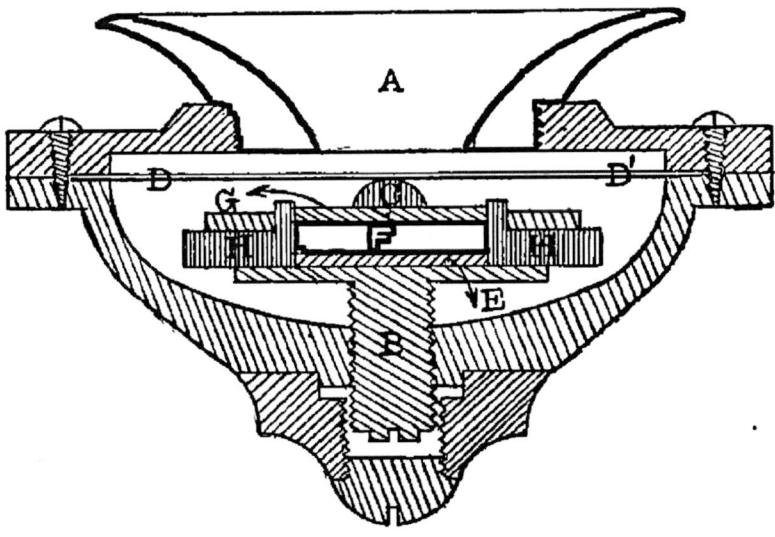

FIGURE 4.

of carbon so arranged that sonorous vibrations will cause varying degrees of pressure upon it. The electrical resistance of carbon decreases under pressure, and upon this fact it was thought that the action of the instrument depended. A ferrotype diaphragm DD^1 is used to receive the sonorous vibrations. These vibrations are then communicated to a platinum plate G by means of the ivory button C. Between the platinum plate and the table BE is placed a circular disc of lamp black F. The table B is capable of adjustment by means of a screw thread which is cut upon its longer extremity. In this way the pressure upon the carbon disc can be varied at will The circular ring H, which is screwed on the table B, serves to keep the carbon button in position. The case of the instrument is made of iron, and forms one terminal and G the other When the diaphragm DD_1 is thrown into vibration, these vibrations are communicated to the platinum plate G, which in turn alters the resistance of the instrument. It is now considered that it is merely the resistance of the contact between the platinum plate and the carbon which is altered, and not that the resistance of the carbon itself is reduced by being alternately compressed and relieved of compression However, this is a point to which it will subsequently be necessary to return

The Edison transmitter, then, so far as we have now considered it, consists in an apparatus the resistance of which will vary in exact synchronism with the sonorous vibrations which we cause to impinge upon its diaphragm If now a battery and a Bell telephone be joined in circuit with this instrument, and we speak on to it, we shall have varying currents passing through our receiver. These currents are in every way proportional to the effects producing them, consequently we shall have speech perfectly reproduced. It should be noted that in this case we do not employ the energy of the voice to produce the distant effect It merely directs the movement of the diaphragm, and the battery which we employ furnishes the energy utilised at the distant end, so that it is theoretically possible to have the effects produced at the distant end greater than the original effects Now let us consider what the proportions of this circuit should be as regards resistance, in order that we may obtain maximum variations of current from changes in the resistance of the transmitter Ohm's law states that the current in any circuit varies directly as the E M F , and inversely as the resistance With a constant E M F , then, the current through a circuit varies inversely as the resistance of that circuit Now, in order that the variation of resistance of *one part of that circuit* may produce a large variation in the value of the current, we should desire that the remainder of the circuit should have as little resistance as possible. For instance, let us suppose that the resistance of our transmitter in its normal condition, battery, and receiver amounts to 20ω, of which the transmitter is responsible for 10ω. If now the note C is sounded, let us suppose that the resistance of the transmitter varies between 9ω and 11ω at the rate of 240 variations per second Consider now one of these variations—for instance, the decrease in the resistance of the transmitter to 9ω. In this case the resistance of the circuit is 19ω, as against 20ω when normal. This represents a variation of 5 per cent. of the original current. Had the resistance of the remainder of the circuit been nil, the variation would have been 10 per cent. On the other hand, if the line were of considerable length the variation would have been far less. Had the resistance of the circuit been 1000ω, the variation would only have been 1-10th per cent., or the percentage variation of current would only have been one hundredth of the percentage variation of resistance of the transmitter. Thus we see that the longer the line the weaker is the speaking, since the speaking depends not upon the current flowing through the telephone, but upon the extent of the variations produced in the value of the currents passing through the instrument. If the line is of any length, then such an arrangement as has been depicted would be utterly useless.

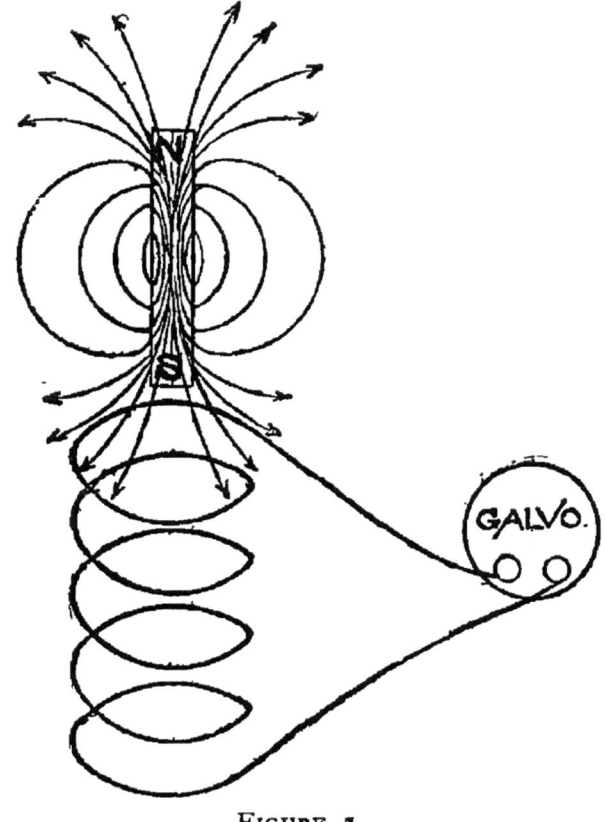

FIGURE 5

The solution of this problem was found in the induction coil. The induction coil consists of an electro-magnet around which a second set of windings are placed. The first set of windings is termed the primary coil, and the second set the secondary coil, and the currents sent through the primary induce currents in the secondary. In order that we may appreciate the reason of this we must refer back a little.

It was previously stated that whenever a line of force cut a conductor an E.M.F was generated in that conductor. Figure 5 illustrates a coil of wire joined to a galvanometer. A magnet N S is placed above, and a few lines have been drawn to represent lines of force If the magnet is moved down into the coil of wire the magnet's lines will cut through the various turns of wire; thus an E.M.F. will be generated in each These E M Fs add together and produce a kick upon the galvanometer, but the effect is only a transient one—it lasts only while the magnet is moving. Immediately the magnet ceases to move the lines cease to cut through the conductors and the E.M.F. ceases. When this magnet is withdrawn the lines of force again cut through the several conductors, but in the opposite direction, viz , from bottom to top, and a current in the opposite direction, lasting only so long as the magnet is moving, is the result. It will at once be remarked that in order to prolong the current the magnet should be moved very slowly. That is so, but the E.M F. induced varies directly as the rate at which the conductors are cut, consequently if we do this the current produced will be correspondingly small, though lasting longer. If now we wished to produce a series of currents in opposite directions we might devise an arrangement by means of which N S is moved rapidly up and down. The essential point is that the lines of force shall cut and re-cut the coil of wire.

If the magnet N S be replaced by an electro-magnet, we may magnetise or demagnetise it at will by making or breaking the circuit of a battery connected to it. In this case we should prefer to place the magnet actually inside the coil in order that a maximum number of lines shall cut through the windings of the coil on making and breaking the circuit. On making the circuit it is obvious that these lines of force have to spring into existence, and that in doing so they will cut the windings of the coil, thus generating an E.M F When the circuit is broken the lines have to collapse, as it were, back into the iron again, cutting through the coil, but in the opposite direction, thus generating an E.M.F. in the opposite sense If now the current is increased in strength more lines of force are added to the magnet, and these lines in springing into existence cut through the coil, thus generating an E.M.F. When these lines fall back into the iron a current in the opposite direction results. If an Edison transmitter and battery be included in the circuit with the electro-magnet (or primary circuit), currents will be generated in the secondary coil which, by their direction, indicate increase or decrease in the resistance of the transmitter and by their strength indicate the amount of variation which takes place. The advantage of this system is that the transmitter, battery and primary coil only are in circuit The line circuit is quite separate

We may make the resistance of our battery low, and we may also make the resistance of our primary coil low, since we can provide a heavy current One quarter of an ampere through 40 turns produces the same magnetic effect as 10 milliamperes through 1,000 turns. At the same time we can employ thicker wire for our ten turns than we could possibly do if we had to provide a thousand. The E.M.Fs. generated in the secondary coil are directly proportional to the current variations in the primary. The resistance of the secondary circuit, which includes the lines and receiver, is constant, therefore the current produced in it will be directly proportional to the E.M Fs induced in it We have thus accomplished our object, for we have made the primary circuit of low resistance, the transmitter itself being the principal item, and thus variations in the resistance of the transmitter are not masked by a large constant resistance. To put the matter plainly and simply, the difference is something like the difference between throwing a cup of water into a small basin of water and throwing it into a pond In the latter case we do not observe any very large altera-

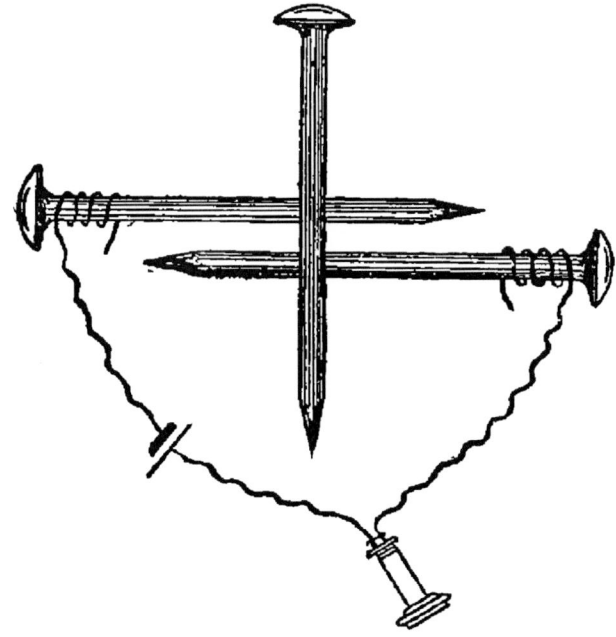

Figure 6.

tion in the quantity of water in the pond, whereas in the former case we may cause the small bowl to overflow.

Professor Hughes, in May, 1878, read a paper before the Royal Society which greatly added to our knowledge of the subject of telephony. Professor Hughes discovered that any system of loose contacts acted as a telephone transmitter He discovered that three iron nails laid upon one another, as indicated in Figure 6, would transmit speech perfectly, and gave to all such instruments the name of "microphone" This was done as it was thought that these transmitters actually amplified the original sounds, but this is an exceedingly doubtful point. An explanation of the action lies in the fact that these loose contacts vary in resistance when shaken by sound waves which are directed towards them—*i.e.*, the resistance of the arrangement varies in exact synchronism with the sound waves. Now, whether the explanation of the phenomenon lies in the fact that when the joints are shaken the pressure on the nails is varied, and that, therefore, the resistance is varied, is somewhat doubtful. The nails are not very efficient as a transmitter, but such sounds as the ticking of a clock and the pitch of a note are reproduced, but the *timbre* is not. Professor Hughes experimented with various substances, but finally found that carbon acted far better than any other substance. The most common form of carbon instrument is shown in Figure 7. It consists of two carbon blocks, between which is fitted a third carbon rod with tapering points. The carbon pencil is fitted loosely, touching both blocks. Sound

FIGURE 7.

is perfectly reproduced by this instrument, notwithstanding its simple and primitive look. The question now arises—Why should carbon behave so much better than iron? Shelford Bidwell investigated this subject, and came to the conclusion that the effect was not solely due to the improvement and deterioration of the electrical contact between the two conductors. The electrical resistance of carbon, unlike that of all metals, decreases when the temperature is increased. The passage of a current through carbon decreases its resistance by increasing its temperature. The increase of temperature is obviously greatest at the points of contact where the resistance is greatest. Let us consider what would take place when the contacts were slightly shaken apart by a sonorous vibration. Firstly, the contact is rendered worse, and the current is thereby reduced, therefore the temperature at the points of contact is reduced. The effect of the variation of contact is thereby greatly enhanced. When the current is increased the temperature is increased, and the resistance of the contact thereby reduced. It is also thought that some of these effects are due to the formation of minute arcs at the points of contact. These theories are supported by the fact that a microphone grows sensibly warm under continued use, and, further, that if the battery power is increased beyond a certain point hissing sounds result.

We thus see that a microphone consists in any apparatus which will, when subjected to sonorous vibrations, vary in resistance. To such contacts Professor Hughes gave the name of "*microphonic joint.*" They may be formed in hundreds of ways, both by intention and by accident. A telephone switch arm with a defective spring, or a loose joint in a gutta-percha covered conductor, will occasionally form such a joint. Carbon is infusible, inoxidible, a bad conductor, and its resistance decreases with increment of temperature; and to these properties it owes its special utility.

It has been pointed out that the core of an induction consists of a bundle of thin iron wires. The object of this form of core is to meet two difficulties, the first being that due to residual magnetism, and the second that due to a solid core acting as a secondary circuit. The current in the primary is uni-directional, and thus residual magnetism is very much in evidence. Residual magnetism tends to mask and reduce the changes in the magnetisation of the core and thus to reduce the values of the E.M.Fs. generated. If the magnetic circuit were completed as in a transformer (see Chapter XXIII), the values of the residual magnetism would be far higher.

When a current is induced in the secondary of an induction coil, a magnetic field is created due to that current in such a direction as to weaken the inducing field (viz, that due to the primary). If a heavy copper cylinder is placed around the primary of an induction coil little or no current will be induced in the secondary, as our copper cylinders will take up the majority of the available energy. Now the core of the primary circuit acts like a closed secondary circuit if composed of solid iron. The iron wires, owing to a thin coating of oxide, are not in good electrical contact, and therefore their effect in taking up energy which we desire only in the secondary circuit is not considerable. In a *perfect* induction coil the energy given to the primary circuit will all be reproduced in the secondary circuit or circuits, and if one of these circuits is taking up energy, the smaller is the amount of energy at our disposal in the other circuit.

CHAPTER IV.

Modern Receivers.

The Bell receiver is very much to-day as it was in 1876, when invented. Of course, the instrument has been vastly improved, but the improvements consist rather in matters of detail than in the essential parts. One of the earlier modifications was the receiver of the Swiss administration. In this instrument the simple bar magnet was replaced by a compound magnet formed by placing eight thin bar magnets side by side. Into the end of the magnet was fixed a soft iron core, and over this a small bobbin, containing about 2,500 convolutions of No 38 wire, was placed. The resistance of the instrument was 100 ohms.

Now let us consider in what respect this receiver differs from the original Bell receiver and what is the effect of such differences. Firstly, a compound magnet can always be magnetised to a higher degree than a bar magnet of equal size This improvement then results in a stronger magnetic field Next the iron core upon which the wire is wound is only 3-16ths of an inch in diameter, and the coil of wire round it has a diameter of 5-8ths of an inch The lines of force are concentrated in the iron core, as nearly the whole of the lines of force from the compound magnet pass through it. Thus we have a very intense magnetic field round the coil of wire, and the slightest motion of the diaphragm modifies the distribution of the lines. The coil is very small, and therefore a large number of lines cut through it at every movement of the diaphragm. The receiver is an excellent one, though not used so much now as formerly, it having given place to the double pole receivers.

The idea that increases in the strength of the magnetic field always resulted in increased efficiency in the receiver led to the construction of Phelp's "Pony crown" receiver, in which six magnets were used. These magnets were bent into circular form, the similar poles being attached to the iron core round which the wire was wound, and the other poles touching the edge of the diaphragm The instrument was, however, not a great improvement upon the original Bell, and is certainly inferior to many simpler modifications in use to-day Besides, the shape of the instrument is objectionable

A telephone was constructed by Gouloubitzky with four coils and two circular magnets. The two ring magnets terminated in four coils, the opposite cores being of opposite polarity; in short, the instrument consisted of two telephones with four coils acting on one diaphragm. The reasoning which led to its construction was based upon the fact that when several receivers are joined up together to receive music, etc., the sound is quite as loud on any one of the telephones as when only one is joined up. It was thought that the combining of two receivers in one would result in double the volume of sound. This was not the case, however, and this and many kindred forms of receiver have now disappeared from the region of practical telephony.

The Ader receiver is one of the most sensitive receivers in use to-day, and though not very extensively used in England certainly merits description. It consists of a ringed-shaped circular magnet (E, Figure 8)

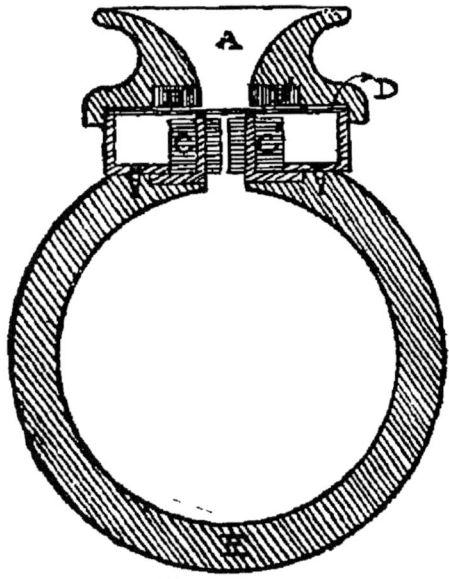

FIGURE 8.

the poles of which terminate in soft iron cores round which two coils C and C^1 are wound. Above the diaphragm D is placed a circular ring of iron B B^1, the object of which is to concentrate the magnetic field. This ring is termed the "*sur excitateur*" (over exciter). The term is a somewhat awkward one to translate, but its general meaning will be gathered from the foregoing. This ring reduces the magnetic resistance of the magnetic circuit and consequently increases the number of lines of force passing through it. Du Moncel found that the nearer the mass of an armature approached that of its magnet the greater was their mutual attraction—*i.e.*, the greater is the magnetic field between them, consequently if having designed our ring and magnet upon these lines we place our diaphragm between them we shall have it placed in the strongest

Ader Receiver.

magnetic field which it is possible to obtain with this particular magnet. If the diaphragm itself is made heavier it loses much of its flexibility.

FIGURE 9.

The ring answers precisely the same purpose without affecting the flexibility of the diaphragm, and to this may be traced its greater efficiency. The magnet is usually nickel-plated, and thus presents a very good appearance.

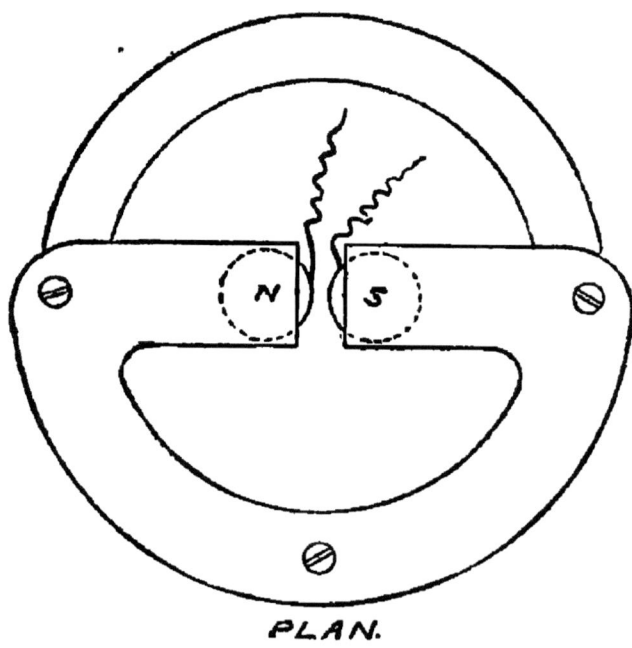

PLAN.
FIGURE 10.

Figure 9 shows the external appearance of the Ader receiver made by the Consolidated Telephone Company.

Gower Receiver.

Another most successful modification of the Bell telephone is the Gower receiver. It consists of a large semi-circular magnet, NS (Figure 10), the poles of which terminate in two soft iron cores turned downwards and fixed into the magnet at right angles to it. The diaphragm is placed above the cores, but instead of having the instrument separate and distinct from the transmitter it is usually fixed, as shown in Figure 11, and the sounds are conveyed to the ears by means of flexible tubes In the construction of the instrument we shall notice several features in which the instrument differs from other modifications of the Bell telephone The diaphragm is very large, being three and a half inches in diameter, and is correspondingly thicker The magnet is very massive and compact, being half an inch in thickness, three-quarters of an inch broad, and nine inches in length. The receiver is a most efficient one, the speaking being very loud, but the flexible tubes are somewhat expensive to maintain. This instrument was formerly used by the Post Office to the exclusion of all others, but now the Gower receiver is replaced by two double pole Bell receivers. The complete Gower Bell Telephone Station will be described subsequently

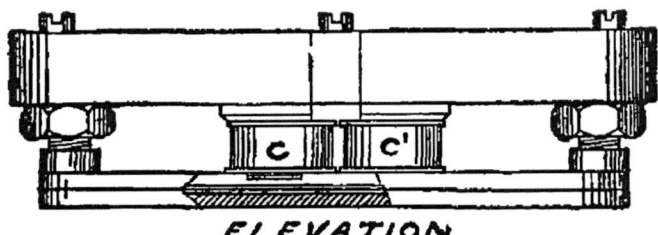

FIGURE 11.

The double pole receiver was invented by Bell, but there is a vast difference in detail, though not in principle, between his instrument and those in use to-day. The Bell instrument was large and heavy, and was fixed upon a stand. Siemens modified this further, rendering it lighter and handier, and from this instrument the present form of double pole receiver has been evolved. This instrument is used by the Post Office, for whom it is frequently manufactured by the General Electric Company. A section of the instrument is shown in Figure 12

The magnet A A is of the horseshoe shape with parallel limbs, and terminates in two soft iron cores P P, which are secured to it by means of two screws. Upon these cores the coils B B are wound They are wound with No 38 silk-covered wire, and have a resistance of 120^ω. The diaphragm D D fits on to the top of the metal case, and is held firmly in its position when the mouthpiece E is screwed down, as shown in the above diagram. The position of the magnet with respect to the diaphragm

Double Pole Bell Receiver.

D D is readily adjustable by means of the screw S. The instrument illustrated is the metal-cased receiver, the shaded portion of the case being metal and the black part ebonite, but the receiver specially made for the Post Office does not in any essential feature differ from this. It is, however, encased completely in ebonite, as shown in Figure 13, and is much lighter. Prior to the adoption of this latter form the metal-

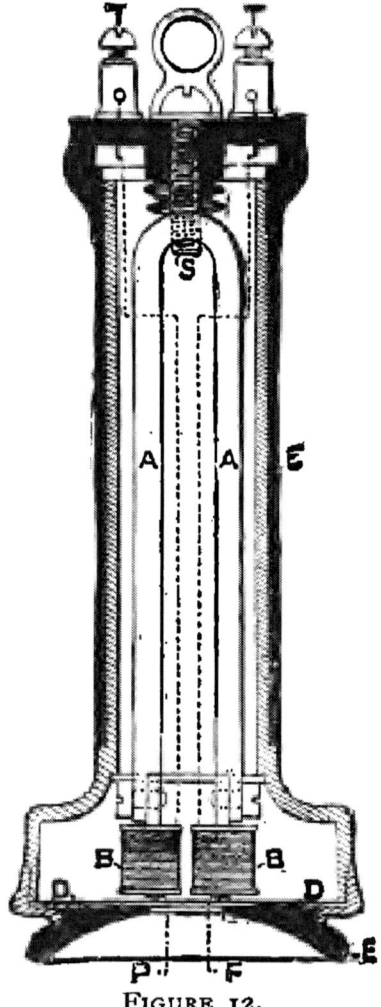

FIGURE 12.

cased receiver was employed. The double pole receiver is certainly one of the most successful and efficient modifications of the Bell instrument, and it is light and of a convenient shape and size.

The Collier-Marr receiver, which has two diaphragms, is more sensitive but its somewhat awkward shape and heavy weight has prevented its general adoption for commercial purposes. It consists of a large horseshoe magnet terminating in two soft iron pole-pieces. A diaphragm is placed close to each pole-piece, and between these diaphragms is the somewhat large coil of wire. This coil of wire is wound upon a bundle of iron wires, the centre portion of which is replaced by a round rod of ebonite The powerful action of the instrument may be due to a resonant action between the two diaphragms. It is wound with a very large number of turns of wire having a resistance of 350ω The efficiency of this instrument may be gathered from the fact that upon one occasion it was found possible to speak to the Head Post Office from an underground box 800 yards distant through a pipe containing some thirty wires, many of which were actually

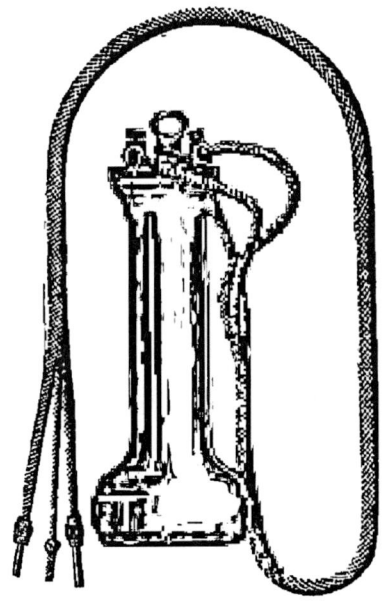

FIGURE 13

working Wheatstone, and this with an earthed return wire! This experiment was tried almost as a joke, but since then the instrument has been much used in Manchester for this purpose It is, however, true that no double pole receivers have been wound to this resistance with the other parts on a large scale, so that it is scarcely fair to term it *the* best receiver.

There are many receivers of the "watch" pattern in use to-day. They are exceedingly small and compact, being, as their name implies, about the same size as a watch. The receiver adopted by the Post Office for the use of linemen is of the watch pattern The instrument is used by the linemen to speak from a pole to the Telephone Exchange, so as to locate faults with certainty where there is no intermediate test-box. A watch receiver is shown in Figure 14. The magnet consists of a ring of steel, from opposite sides of which come pole-pieces around which are wound two coils of wire. The circular magnet may be regarded as two bent bar magnets placed with similar poles together.

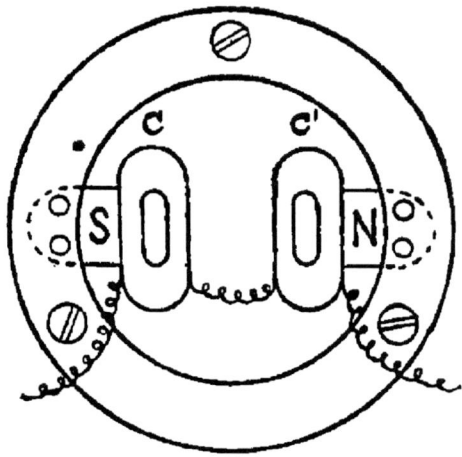

FIGURE 14.

The instrument is very efficient, and is frequently provided with an oval ring fixed at right angles to the back of the case, thus making it somewhat resemble an Ader receiver. In some forms of this instrument a *sur excitateur* is also added.

CHAPTER V

MODERN TRANSMITTERS

There are many different forms of transmitters now in daily use, but they may be readily divided into three classes:—
  I. Modifications of the Hughes Microphone (carbon only).
  II. Modifications of the Edison Transmitter (carbon and metal).
  III. Granular Transmitters

The first two classes are very nearly identical—in fact, every transmitter might with propriety be regarded as a modification of the Hughes instrument. The third class is very different in form to the first two, and to it belong many of the most efficient instruments now in use.

CLASS I.—MODIFICATIONS OF THE HUGHES MICROPHONE.

The first transmitter of this class was probably the Crossley, in which four carbon pencils were used. It was for a time used by the Post Office,

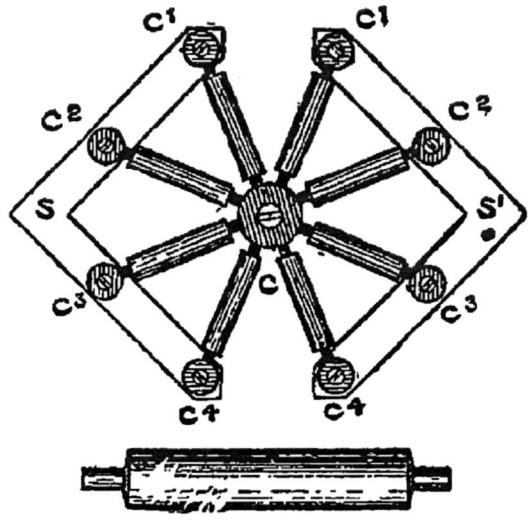

FIGURE 15.

but rapidly gave way to the more powerful Gower. The Gower consists of a central block of circular carbon C (Figure 15), from which radiate eight carbon pencils, each terminating at a carbon block. The four right hand blocks are connected by a strip of copper, and form one terminal of the instrument, and the left hand four blocks form the other. This system of pencils and blocks is fixed upon a pine board nine inches wide by five inches deep and one-eighth of an inch in thickness. This pine board acts as a diaphragm, and is fixed inside the box immediately below the porcelain mouthpiece. The action of the transmitter is precisely similar to that of the original Hughes microphone, save that as more contacts are employed its action is rendered more uniform and more reliable. Movement of the diaphragm causes disturbance of the contacts, and thus increases or reduces the resistance of the instrument. For instance, when the diaphragm moves downwards the centre blocks and the outside blocks move downwards, but owing to inertia the carbon pencils do not immediately follow, and this causes a looser contact, which results in increased resistance. When the diaphragm moves upwards the pencils tend to remain in the position they occupy; thus pressure is caused between the blocks and the pencils, and thus the contact is improved—*i.e.*, its resistance is decreased.

There are a very large number of carbon pencil transmitters in use, of which the Gower may be taken as a prototype. The Ader transmitter consists of three parallel blocks of carbon, between which are placed twelve parallel carbon pencils, six on each side, the two outer blocks forming the terminals. It, however, possesses no advantage over the Gower. A pencil transmitter much used in Germany is that made by Mix and Genest, in which two parallel carbon blocks are bridged across by three carbon pencils. In this case the transmitter is placed in a vertical position. The pencils are held up by means of a sort of felt brake, which prevents the pencils from remaining on the bottom contacts of the two carbon blocks. This is a great advantage, as it entirely eliminates the jarring sounds present in all other pencil transmitters when placed in the vertical position. The jarring is due to the pencils rolling along the contacts. The brake effectually prevents revolution of the pencils, yet leaves them sufficiently free. Of the carbon transmitters this latter instrument is the only one which presents any very novel feature. Many modifications have been introduced merely for the sake of avoiding patents, etc. If the process of cutting bread with a knife were patented someone would immediately discover that the process of cutting was more neatly and effectively carried out by means of a saw, which he would be happy to supply at a cheap rate. Similar remarks apply to many transmitters. If we thoroughly understand our prototypes we shall have no difficulty in realising the *modus operandi* of any instrument which we may chance to come across.

There is yet another class of transmitter used somewhat upon the Continent, known as pendulum transmitters. The Berliner microphone may be taken as the prototype of these instruments. It consists of a ferrotype diaphragm, to which is secured a cylindrical carbon button. A second button rounded off at the end and carried by an articulated lever is held against the first button by its own weight. The diaphragm is contained in a circular indiarubber ring, and a spring coated with indiarubber is also employed to prevent persistent vibration

CLASS II.—CARBON AND METAL TRANSMITTERS

The Edison was the first of this class. Usually a ferrotype diaphragm is employed to collect and mechanically transmit the sonorous vibrations to the electrical system of the transmitter. The Blake transmitter, which belongs to Class II., is even to-day in very extensive use in this country. It consists of

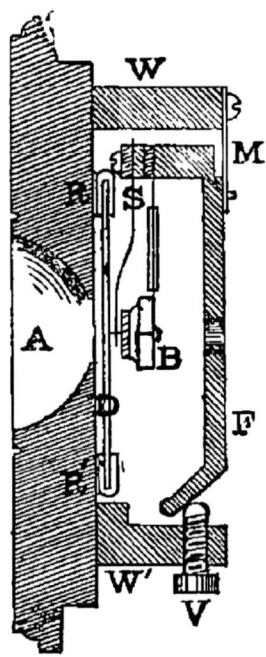

FIGURE 16.

a carbon button (Figure 16) carried by a spring and holder B, and held opposite the centre of a ferrotype diaphragm D, the vibrations of which influence the contact between the carbon button and a platinum point carried by a second spring S. The two springs are mounted on an adjustable frame F, which is secured to the two pillars W and W'. It is secured to W by means of a spring M fixed to both. The screw V serves to regulate the amount of pressure between the platinum point and the carbon button. The diaphragm is fitted into the indiarubber ring RR', and is held in position by means of two springs E and E' (Figure 17) fixed to the circular ring which carries the two pillars to which M and V are secured. It should be noted that the various parts in Figures 16 and 17 are labelled to correspond. The action of the instrument is explainable upon the

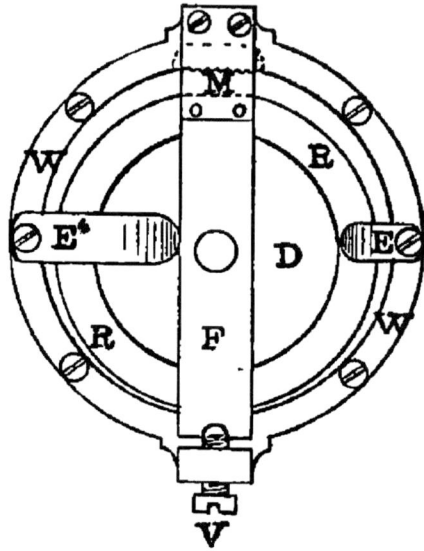

FIGURE 17.

ground that the contact between the carbon button and the platinum point is improved and deteriorated by movement of the diaphragm The indiarubber ring is most useful in that it prevents a vibration from con-

FIGURE 18

tinuing after the originating sound has ceased. If a long loose chain is shaken from one end the movement travels slowly to the end. The chain is, in fact, moving after one has ceased to shake it. If our diaphragm vibrates after we have ceased to send sound waves on to it, we shall have jarring and blurring of sounds, and to get rid of this the indiarubber ring is employed. It effectually damps out these after-vibrations. Our diaphragm must be the exact converse of a tuning fork, which latter is a persistent vibrator. The whole transmitter is contained in a square box, the front of which is hinged, and a hole is cut and turned to serve as a mouth-piece. The external appearance of the Blake transmitter, as manufactured by the Consolidated Telephone Company, is shown in Figure 18.

For short distances the Blake is very efficient, but is by no means satisfactory for long distances. It was used by the National Telephone Company until recently to the exclusion of all others.

Class III.—Granular Transmitters

The granular transmitters are instruments in which carbon in granular form is used. The great trouble with transmitters of this class is that they become practically useless when the granules become damp and clogged. The Hunnings transmitter was the first of this class, but it is not at all satisfactory as a practical instrument. It consists of two platinum plates D and B (Figure 19), the space between which is filled

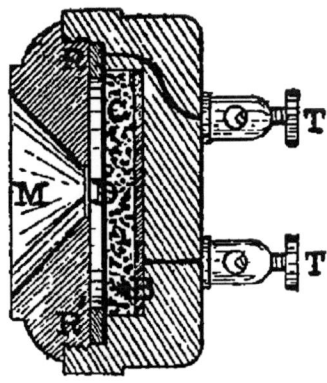

Figure 19

with little carbon granules. The front plate D, held in position by means of the ring RR^1, acts as the diaphragm. The cover carrying the mouth-piece M serves to clamp the diaphragm D in position. A small fine wire grid is put across the mouth-piece to arrest moisture. The principle of action is that when the diaphragm moves inward the granules are brought into closer contact and thus the resistance between the two plates is reduced, and when the movement is in the outward direction the converse takes place. Undoubtedly the Hunnings transmitter is more powerful than any of the transmitters which have been described. Now let us examine its defects and see what remedial measures can be adopted. The transmitter must of necessity be vertical, otherwise the granules would not always be in contact with the diaphragm, since the effect of working the instrument is to cause the granules to settle down into the smallest possible compass When the instrument has been in use some time the granules at the bottom of the diaphragm become closely packed, and correspondingly loose at the top. The part of the diaphragm which moves most under sonorous vibrations is the centre. At the outside all round the diaphragm the movement is inappreciable, consequently we have the granules all round remaining in practically the same condition as regards resistance of contact Further, at the bottom the granules are very tightly packed, and form a sort of short-circuit across the centre part The contact resistance of the granules between the front and back plates at the centre of the diaphragm is varied to a very large extent, but the granules round the edges, particularly at the bottom, do not vary, and therefore we have our variation very much reduced. For instance, let us isolate, say a half-inch circle of granules at the centre of the plate, and assume the resistance offered in the normal position to be, say, 10ω. Let us now start an organ pipe, which causes the resistance to vary from 5ω to 15ω; we have here a variation of 100 per cent., but now if the resistance of this outer set of granules be 5ω we shall merely have the variation between the joint resistance of 5ω and the lower, and 5ω and the higher resistance—*i.e.*, between $2\frac{1}{2}\omega$ and $3\frac{1}{2}\omega$, or $33\frac{1}{3}$ per cent. Thus it will be realised how serious is the "*packing*" trouble, as it is called. In the first case the transmitter is three times as efficient as in the second.

As has already been stated, the Hunnings transmitter originally consisted of a platinum diaphragm, between which and the backplate of carbon is placed a layer of granulated carbon. This granulated carbon consists of oven-made engine coke powdered and sifted free from dust. Many improvements were introduced by Charles Mosley, of Manchester The platinum plate was replaced by a very fine thin board, in the centre of which was fixed a small carbon disc, forming one electrode, the back of the instrument, as before, forming the other electrode The effect of this improvement was to confine the current to the central granules—that is to say, the granules in contact with the small carbon disc attached to the diaphragm Further, the space was made wedge-shaped, the point of the wedge being at the bottom—*i e.*, the diaphragm and the back of the transmitter were inclined together These improvements resulted in very greatly enhanced efficiency, owing largely to the greater uniformity of contact amongst the loose granules. The packing trouble was not even here entirely eliminated The granules became set and wedged together, thus little variation in the degree of contact took place. The packing trouble does not manifest itself until the transmitter has been in use some little time. The transmitter must always be in the vertical position, otherwise the granules will settle down, and the diaphragm will not always touch them when at rest—a very necessary condition.

The "Hunnings-cone" invented by Deckert is, perhaps, the most reliable of the many granular transmitters. This is the instrument

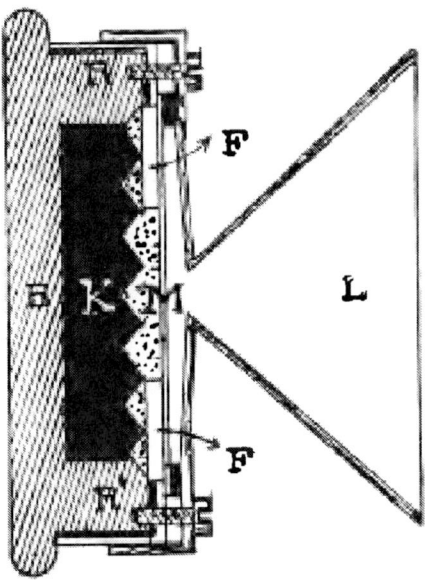

FIGURE 20

adopted by the Post Office, for whom it is manufactured by the General Electric Company. The object of all the improvements which have been

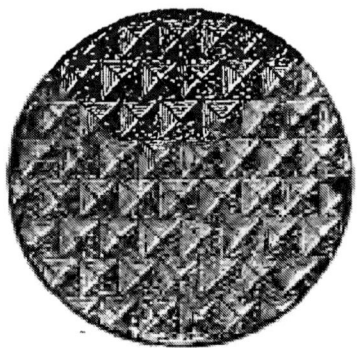

FIGURE 21.

made from time to time upon the original Hunnings transmitter has been to eliminate the packing difficulty. The Deckert transmitter shown in section in Figure 20 consists of a carbon diaphragm M and a backplate of carbon K, which is cut into the shape of little pyramids, as shown in elevation in Figure 21. Further, the space between them is filled with granular carbon. It will be noticed that the ridges between one pyramid and the next fall opposite the centre of the pyramid above and below (Figure 21). This prevents the granules from running from the top to the bottom along the ridges.

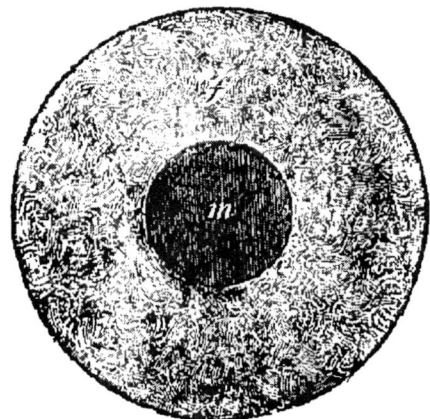

FIGURE 22.

The cones keep the granules well distributed, and thus uniformity of contact is secured. In order to prevent the trouble which arises from the granules becoming packed at the bottom of the cones, the diaphragm is fitted with a woollen ring F F, so that only the granules in the centre of the transmitter are active. A plan of the diaphragm is shown in Figure 22. The central set of pyramids opposite m in Figure 22 are

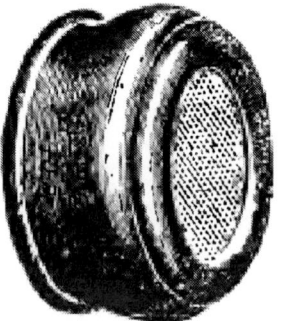

FIGURE 23.

fitted with little tufts of silk at their points, and tend to damp out any vibrations which are not continuously sustained, and, as we have seen, an efficient transmitter must on no account be a persistent vibrator. One terminal of the instrument is formed by the metal ring R R', upon which the polished carbon diaphragm is mounted, the backplate of carbon forming the other terminal. The external appearance of the Post Office form of this transmitter is indicated in Figure 23.

A new Deckert transmitter works admirably and leaves but little to be desired, but after it has been in continuous use for some time, say three or four months, its efficiency becomes much impaired, due to bad connection between the ring R R' and the diaphragm, also to the granules becoming wet and packed; but this can easily be remedied by a skilled mechanic The Deckert, or, as it is more commonly termed, the

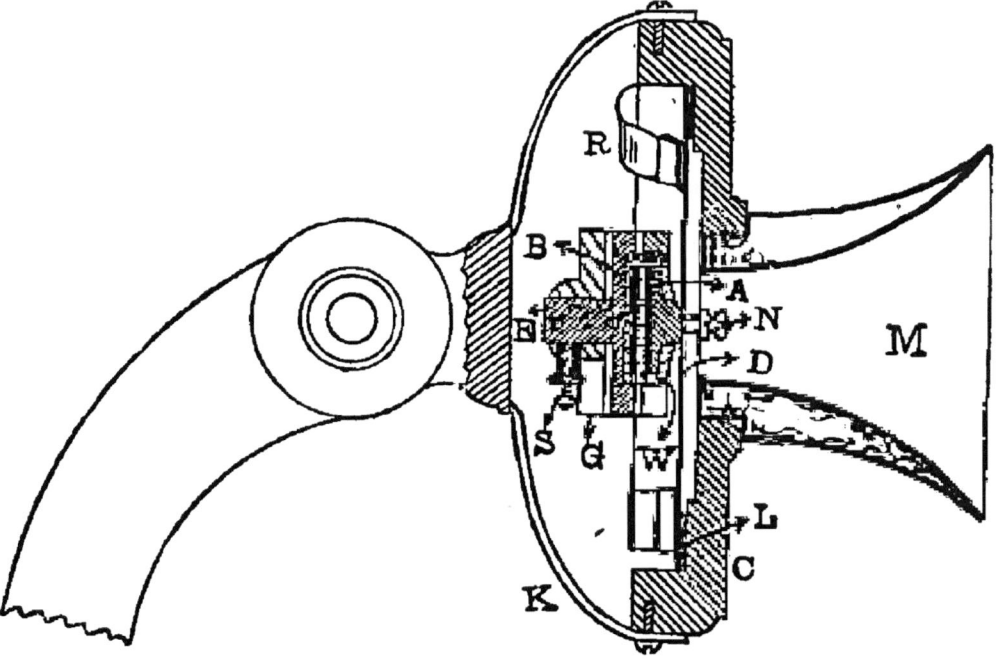

FIGURE 24.

Hunnings cone transmitter, is certainly one of the best long distance transmitters in the market. The National Telephone Company are fitting these transmitters in connection with their new systems, and it is hoped that this course will result in increased efficiency when speaking over long distances.

Another form of transmitter, very much used in America, is the solid back. It consists of two very small discs of carbon A and B placed in a small chamber or cell filled with carbon granules. The movement of the diaphragm D causes the nearer approach of the discs and thus more intimate contact between the granules. The instrument is shown in

Solid-back Transmitter.

section in Figure 24. The diaphragm, which is of ferrotype, carries the carbon disc A, bolted to it by means of a small screw N, and is clamped around its periphery. The second electrode and containing cell is carried by the mica washer, and is adjustable by means of the screw S. The interior of the cell, which is lined with insulating material, is filled with carbon granules. It will be noticed that the electrodes are somewhat smaller than the chamber, and the object of this is to cut the granules out of circuit at the bottom of the chamber. This gets rid of the packing difficulty in this case. The current passes through the granules directly between the electrodes. This, of course, tends to render the transmitter very efficient. A small spring R coated with indiarubber serves the purpose of damping out any vibrations which tend to persist after the originating cause has ceased to act. The ferrotype diaphragm forms the one and the back electrode the other terminal of the instrument.

This instrument is undoubtedly one of the most efficient transmitters in use to-day, but unfortunately it is somewhat delicate, and will not stand rough usage. From the above description it will be gathered how very small the working parts are, and hence how liable to damage. It is, however, used somewhat extensively by the American Bell Telephone Company.

The Breastplate transmitter used by the Post Office is of the Ericsson form, and a full and detailed description will be found in Chapter XIII., when the various switch-board accessories are dealt with.

CHAPTER VI.

BATTERY TELEPHONE STATIONS.

Having examined some of the leading types of transmitters and receivers, it now becomes necessary to consider what arrangements will have to be made in order that the instruments may be put to practical uses. First of all some means of calling attention to the instrument must be arranged, as a telephone is not usually required sufficiently often to justify continuous attendance, and a bell and a key must therefore be added at each end for calling purposes.

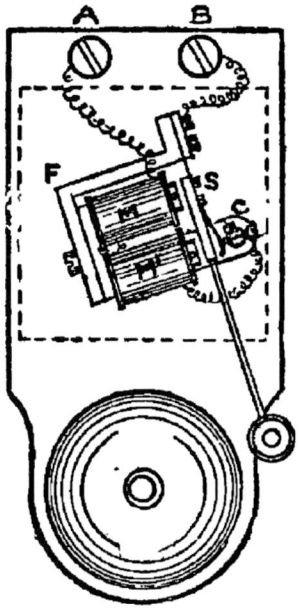

FIGURE 25.

The trembler bell electrically consists of an electro-magnet, the circuit of which is completed through its armature. The electro-magnet MM¹ (Figure 25), consisting of two coils, is fixed to a brass frame F, which is in turn secured to the wooden base. To the top of the brass frame a steel spring S, carrying the armature, is secured by means of screws

It will be seen that the spring is prolonged beyond its junction with the armature and rests upon the platinum pointed screw which is carried by the binding pillar C. This pillar is insulated from the brass frame of the instrument by means of an ebonite washer. The bell-hammer is screwed into the end of the armature.

The path of the current is from the terminal A, through the electro-magnet, on to the contact screw C, and along the steel spring S, out on to the brass frame of the instrument, thence to the second terminal B. Thus the circuit is only complete so long as the spring touches the contact screw. The connection of a battery between the terminals A and B will cause the hammer of the bell to vibrate backwards and forwards. The current, in passing through the coils of the electro-magnet, causes it to become a magnet, and the armature is attracted towards it, causing the hammer to strike the bell. Immediately the armature moves towards the coils the spring S is pulled from the contact C and the circuit broken. This causes the soft iron cores to become demagnetised, and the steel spring then restores the armature to its normal position, when the contact is again made. This alternate make and break goes on, and the armature is thus kept in a state of vibration.

It will be equally obvious that we might arrange our bell so that when the armature was attracted the coils of the electro-magnet would be short-circuited. For some purposes, where it is undesirable that the circuit should be broken, this arrangement is preferable, but ordinarily this is not important, and the disadvantage of running the battery the whole time and the risk of bad contact at the short-circuiting points far outweigh any advantage. Unless the contact is perfect the arrangement is most inefficient, far more so than would be the case in the ordinary form.

The spring contact screw is tipped with platinum at the point of contact in order that the sparking, due to self-induction when the circuit is broken, may not impair the contact. Platinum is selected, as it is inoxidible and infusible at all but enormously high temperatures. It should be noted that the distance between the armature when down and the electromagnet is never less than 1-32nd of an inch. This distance can be adjusted by means of the pole pieces which are screwed on to the cores. The magnetic circuit is completed through the armature and through the piece of iron which joins the lower extremities of the cores. The mechanism is usually protected by means of a wooden cover. The resistance of the bell varies with different makes from about 15^ω or 20^ω to 100^ω, which latter figure represents the resistance of the Post Office form. In this pattern of bell the ends of the coils are brought to four brass connection plates, so that the coils may, if desired, be connected in parallel, thus reducing the resistance from 100^ω (in series) to 25^ω for short or local circuits.

An arrangement must also be introduced by means of which the bell, ordinarily connected to the line wires, is cut out of circuit and the speaking apparatus joined up. The key for calling the distant station must cut out both the telephone and the bell and put a battery direct on to the lines. Our key must then have two positions. Firstly, at rest one line wire must be joined through to the second switch, the purpose of which is to insert either the bell or the telephone as required. Secondly, on depression a battery must be joined up between the lines. Lastly, a third switch must be provided, by means of which the microphone battery is cut off when the instrument is not in use in order to prevent unnecessary waste. The two lines necessary for satisfactory telephone working are termed the "A" and "B" wires respectively for purposes of distinction. A double wire circuit is termed a "*metallic circuit*" in contradistinction to an earthed or single wire circuit (see Chapter XXII.)

The A wire (Figure 26) is led to the end of a brass spring A, which normally rests upon the top contact. The depression of the brass spring establishes a contact with the bottom stop, to which is joined the positive pole of the battery B', the negative being joined to the B wire. The top contact is joined to the centre of the switch-arm D, which is very similar

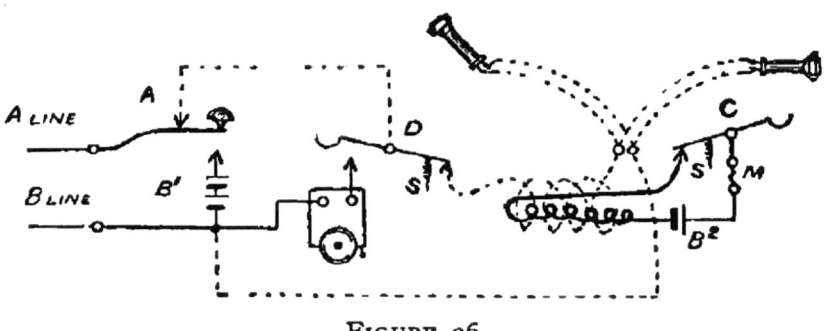

FIGURE 26.

to an ordinary single current Morse key. The end of the switch-arm is shaped so that the receiver may be hung upon it. The weight of the receiver holds the arm down in opposition to the spring S, thus establishing contact between the lever and the front stop. Raising the receiver from the arm allows the spring to raise the lever, and thus establishes contact with the back stop.

The instrument is only in use for speaking purposes when the receivers are lifted off the rests, consequently the back stop is joined to the secondary of the induction coil and the receivers (which are joined in series), the other end being connected to the B line. The front stop is connected to the bell, the other terminal of which is joined to the B wire. The right hand switch-arm is arranged to join up the speaking battery through the microphone and primary circuit of the induction coil by completing the circuit between the back and central contact of the lever.

In the case which we have been considering two switch-arms were employed, and this necessitates the use of two receivers The two receivers are always joined in parallel, but in series with the induction coil, as shown in Figure 26 When both receivers are raised from the rests the microphone and receivers are joined up. Speaking on to the diaphragm causes variations of the current strength in the primary coil which leads to the production of E.M Fs. in the secondary. The currents sent out flow through both receivers on the B line, thence through the distant station's receivers and secondary of induction coil on to the A line, thence to the ringing key A, through the top contact to the left switch-arm, and through its back contact to the secondary coil where the E.M.F. originated This is the speaking circuit. The receiving speaking circuit is from the A line through the ringing key, left switch-arm, receivers and secondary of the induction coil to the B line, as shown by the dotted lines When the diaphragm of the transmitter is quiescent no E.M Fs are produced in the secondary, consequently the received speaking is not interfered with. The speaking currents sent out pass through your own receivers, and this fact may be demonstrated by tapping the microphone or by blowing upon it, when a distinct sound will be observed. By depressing the ringing key or push A, the battery B' is connected between the A and B lines, no matter what position the switch-arms are in   A current received when the switch-arms are down passes from the A line through the top contact of the ringing key to D through its front stop, thence through the bell on to the B   A current of from 20 to 30 milliamperes will be required to ring the bell.

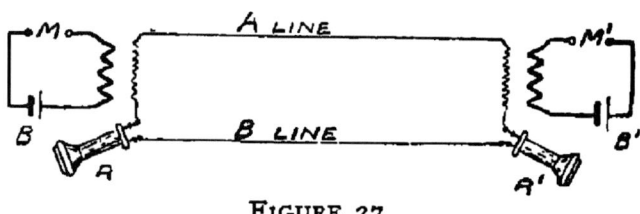

FIGURE 27

A diagram (Figure 27) shows the connections of the speaking circuits when two stations have raised their receivers from the rests The line circuit consists of two sets of receivers, R and R', two secondary coils, and the A and B lines themselves. The primary circuits are quite separate and distinct from the line circuit, and it is thought that this diagram renders the matter sufficiently clear.

It is preferable to use two receivers so far as the speaking is concerned, as the addition of the second receiver does not sensibly reduce the volume of sound produced in the first, and, further, both ears are closed by the receivers, and are thus less influenced by external sounds. One receiver is, however, quite sufficient, and it can be held to the ear whilst writing down a message. When only one receiver is used a switch-arm of a somewhat less simple character is required. In addition to joining up the receivers and secondary or the bell, according to its position, it must also complete the microphone circuit. In the Crossley telephone an ordinary switch-arm, with the addition of an insulated metal plate and two springs, is used. The switch-arm (Figure 28) has two positions When down,

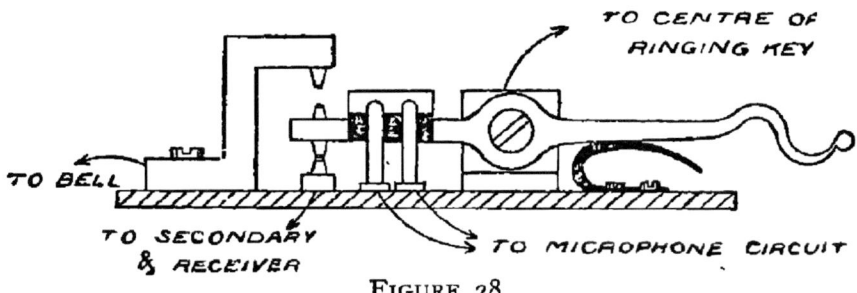

FIGURE 28

the lever makes contact with the top stop, thus joining up the bell The two springs, which are the extremities of the microphone circuit, rest upon the ebonite plate, and are disconnected. When the receiver is lifted off, the steel spring causes the lever to rise, making contact with the bottom stop, and thus joining up the receiver and secondary coil The two springs now rest on the insulated metal plate, and are thus connected, completing the microphone circuit It was soon discovered that this insulated plate was quite unnecessary, as the switch-arm itself might be used for the purpose of completing the microphone circuit, and in many modern single receiver stations this is accordingly done.

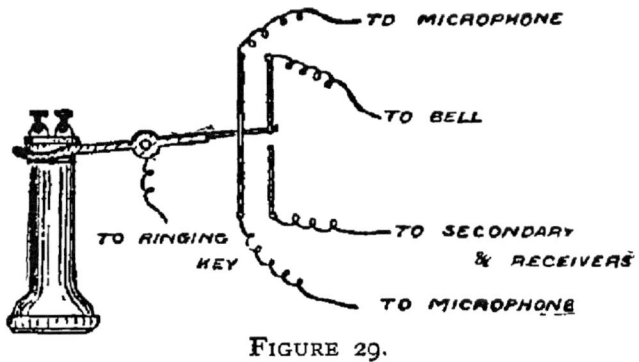

FIGURE 29.

In the Post Office form of the instrument the two circuits are kept distinct, two springs being provided. The switch-arm (Figure 29) consists of a brass lever, the end of which is in the form of a circular rod. The two right hand springs correspond to the top and bottom contacts of the Crossley form. A small ivory stud projects from the side of the arm, and when the receiver is taken off pushes the two microphone springs together, thus joining up the speaking battery. In the double receiver form two similar switch levers with two separate pairs of springs are employed.

Nearly every telephone has a different form of switch-arm, but only three forms have been described A very superficial examination of actual apparatus wi l at once render the particular device adopted and the object of each part perfectly obvious. The differences are purely mechanical in the majority of cases The three types described are three forms used at various times in the Post Office

Instruments of this class with trembler bells present some disadvantages. In addition to the two cells required for speaking, a ringing battery has to be provided, and this battery has to be maintained. In the case of a private wire from residence to manufactory this is not a very serious consideration to the owner of the wire, but where perhaps a couple of thousand subscribers have to be joined to a central exchange the matter becomes all important. The batteries require periodical examination, whereas a magneto generator does not This at once resolves itself into a commercial question of pounds, shillings, and pence.

CHAPTER VII.

THE LECLANCHÉ CELL.

For battery telephone stations the Leclanché cell is found to be most suitable on account of the absence of local action and the small amount of attention required. The cell consists of a square glass containing vessel in which is placed the zinc rod. The porous pot carries the carbon plate packed round with manganese dioxide. The exciting fluid is salammoniac, which has no effect upon the zinc until the circuit is closed, when the following reactions take place:—

Outer cell:—

$$Zn + 2NH_4Cl + 2H_2O$$

One molecule of Zinc, together with two molecules of Salammoniac, and two molecules of Water

$$= ZnCl_2 + 2NH_4HO + H_2$$

form one molecule of Zinc Chloride, together with two molecules of Ammonium Hydrate, and two atoms of Hydrogen

Inner cell —

$$H_2 + 2MnO_2 = Mn_2O_3 + H_2O$$

Two atoms of Hydrogen and two molecules of Manganese Dioxide form one molecule of Manganese Sesquioxide and one molecule of Water

The manganese dioxide is frequently made into a solid block and placed next the carbon, thus doing away with the porous pot.

A battery used for telephonic purposes must be free from local action, as the time during which the instrument is in use is very small as compared with the time it is idle. The battery is usually employed only for a very short time, and is then given plenty of time in which to recover before it is again used. The Leclanché cell possesses no local action, but polarises somewhat rapidly if the current is kept on for any length of time, because the hydrogen arrives at the carbon plate faster than the depolariser—i.e., the manganese dioxide—can get rid of it. This is particularly the case with the ordinary porous pot form in which the manganese is packed round the carbon plate in the porous pot. An illustration of this type of cell as manufactured by the Consolidated Telephone Company is shown in Figure 30. The agglomerate form represents a distinct advance in that the internal resistance of the cell is greatly reduced by the absence of the porous pot. The manganese dioxide is mixed with carbon and is pressed into the form of a solid block. The blocks are held in position on the carbon plate by means of indiarubber rings. Sometimes the zinc is held in a small porous pot, as shown in Figure 30. This precludes all possibility of the zinc touching the carbon and thereby causing a short-circuit.

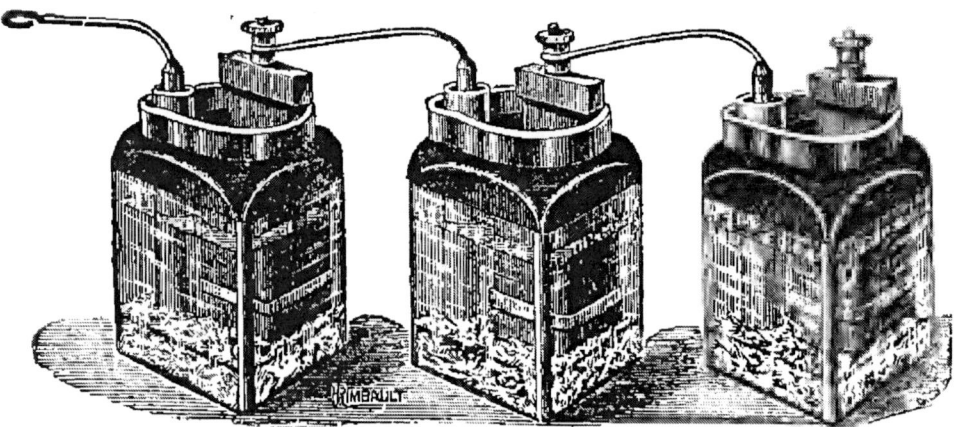

FIGURE 30.

In the form of cell used by the Post Office the zinc rod is provided with indiarubber rings at top and bottom, and thus the same object is accomplished without the resistance introduced by the porous pot.

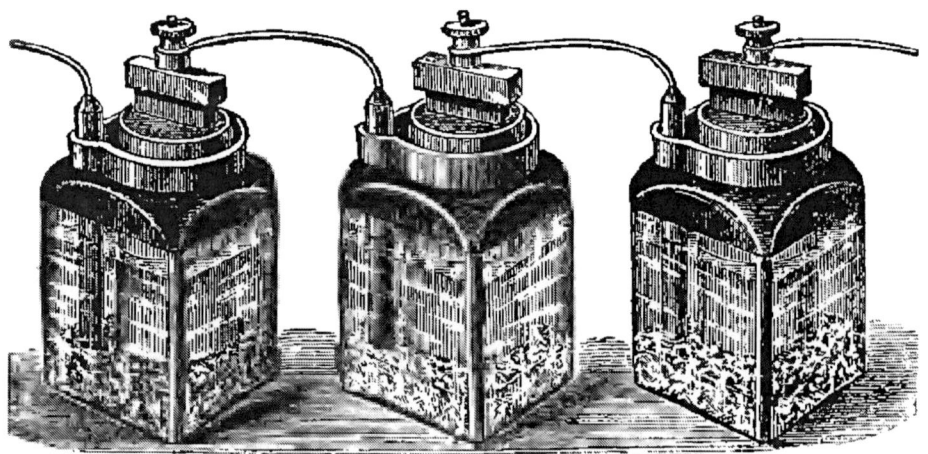

FIGURE 31.

There is far less polarisation in this form of cell than in the ordinary type, and it is therefore more efficient. A special form of agglomerate cell is used for speaking purposes. It consists of a thick carbon rod grooved to receive the edges of six agglomerate blocks composed chiefly of carbon and manganese dioxide (Figure 32) The blocks are placed in position, and coarse cloth of a canvas nature is wrapped round the arrangement, and the whole is then held in position by means of two indiarubber rings. A circular zinc plate surrounding the negative element reduces the internal resistance of the cell by distributing the current through a very much larger quantity of the liquid than is the case with a zinc rod These large zinc plates were found to be very wasteful, as the current is not evenly distributed throughout the area of the zinc, the result being that the zinc is worn away very

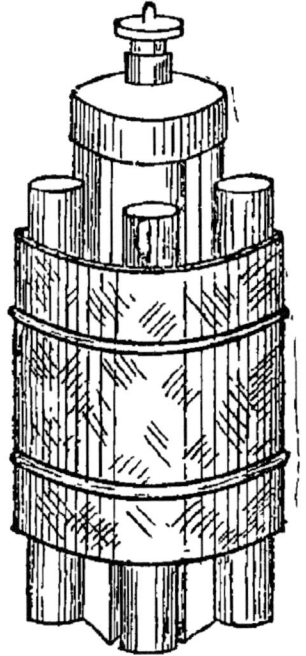

FIGURE 32.

unevenly. A hole occurred about an inch and a half from the bottom and also at the point where the liquid ceases at the top It was found by experiment that the size of the zinc might be greatly reduced without proportionately increasing the resistance of the cell by using the form of shallow circular zinc shown in Figure 33 This zinc, instead of resting on the bottom of the cell, is suspended from the top by the lug, which is bent backwards. The whole of the zinc is immersed below the liquid The complete cell is termed the six-block agglomerate Leclanché, and is contained in a circular earthenware jar. Two cells are used with the Deckert transmitter and give most excellent results, but, in the Post

Power Necessary for Speaking and Ringing.   43

Office exchanges, it is found that, with a new and carefully adjusted breast-plate transmitter, one cell gives better results, as the speaking with two cells is exceedingly heavy and muffled, a man's voice coming through in the form of an indistinct roar For ringing purposes a cell

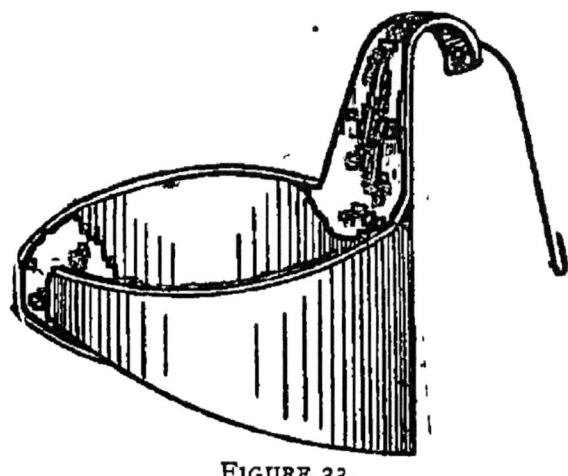

FIGURE 33.

with a higher internal resistance answers the purpose equally well. The two six-block cells are usually supplemented by sufficient cells of the ordinary form to provide the ringing current. The six-block cell does not polarise to so great an extent as the ordinary cells.

CHAPTER VIII.

Magneto Telephone Stations.

The magneto generator and bell is used by the National Telephone Company upon all their systems, and in order that the working of both the trunk and local systems may be apprehended it is necessary to discuss this apparatus. The object gained is to reduce the battery necessary at the subscribers' offices. The generator provides alternating currents in return for the mechanical energy expended in turning the crank handle. The bell is designed to ring with these currents and will be described first. It consists of an electro-magnet A B, with a pivoted armature J rendered

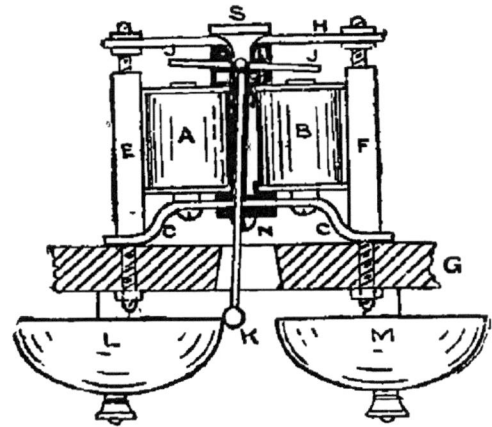

Figure 34

magnetic by induction from a permanent magnet N S (Figure 34) A thin steel rod carrying a brass ball is screwed into this armature at right angles to it, and plays between the two bell domes L and M. The diagram sufficiently illustrates the mechanical construction.

The south pole of the permanent magnet is immediately above the centre of the armature, thus rendering the centre north and both ends south. The electro-magnet is joined up in the ordinary way; thus a current in one direction flowing through it will cause A to become north and B south. The armature is repelled at B and attracted at A, thus holding the hammer upon the right dome. Reversal of the current makes A south and B north; the armature is therefore attracted at B and repelled at A, the result of which is that the hammer passes over to the left hand dome. It will be seen that a succession of currents in opposite directions will cause the hammer to vibrate between the two domes, thus giving a ring. Adjustment of the play of the armature is made by moving the domes bodily, screws for that purpose being provided. The distance between the armature and the electro-magnet is adjustable within small limits by means of the nuts on the screwed pillars of the frame work.

FIGURE 35.

The external appearance of a magneto bell is shown in Figure 35. Its resistance is now 1,000 ω, though formerly many of lower resistances, 100 ω to 500 ω, were used. The high resistance bells require far less current, and in a large exchange this is an important matter, as the pulling up of the generator is very serious. During the busy hours of the day the generator would almost stop were 100ω bells universal, and it is obvious that the lower the speed of the generator the less is its E.M.F., and thus many of the bells would not be rung at all. In order that the principle of the magneto generator may be clearly comprehended, it will be well to refer back to the theory of the induction coil. It has previously been stated that whenever a conductor is cut by magnetic lines of force E.M.Fs. are generated in that conductor. It would, however, be more accurate to say that whenever the number of lines of force passing through a system of conductors is altered, an E.M.F. is generated. The magneto generator takes advantage of this fact. A coil of wire is twisted round in a strong magnetic field in such a way that the number of lines of force passing through the coil is continuously changed. The magnetic field is produced by the strong permanent magnet (Figure 36). The system of conductors, together with its mechanical support, is termed the armature. The form of armature now universally adopted is that used in the dynamo invented by Dr. Werner Siemens in 1858, and consists of a bar of iron wrought into the shape of the letter "H." The two sides of the H are curved, as shown in Figure 36, in order that they may the more closely fit the pole pieces. In fact, it consists of an iron cylinder into which are cut two wide deep slots so as to leave only a relatively small central bar, around which a large number of turns of wire are wound. This is the shape of the armature in section. It is usually about an inch in diameter and from three to four inches long, and is wound with silk-covered copper wire of about 40 S W.G —i.e., ·0048 inch in diameter. When the curved ends of the armature are at the top and bottom the lines of force nearly all pass from the north pole of the magnet through the curved ends of the armature to the south pole, scarcely any

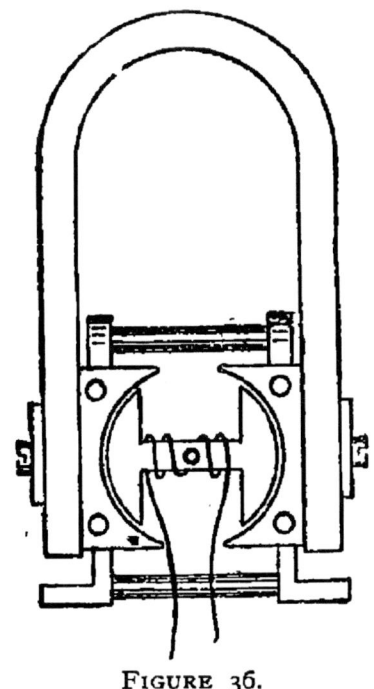

FIGURE 36.

lines of force passing through the central or cross portion of the H—*i.e.*, there is the minimum number of lines through the conductors. Imagine now that the armature is revolved until the curved ends of the armature are precisely opposite the two pole pieces, as shown in Figure 36. The lines of force all crowd through the small air-gap into the curved end and through the central portion out on to the other curved end, thence through the small air-gap to the south pole. Here, then, nearly all the lines pass through the conductors. In moving from the first position, where very few lines passed through the conductors to this one, where a very large number pass through the conductors, E M.Fs. have been induced as the number of lines through the conductors have been gradually increased

Magneto Generator.

from none to the maximum. This represents a quarter of a revolution, and at this point the E.M.F. falls to zero. On moving forward till the first position is reached there are again no lines through the conductors. The lines, on threading out of the circuit, produce an E.M.F. in the opposite direction to that produced when threading in. On moving forward to the second position, lines have again been threaded through, but in the opposite direction, as the faces of the armature have been reversed; this produces an E.M.F. in the same direction as the decaying lines. At this point the E.M.F. again falls to zero, and on turning to the first position is again at its maximum value, but in the opposite direction, falling to zero as the second position is reached. Hence it will be seen that in

Figure 37.

one revolution of the armature fresh currents in opposite directions are induced.

A very small movement of the armature from the first position causes a much larger alteration in the number of lines passing through the armature than an equal movement from the second position. A consideration of these facts will show us that the largest E.M.Fs. are produced when the movement is from the first position, and smallest when from the second. The number of lines through the armature is continually changing as it revolves; consequently E.M.Fs. are continuously induced.

These E M.Fs. rise to a maximum at the first position, fall to zero at the second, then rise to a maximum in the opposite direction, and again fall to zero as the second position is reached; hence we see that the current is reversed in direction twice per revolution. The external appearance of a combined magneto generator, bell, and switch lever is indicated in Figure 37.

There is yet another point which will have to be considered in the design of our magneto generator, and that is as to how it should be joined up with the bell. It is not desirable that we should have the bell and the generator in series, since we should have to waste a goodly proportion of the energy of our distant generator in overcoming its resistance. A switch is therefore placed on the armature of the generator, by means of which the generator is short-circuited when not in use, but immediately the handle is turned the short-circuit is removed. There are many forms of switch for this purpose, but the one most generally used is the one illustrated below in Figure 38. It consists in so arranging the spindle, upon

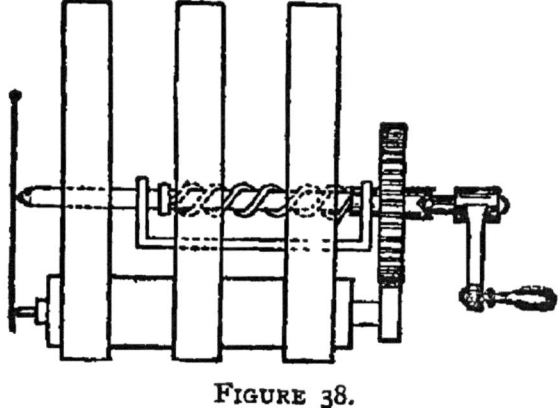

FIGURE 38.

which the wheel driving the armature is fixed, that when rotated it moves over slightly to the right, thus breaking a contact   The spindle has a pin put through it, and this pin rests in two triangular grooves   It is held to the narrow end by means of a spiral steel spring. When the handle is rotated the pin rides to the top of the groove, where it catches the top edge, and the armature then begins to rotate When the pin rides to the top the spindle inside the tube upon which the wheel runs moves forward, thus breaking contact between this spindle and the spring which rests upon it at the end.

The ends of the armature coil are connected to the spindle and spring, which are in turn connected to one side of the magneto bell and the switch-arm. It will be seen that a current from the distant station passes from the spring to the spindle, thence on to the magneto bell without

Connections. 49

traversing the resistance of the armature. On rotating the armature the short-circuit is broken, and alternating currents pass out through the bell to the distant station, there actuating the distant bell. The bell at the calling station rings, and this gives an indication that the circuit is com-

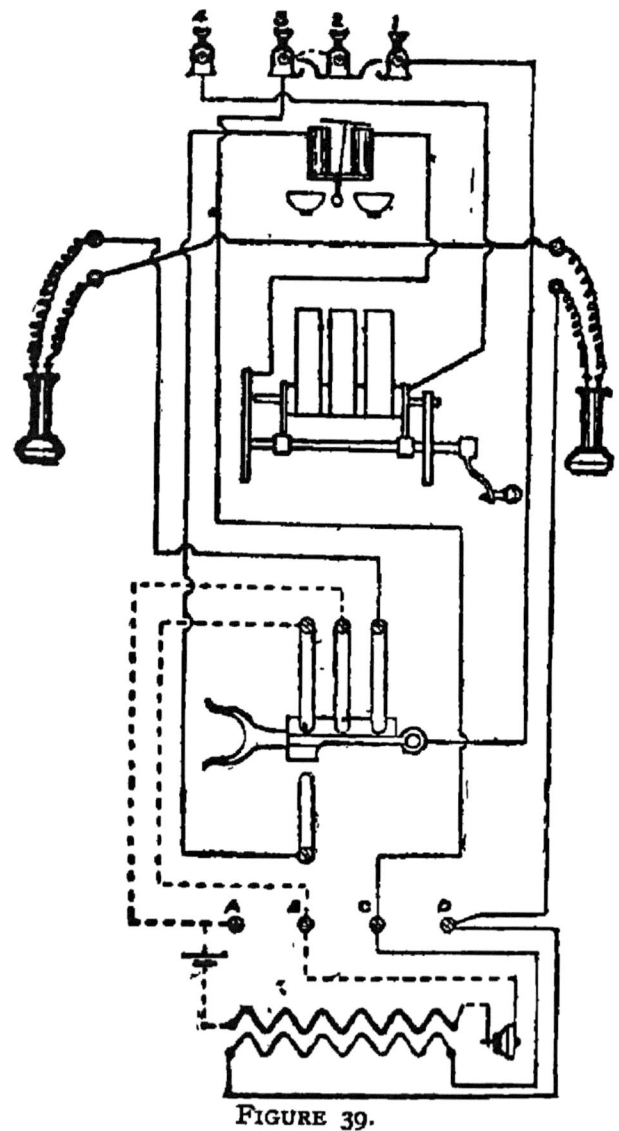

FIGURE 39.

plete. It corresponds somewhat to the galvanometer which is used in the case of telegraph circuits. If the wire is disconnected the bell at neither station rings.

E

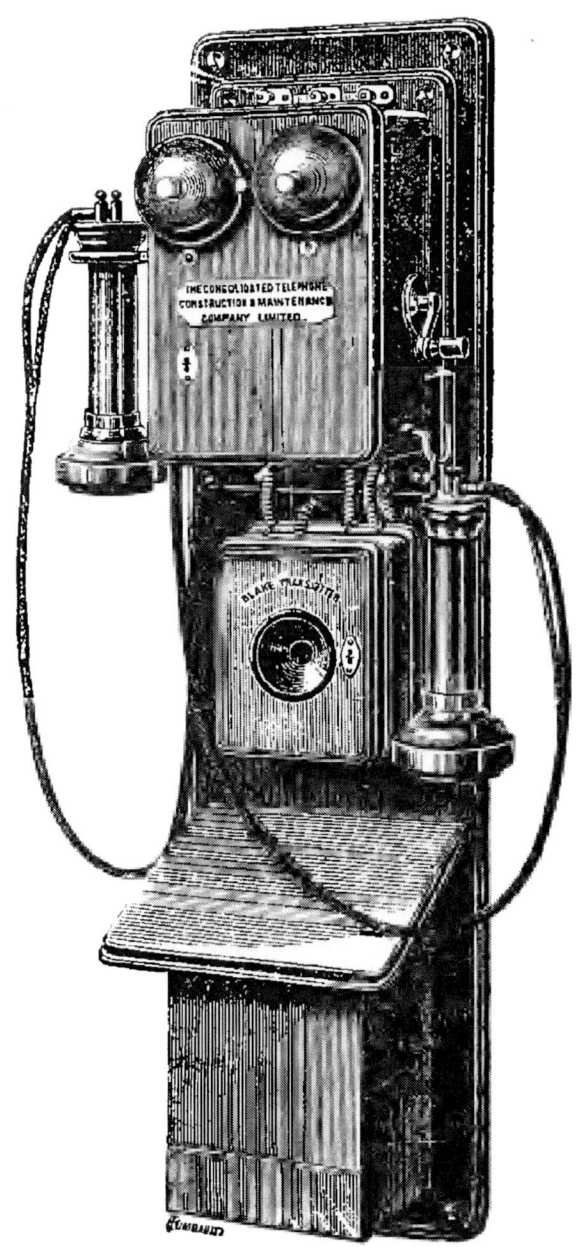

FIGURE 40.

There are some magneto-generators which are joined up so as to cut out the magneto bell and ring direct on to line, but it is very questionable whether this is altogether an advantage. The amount of force required to turn the handle when the wire is disconnected and when the circuit is complete is very different, so that perhaps this indication might be deemed sufficient. This plan is adopted in connection with the call wire system in operation at Manchester.

Another plan for bringing about this short-circuiting of the armature is to place a disc of brass upon the spindle. Near the edge of this disc a hole about half an inch long is cut. A sleeve is placed upon the spindle, and upon this sleeve is placed a crank which carries a pin fixed at right

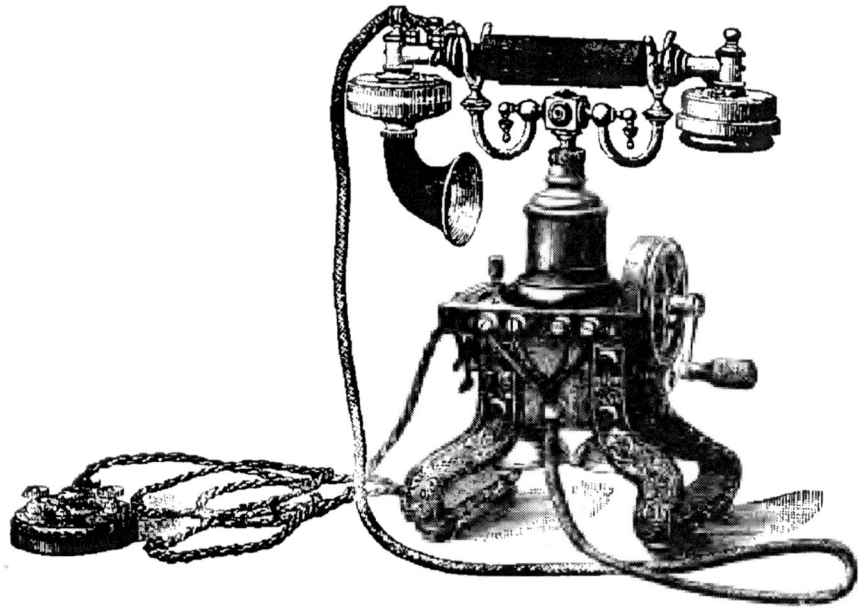

FIGURE 41.

angles to it and passing through this slot. The pin is held to one end of the slot. The other end of the slot is insulated with ebonite. On revolving the crank the pin moves from the metal on to the ebonite at the other end of the slot, and then begins to rotate the armature. It will be seen that the disc and pin are in contact when the generator is at rest, and are disconnected when the pin rests upon the ebonite. In the former position the armature is short-circuited.

In yet another form of generator, a spring with a small weight or bob fixed to the end of it is screwed on to the armature. The spring rests upon a contact. When the armature is rotated the bob, owing to centritugal force, flies away from the contact, thus breaking the short-circuit. This form of instrument is very little used, and is not so reliable as the first-mentioned device, which is now almost universally adopted.

We have now considered all the essential parts of a magneto-generator station The only other point which needs consideration is the method of joining up This does not greatly differ from that adopted in the case of battery stations. The press button is not required in the case of the generator. One switch-arm only is necessary, and serves the double purpose of completing the microphone circuit and joining up the receivers. When the arm is held down the bell and generator in series are connected between the two lines The full connections are indicated in Figure 39, and should require no further explanation.

The appearance of a Bell-Blake set is indicated in Figure 40, and it may be remarked that this instrument is in very general use in this country. The Blake transmitter is, however, now being replaced by a form of Deckert which fits into a Blake case.

For table purposes the Ericsson set shown in Figure 41 is very popular. The generator and bell are contained in the lower part of the apparatus, and are very compact The transmitter and receiver are mounted upon an ebonite handle with a press lever to complete the microphone circuit. The cradle upon which the telephone rests actuates the switch lever, and it must be admitted that the instrument presents a very pleasing appearance.

CHAPTER IX.

Post Office Telephones.

In 1882 the Gower-Bell was pronounced to be the best and most reliable telephone in use. Its great advantage was that, in addition to

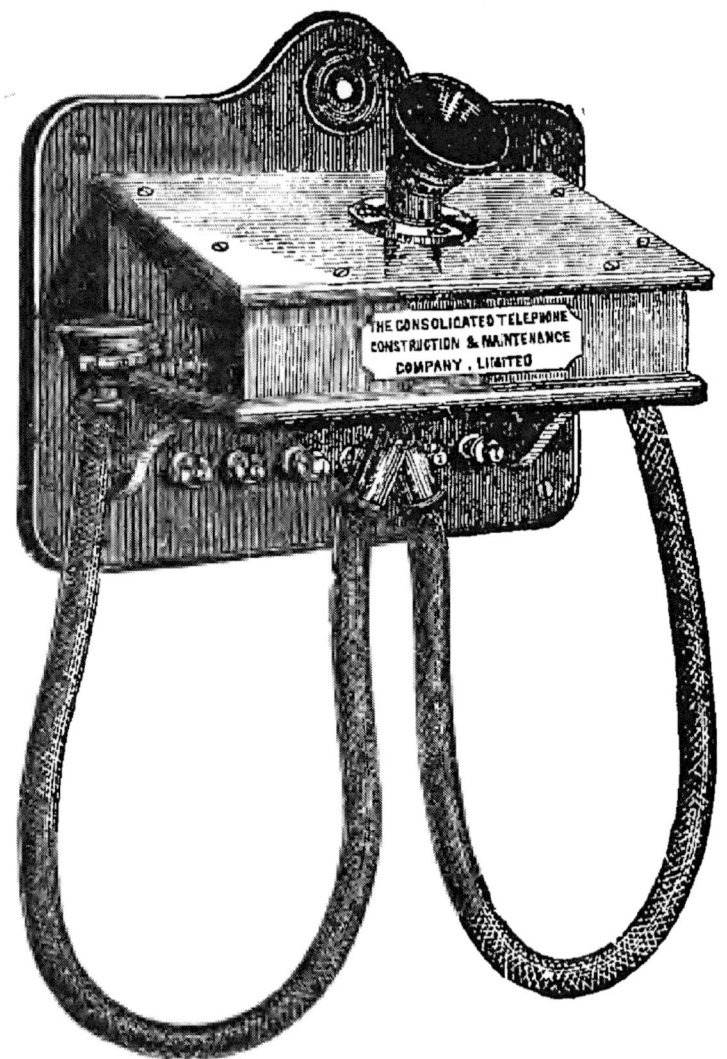

Figure 42.

being efficient as a telephone, it required no adjustment, and when once fixed remained in working order without attention. Indeed it held its place in the Post Office until very recently, when the Deckert transmitter was introduced. Figure 42 shows the external appearance of this telephone as manufactured for the Department by the Consolidated Telephone Company. The wooden diaphragm is covered by the top board of the instrument. In the centre of this board a hole is cut, and a brass tube carrying a china mouthpiece is fixed. This mouthpiece concentrates the sounds of the voice, bringing them more forcibly upon the transmitter than if the diaphragm were left open. Care is of course taken that the diaphragm is left free to vibrate.

It has previously been remarked that the tubes and receiver are now replaced by two Bell receivers. In this form there are a great many

FIGURE 43.

instruments in use by the Post Office to-day. A much neater and more compact Gower-Bell telephone was designed, and this instrument is known as the Post Office Telephone. It is considerably smaller than the ordinary form, measuring 7 inches by 5 inches and projecting 6 inches. The diaphragm is stained black. The great objection to the china mouthpiece arrangement lies in the fact that moisture is condensed upon it, and when the telephone is much used most unpleasant odours are present. The transmitter is of the ordinary Gower pattern. Its external appearance is indicated in Figure 43.

Connections. 55

The internal connections of the Post Office telephone are shown in Figure 44. The transmitter is connected to two flanges upon the inside of the case A screw passes through the flange on either side, thus joining the microphone to the connections on the back board of the instrument.

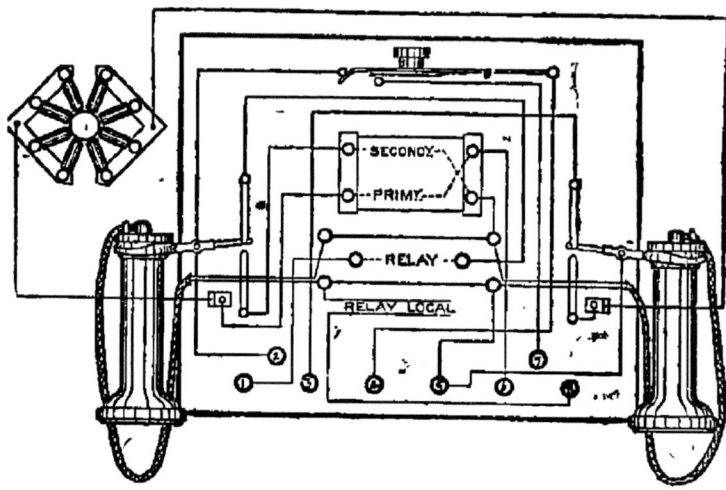

FIGURE 44

In this instrument two Bell receivers are shown joined up in parallel. The induction coil is fitted beneath the case, and formerly had a resistance of 5ω and 150ω respectively for primary and secondary. A coil having from $\cdot 9\omega$ to $1\cdot 2\omega$ and 25ω is now used.

The instrument is fitted with eight external terminals, which precisely correspond with the eight terminals fitted to the old Gower-Bell telephone. The two central terminals are connected to the lines From terminal 4 the current passes to the end of the lever button, along it to the left switch lever through the upper contact to terminal 1; from terminal 5 to the centre of the right switch lever, through the upper contact to 3. Thus the bell must be joined between 1 and 3. When the receivers are raised the left switch-arm joins them up, and the right switch-arm joins up the microphone battery, which is connected between 5 and 6. Terminal 7 is used for the ringing battery, which is joined up in series with the microphone battery, which unites with it.

It will be seen that two terminals are joined together by a dotted line, and are marked "relay." Where a relay is not used these terminals are strapped across, but when a relay is used this wire is removed, and the relay is joined between them. The local contacts of the relay are joined to the two wires marked "local" The relay is described in Chapter X

The Post Office Telephone is also fitted with one receiver in some cases, and in this instrument the terminals also correspond with those of the

Gower-Bell and Post Office telephone with double receivers. The adoption of this uniform system of connecting telephones up prevents any confusion when changing from one class of instrument to another. More recent telephones, fitted with Deckert transmitters, are joined up in exactly the same manner.

A table telephone has recently been designed for the use of subscribers, etc. It consists of an Ericsson switch-board telephone which rests upon two curved switch-arms. It is surmounted by a trembler bell, which, it may be remarked, is of the short-circuiting type. The gong covers the whole of the mechanism of the bell. Space is provided for the insertion of a relay inside the square wooden cover of the instrument. The instrument is of the universal type, and the bell may be replaced by a magneto-bell and generator for use upon telegram circuits.

It is frequently necessary to group three or more stations upon a single circuit, and for this purpose a switch having eight terminals is used by the Post Office. Four of these terminals are used for the two circuits, two for the telephone at the intermediate office and two for an extra bell. The switch has three positions, viz: 'up, down, and through.' In the through position the two circuits are connected together with the telephone, together with the trembler bell attached across the two lines in leak. The extra bell is in this case disconnected. When the switch is turned to down, the telephone is placed upon the down side and the bell upon the up side; turning to up, places the telephone upon the up, and the bell upon the down side. Here it should be remarked that telephones should always be connected in bridge or leak, as otherwise inductive disturbances will arise (see Chapter XXII). Not only that, but a bell in series with a line will greatly impede the speaking, on account of the self-induction introduced. This will, however, appear more clear when the later chapters have been considered.

CHAPTER X

THE LOCAL EXCHANGE SYSTEM.

The great utility of the telephone system consists in the fact that by special arrangements at a central office any subscriber's telephone line can be connected to any other.

The first exchange was a telegraph exchange at Newcastle, where the subscribers were all furnished with ABC instruments and arrangements were made so that any line could be connected to any other line. The Telephone Exchange is precisely similar, but in the course of time has become somewhat complicated to meet the various requirements

In providing for the inter-communication of subscribers the first requirement is some means of calling the attention of the exchange to the subscriber's circuit when necessary. Secondly, a means of joining up the exchange operator's apparatus to the line, in order to ascertain the nature of the service required and to call a subscriber up. Thirdly, a means of connecting one subscriber to another. Fourthly, some arrangement by means of which a subscriber can indicate that the connection should be severed.

First, let us consider the systems generally, and gain an idea of the *modus operandi*, and then consider the practical details. Clearly, an indicator of some kind must be placed upon each circuit, and also a special series of contacts by means of which that line can be joined up to the connecting apparatus The simplest form of indicator would be a galvanometer; but for various reasons this instrument would not be suitable for practical purposes. For the present, however, it will serve the purpose of indicating the general scheme. Therefore, imagine a galvanometer connected between the two lines from each subscriber. The lines must now be continued to some form of terminals. The terminals consist of specially-arranged springs termed "jacks" or "switch-springs" The connecting apparatus usually consists of two pegs joined by two connecting wires. The pegs are so arranged that when put into a switch-spring the lines are connected to the two conductors and thus to the second peg If now this second peg be inserted in any other switch-spring these two lines will be joined straight through There will be a galvanometer bridged across each of the two lines, and any ring will be indicated upon them This will provide for a completion or "ring-off" signal If, after the subscribers have spoken, one or both of them turn their generators or depress their battery ringing keys the needles at the Exchange will be vibrated, and thus indicate to the Exchange operator that the conversation is finished, when the pegs will be removed and all left as at first. In order to provide for the operator's apparatus we may arrange a second peg connected to a telephone, which, when inserted into a switch-spring, will join that line to the telephone. We might also so arrange matters that by turning a switch the operator's telephone is thrown across the two conductors of the cord This plan possesses a very great advantage in that it reduces the switching operations. Under the first arrangement the operator would have to insert her telephone peg to ascertain who is wanted, place it in the wanted subscriber's switch-spring, gain his attention, remove her peg, and then make the connection from switch-spring to switch-spring. Under the second arrangement she would insert one peg of a pair in the wanted subscriber's switch-spring, depress a key or switch joining up her telephone to the pair of pegs, and ascertain who is wanted. She would then remove this peg to the wanted subscriber's switch-spring, and immediately upon gaining his attention would place the other peg of the pair in the calling subscriber's switch-spring, thus completing the connection This is much quicker, and allows the operator to listen and see that they are able to speak to each other. This is considered a disadvantage by some authorities, on the score of lack of secrecy; but, in the writer's opinion, a telephone operator is usually too much occupied to spare time to listen to conversations on business matters, which frequently would be quite unintelligible. Supposing, however, that operators heard every conversation, they would not be likely to repeat them in view of their undertaking not to do so (as in the case of telegraph messages).

There is a disadvantage in the systems outlined above, and that is, that when two subscribers are speaking two indicators are in circuit, thus reducing the clearness of the speaking In order to avoid this the springs are frequently so arranged that the insertion of a peg cuts out the indicator altogether Where this is done it is necessary to provide for an indicator for ringing-off purposes. This is done by joining a special indicator permanently across the two conductors joining the two pegs of each pair We now have one indicator in circuit in place of two, and this is a desideratum.

Having considered the scheme of a telephone system in skeleton, we shall now be in a position to follow the details involved.

The system adopted by the Post Office is remarkable on account of the method of obtaining an automatic call and ring-off. The subscriber's telephone is of the universal pattern, and is so arranged that when both receivers are placed in the switch-arms a current is sent out to the exchange. This current passes through an indicator bridged permanently across the lines, so arranged that the current through its electro-magnet holds up an iron shutter. When the current is stopped this shutter falls, calling the operator's attention to the circuit A small magnetised needle is also added, and this indicates when a current is flowing through the electro-magnet, and it is upon this that the ring-off or finished signal is observable The placing of the receivers upon the rests automatically restores the permanent current. In this system the operator is furnished with a separate peg for answering

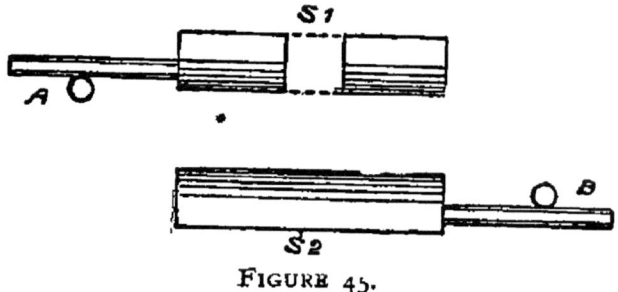

FIGURE 45.

The switch-springs consist of two springs S_1 and S_2 (Figure 45), resting upon two contact points, A and B The upper spring S^1 is cleft in order to permit the insertion of the peg. The springs curve backwards, and are fitted upon the back of the board by means of screws.

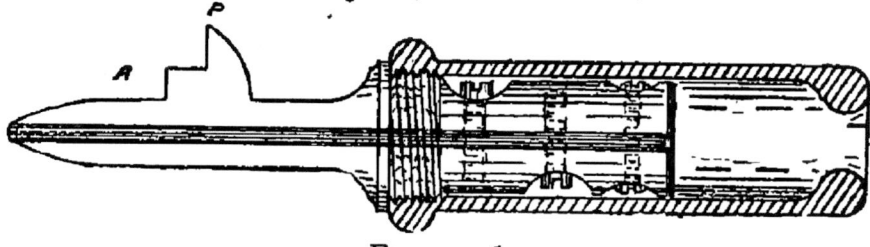

FIGURE 46.

The pegs consist of two flat pieces of flat brass A and B (Figure 46) insulated by ebonite, fitted with a handle. One of the brass pieces carries a projection P, which fits the cleft in the upper brass spring This ensures that the peg shall be inserted the right way up, and this, as will be seen later, is an important matter.

The indicator employed consists of an electro-magnet C and C^1 (Figures 47 and 48), in front of which is a circular iron ring R, pivoted at its lower extremity Between the two poles of the electro-magnet a magnetised needle N is hung. The protruding iron cores are covered with ebonite, in order that the needle may not stick to the pole pieces The back of the iron shutter is covered with paper, in order to prevent its sticking—due to residual magnetism. When the shutter drops, the small insulated spring S is brought into contact with the pin P, which is connected to the base or brass foundation of the instrument, and this contact is employed to ring a bell at night. It will be seen that the ends of the pole-pieces are connected by a piece of iron, which also serves to secure the electro-magnet to the base. The limbs of the electro-magnet are cased in by two

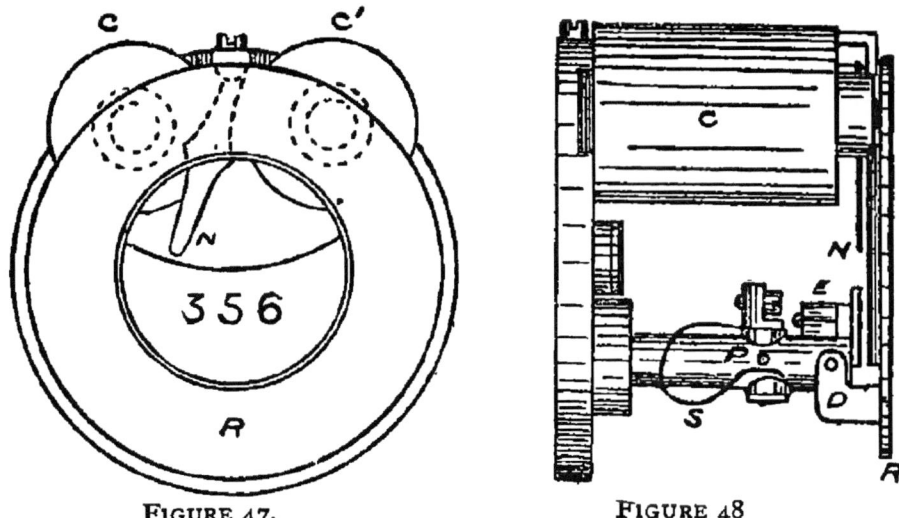

FIGURE 47.   FIGURE 48

thin sheets of iron, in order to prevent lines of force from straying out into the surrounding air. This prevents induction from one indicator to adjacent ones. If this were not done it would be possible to overhear conversations from one circuit to another whose indicator was next to it on the switch-board.

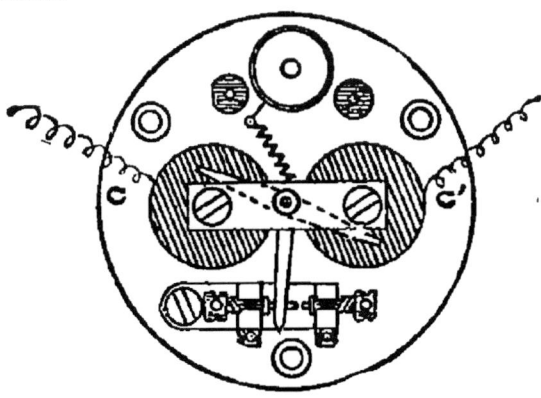

FIGURE 49

At the subscriber's end the permanent current passes through a relay which is biassed against it. The ring is thus produced by augmenting the current through the relay by joining up a battery at the exchange.

The relay employed is shown below in Figure 49. It consists of an electro-magnet with a pivoted soft iron armature held away from the

Subscriber's Instrument.   61

pole-pieces by means of the spiral spring, the tension upon which may be regulated by revolving the screw at the top of the instrument. This screw carries a hook about a quarter of an inch long, to which the spiral spring is attached. The tongue of the relay is provided with a platinum tip, which is brought into contact with the contact screw on the right when a sufficiently strong current is passed through the relay. The contact screw on the left, upon which the tongue rests, is furnished with an ivory tip.

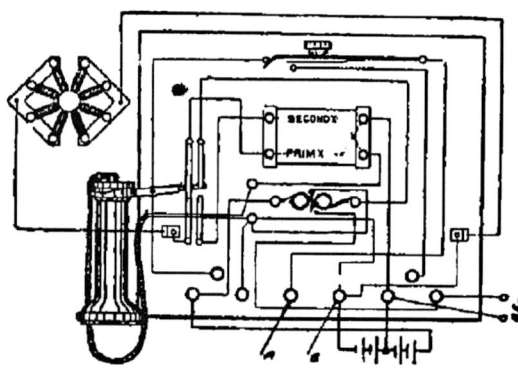

FIGURE 50.

The telephone at the subscriber's end is joined up as shown in Figure 50. It will be seen that the battery employed consists of four cells, two of which are used also for the microphone and also as the local battery for the bell. The permanent current, usually about 7 milliamperes, is sent out by the four cells. The resistance of the indicator at the exchange is 1000 ω, hence for reasonable distances the resistance of the line is of little account. The current flows from the positive pole of the battery to terminal 1, through the relay and right hand switch-lever spring, through the back contact of the press-button to the A line, through the exchange indicator along the B line to terminal 5, and back to the negative pole of the battery.

It will thus be seen that the removal of the receiver from the switch-arms stops the permanent current, thus dropping the exchange indicator. This automatic signalling is one of the distinctive features of the Post Office system.

The relay at the subscriber's end is biassed against the permanent current passing through it, and in order to effect a ring the exchange clerk joins a battery to the line, which combines with the subscriber's battery, thus overcoming the bias upon the relay and closing the local circuit. The path of this local circuit is from the split of the battery to terminal 6, thence through the bell to terminal 8, to the contact screw of the relay, and through the tongue back to the negative pole of the battery.

It will now be as well to consider the operator's apparatus The speaking apparatus consists of a Deckert transmitter and a watch receiver mounted upon a suitable handle (Figure 51) This handle is so arranged that when the receiver is placed to the ear the transmitter faces the mouth, and from what has already been said in reference to the

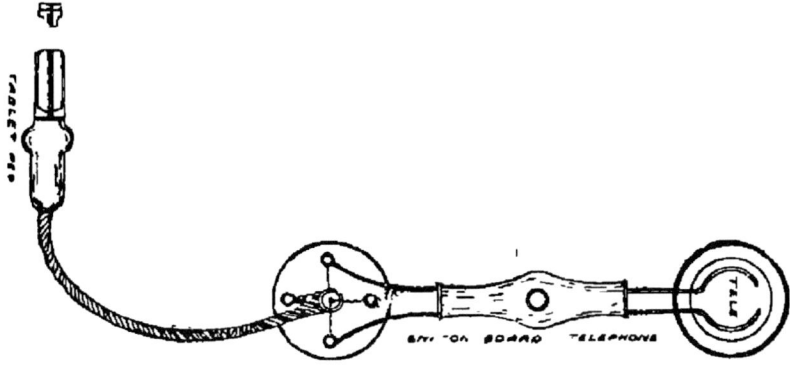

FIGURE 51.

vertical positions of granular transmitters It will be seen that the instrument should be held on a level with the nose, the head being held up. There is also a button placed upon the handle, and this button serves to short-circuit the secondary of the induction coil, thus leaving the receiver in circuit, but cutting out the transmitter, and thereby preventing the operator's breathing or conversation being overheard by subscribers engaged in conversation

It is also necessary to make provision for ringing subscribers, and it will perhaps be most convenient to consider this first A brass lever, pivoted at the back of the tablet and mechanically connected to a divided lever somewhat similar to that of a telegraph double-current key, protrudes from the front of the switch-board Two spiral springs (Figure 52) hold this lever down upon two contact springs, and in this position the divided lever joins up the speaking apparatus to the switch telephone switch-spring When the lever is depressed the call battery is connected to this switch-spring by means of the upper springs and divided lever A peg is usually kept in this switch-spring The insertion of the other peg of the pair into a subscriber's switch-spring allows the call battery to join with the subscriber's permanent current battery, thus overcoming the bias of his relay and ringing his bell

The switch-board telephone is connected to a peg divided into four parts, which in turn fits into the switch-spring upon the tablet. This switch-spring consists of four springs, which are in turn connected to the stationary apparatus. The connection between the telephone and peg is made by means of four conductor flexible cord.

Switch-Board Telephone Tablet. 63

When the lever is at rest the two halves make contact with the two bottom springs. The four-way peg carries a projection which fits the top switch-spring, thus preventing the peg being inserted upside down The primary circuit is from either speaking battery according to which position the two-way switch occupies, through the centre of the two-way switch, through the primary of the induction coil to the left top spring, thence through left top quarter of the peg through the microphone, back

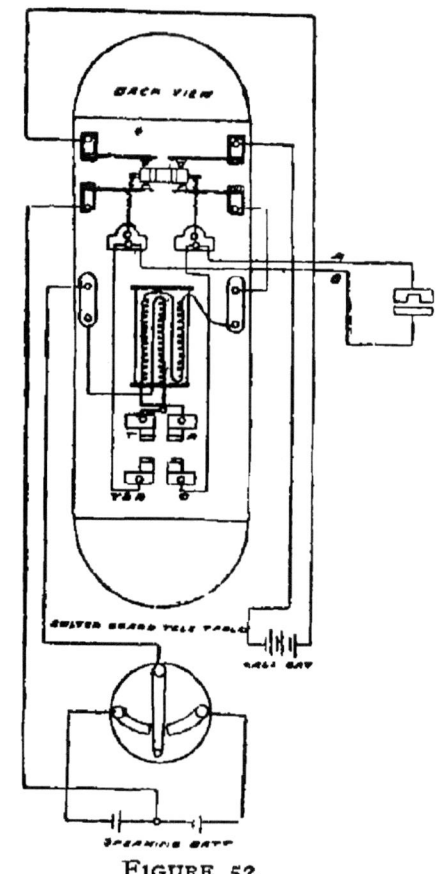

FIGURE 52.

through the bottom left hand switch-spring to the left hand side of the divided lever, through the left hand bottom spring back to the battery. It will be seen that when the lever is depressed the primary circuit is broken, thus preventing the battery from being run down. The secondary circuit is from the upper switch-spring upon the switch board (shown at the side of the tablet) through the right hand side of the divided lever, through the right hand bottom spring, through the secondary of the induction coil to the top right hand spring, through the receiver back to the left hand bottom spring (which we have seen also serves for one side of the microphone) to the bottom spring of the switch-spring from which we started. The button upon the telephone when depressed connects the bottom right switch-spring to the top right spring. The secondary of the induction coil is thus short-circuited from the top right spring, through the bottom right spring, through the right side of the divided lever to the other end of the divided coil.

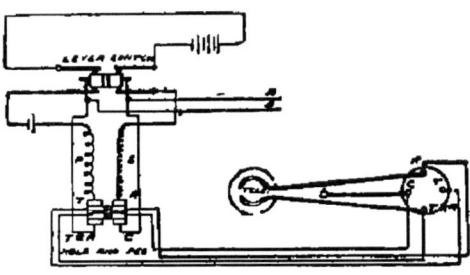

FIGURE 53.

The connections are shown in skeleton (in Figure 53), and the various parts of the apparatus labelled accordingly.

It is usual to hang the telephone upon the lever when not in use. This leaves the call battery always on to the operator's peg, but cuts the primary and secondary circuits

The fact that the operator is unable to listen to conversations might at first sight appear a great advantage, but in reality it is not so, as the operator would not find out that the subscribers were not speaking if the pair of pegs and cords were defective, and this is a very common fault.

A new switch has recently been designed for the larger offices, which is not a secret one. The replacing of indicator shutters takes time, and the tendency of all modern telephone engineers is to make everything automatic Accordingly, in place of the indicator with a shutter a polarised indicator relay is inserted. This instrument (Figure 54) consists of an electro-magnet with a soft iron armature rendered magnetic by induction from a bar magnet which also forms its support. The base of the instrument is of brass, as it was found that the use of iron, whilst improving the magnetic circuit, gave rise to a serious amount of trouble from residual magnetism, etc. The second permanent magnet N carries an iron needle, which it thus magnetically polarises. It will be seen that the needle will take up its position opposite the pole-piece of opposite polarity, and in this way will indicate the direction of the current passing through the electro-magnet. The terminals consist of four insulated brass washers. The left hand top point is connected through the left hand coil to the bottom right hand terminal, thence through the right hand coil to the top right hand terminal The terminal which joins the two coils together is only used for trunk working, and we may therefore leave it out of consideration for the present. The armature is normally held upon the right hand contact point by means of the spiral spring, the tension upon which can be varied at will by turning the screw which works upon the movable ring carrying the hook The left hand contact point, which is insulated, is connected to the fourth terminal, and the body of the instrument to which the armature is attached forms the other terminal. The connections are made by brass screws, which not only hold the instrument in position, but at the same time fit into pieces of brass which are, behind the switch, connected to the various points. A current passing through the indicator from left to right makes the left hand electro-magnet into a south pole, and the right into a north pole, thus deflecting the iron needle

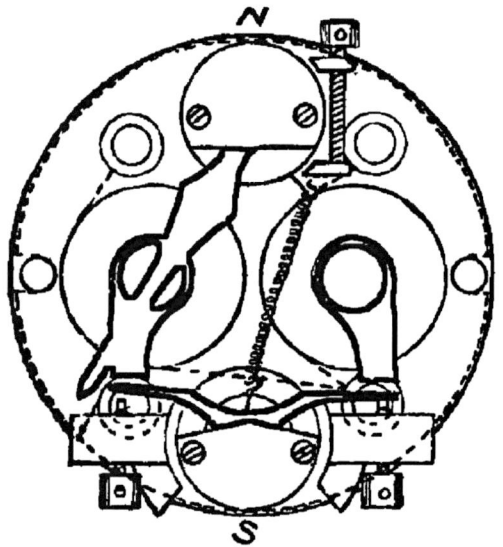

REAL SIZE.

FIGURE 54.

which by induction is made north, to the left At the same time the armature is deflected on to the left hand contact point. Both ends of the armature are made into south poles by induction from the lower magnet; thus the right hand side is attracted and the left hand side is repelled, so closing the local circuit The use of this local circuit is to close the circuit of an electric bell, thus calling attention to the circuit. The instruments are mounted upon a copper strip, thus connecting one side of all the local circuits together.

When two subscribers are put through, their permanent currents are stopped by the removal of their receivers, and they speak through in the ordinary way, the needles thus hanging vertically and indicating that these

F

subscribers are engaged Immediately they put their receivers back upon the rests as in Figure 55 (3 and 4) their permanent currents flow on to the line, where they meet and oppose each other, but each has a path through its indicator, deflecting both to the right and thus indicating that the conversation is finished. As it is only by the act of the subscribers that the needle can assume its normal position, the operator disconnects them without remark When the operator wishes to speak to a subscriber the peg connected to the speaking apparatus previously described is inserted The operator to effect a ring joins the calling battery to line in such a direction as to augment the subscriber's permanent current, thus overcoming the bias of the relay and closing the lock

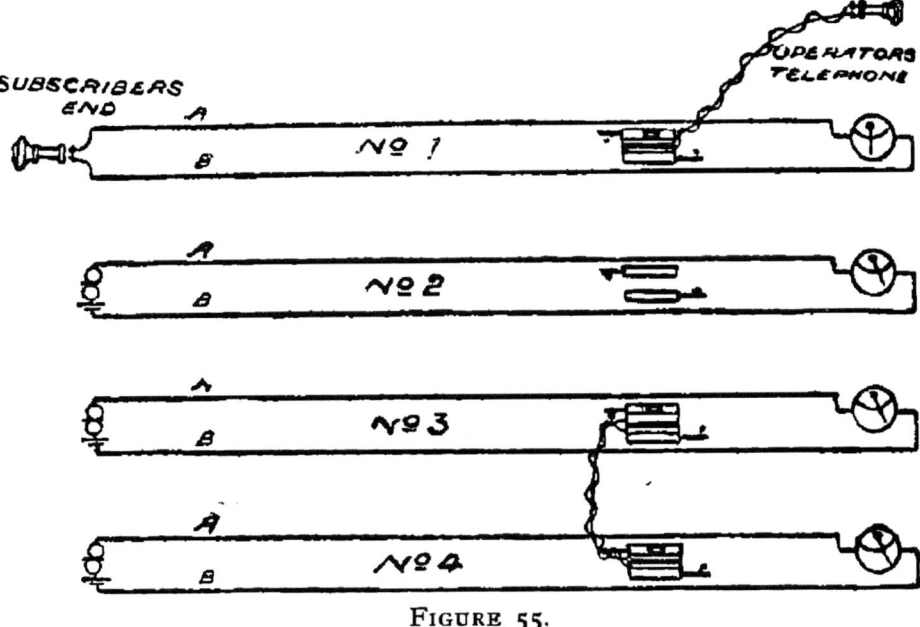

FIGURE 55.

circuit. It should be noted that normally the exchange indicator is deflected to the right.

The acquisition of the trunk lines rendered a new form of local switch absolutely necessary, but before going into its details it will perhaps be advisable to first describe in outline the modifications which have been made, and their object. First, the drop indicators have been replaced by the indicator relays. Secondly, provision is made for junction wires to the trunk switch sections, in order that renters may be put through on to trunk lines Thirdly, each renter's line is also brought to a plug switch-spring placed next to his switch-spring for the purpose of joining up the operator's set. This is accomplished by pulling out the plug a distance of about half an inch. This puts the operator's set across the lines. The pegs and cords are of the circular pattern and have no apparatus connected to them. The operator can listen to any conversation by withdrawing the speaking plug.

A circular peg is illustrated in Figure 56 The metal parts of the pegs are made in three parts. The part A is hollow, and a sleeve of ebonite C is placed inside in order to insulate the rod B Upon the end of this round rod is fixed a small circular ball D. Thus the screw marked E is in connection with the tip, and F with the body of the peg A The cords consist of two twisted tinsel strands insulated with cotton, wrapped round outside with wire; over this is a braided cotton cover The wire gives mechanical strength to the cord, thus preventing its wearing out as quickly as it would do were the wire omitted. The conductors are

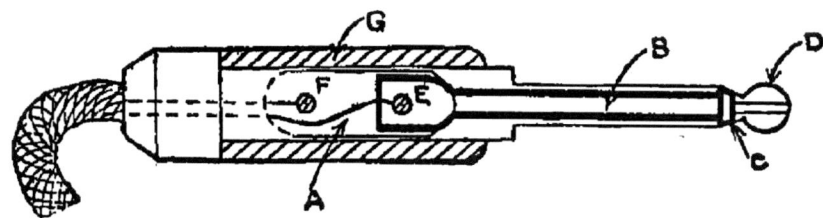

FIGURE 56.

soldered to two small copper tags, which are secured under E and F. The brass peg is covered by a red or black celluloid sleeve, which is held in position by a small screw. The tip of one peg is connected to the tip of the other, and shoulder to shoulder. The pegs and cords have no other connections, and the shoulders of the pegs rest upon brass brackets. The cords are held taut by means of weighted pulleys, in order to prevent tangling. The weights are arranged so as to run up and down guided by thin steel rods. The brackets are removable from the back of the switch; thus in the event of a fault it is not necessary to go to the front of the switch, thereby impeding the operator.

The renter's lines pass through the indicator relays, thence to the switch springs Each switch-spring is also "teed" on to the plug switches, which when withdrawn also " tee " the line on to the operator's set.

In Figure 57 the connection of two renters are indicated. Line 1 passes along to switch-spring No. 1 with the indicator "teed" across. The straight line is the A and the curved line the B line. The two springs are "teed" on to the two inner springs, and the round ebonite plug holds the two outer springs apart and prevents their making contact with the two inner springs. The two outer springs are connected to the operator's apparatus

The withdrawal of the plug allows the two outer springs to make contact with the inner ones, thus joining the subscriber's line to the operator's set, as shown at No. 2. The subscriber's switch-spring consists of two springs, the top spring being slightly longer than the lower one The top spring is slightly curved, and when a peg is inserted the curved end rests upon the tip of the peg The lower and shorter spring makes contact upon the shoulder of the peg. Thus the two lines of the subscribers are connected together by means of a pair of pegs and cords. The tips of the pegs connect the two "A" lines together, and the two shoulders connect the "B" lines

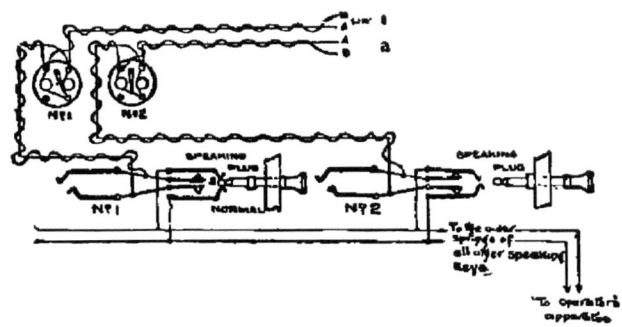

FIGURE 57.

together. The permanent currents behave exactly as they do in the case of the old switch In the normal condition the renter's permanent current from the subscriber deflects the indicator to the right The removal of the receivers stops the permanent current, thus causing the indicator relay needle to hang vertical. This calls the attention of the operator to the circuit, who withdraws that subscriber's plug, thus connecting the speaking set, and obtains the number of the subscriber wanted. The speaking plug of that subscriber is then withdrawn and the operator obtains his attention, and then completes the connection by means of a pair of cords and hears the renters speak. The speaking plug is then pushed back, thus cutting the operator out of circuit. When the renters put back their receivers both renters' needles are again deflected to the right, thus serving as an instruction to the operator to remove the plugs, which is accordingly done It should be noted that the relay tongue is biassed by means of the spring and held on to the right contact; thus the stoppage of the permanent current (which holds it off the left hand contact point) allows the spring to close the local circuit, thus effecting a ring.

The operator's connections are shown in Figure 58. The outer springs from the plug-switch pass through the central springs of the springs labelled "direct," through the inner springs, through the "reversed" springs, through the generator springs to the secondary coil and receiver of the operator's telephone. The receiver is joined to an ordinary peg and is inserted as shown, and the transmitter is similarly connected. The right-hand inner spring is connected through the secondary of the induction coil S to the left spring, through the tip along the shoulder back

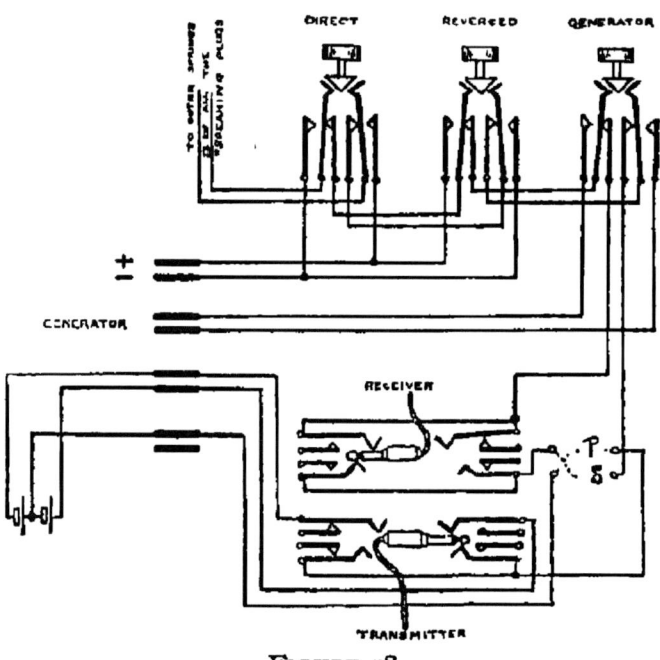

FIGURE 58.

to the inner left spring. The path of the primary circuit is from the right hand battery to the right hand long transmitter spring, through the transmitter back to the other pole. When the transmitter and receiver are reversed the other battery is inserted. The pegs must be inserted diagonally. The depression of the first peg puts a battery to line in one direction, and the second key puts on the battery in the reverse direction. The generator is put on to the circuit by depression of the third key.

CHAPTER XI.

Principle of Permanent Current System.

In dealing with trunk, *i e ,* inter-town wires, we confront quite a new aspect of the question. The National Telephone Company have established exchanges in nearly every town of any size, and subscribers' lines terminate at these centres. The trunk lines connect together the different centres or districts, and terminate at the nearest Post Offices. In order that a subscriber of the Company may be put through upon a trunk line he must be connected to the Post Office, who will put him through to the distant Post Office The distant Post Office in turn puts him through to the distant exchange of which his correspondent is a subscriber

The lines between the Post Office and the Company's exchange are termed "*junctions*" A junction is provided for every trunk terminated at the Post Office, so that should calls for all the trunks be received delay may not occur through there not being a junction at liberty. It has been found advisable to set apart a special wire or wires in addition for passing calls from the National Company to the Post Office and *vice versâ*, thus rendering indicators upon the junctions unnecessary. The apparatus required at the Post Office must be such as to enable the operator to see whether a trunk is calling, engaged, or disengaged , also to connect junctions and trunks together, and to be able to speak on the trunk and on the service wires. Further arrangements must be made for a ring-off signal.

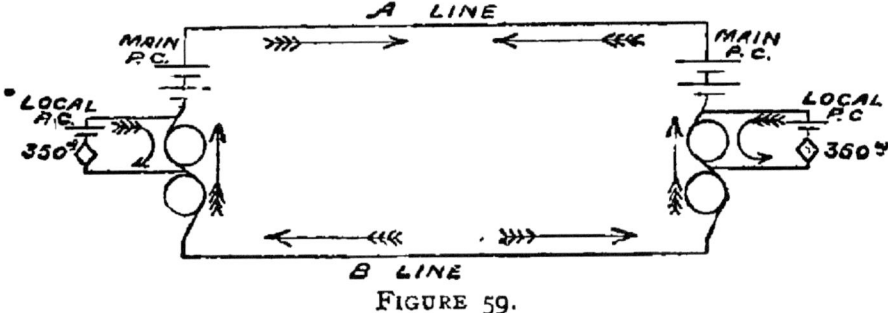

FIGURE 59.

First, it will be well to consider the principle of the automatic signalling upon trunk lines. A polarised indicator relay (described upon page 64) and two sets of batteries are employed, which normally (trunk disengaged) are joined up to the trunk, as shown in Figure 59. The larger battery usually consists of six Leclanché cells, and is joined up in series with the indicator and the trunk line. The battery and indicator are similarly joined up at the other end of the line; thus the two batteries oppose each other, and no effect is produced upon the two indicators. The circuit is thus in a state of equilibrium. The smaller battery consists of three cells, and is joined across the right hand coil at either end, and sends a current through this coil in such a direction as to deflect the needle to the right—i.e., in the opposite direction to the main permanent current. The local permanent current battery has a resistance coil of 350ω joined in series with it. It will be seen that the two main permanent current batteries oppose one another, and that the local permanent current batteries produce a deflection in no way interfered with by the other batteries. In the normal condition, then, both indicators are deflected to the right.

When a peg is inserted into the trunk switch-spring the apparatus, at the end where the peg is inserted, is entirely removed, and the lines are

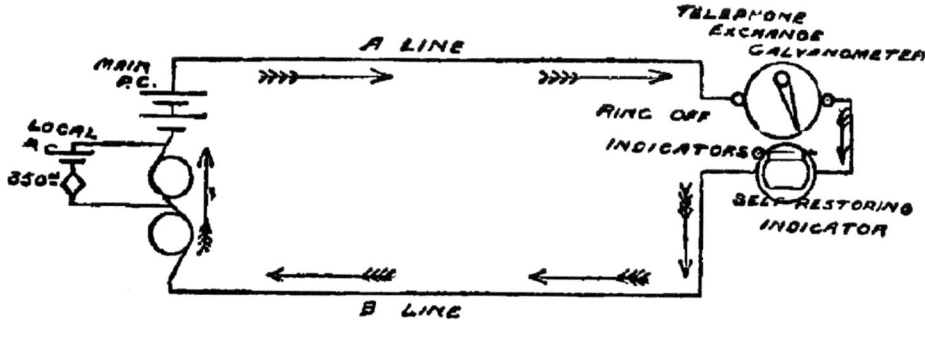

FIGURE 60.

connected through the ring-off indicator (which will be described later) connected across the cords. This condition is illustrated in Figure 60. The main permanent current battery is made sufficiently large to overcome the local battery and send a current through the indicator at the undisturbed end in such a direction as to cause a deflection to the left. The local permanent current flows through one coil only, but the main permanent current flows through both, thus doubling the magnetic effect of the relay upon the armature and needle. The 350ω coil is inserted in preference to using a smaller battery in order that the current due to the main battery may not pass through the low resistance of the battery in so large a proportion as to rob the right hand coil of current. It will thus be seen that the insertion of a peg at the distant end allows the main permanent current to overcome the local, thus reversing the deflection of the needle from the right (disengaged) to the left, which position indicates a call.

72 Connections of Trunk Switch-Spring and Relay.

Next it will be most convenient to consider the form of switch-spring. And here it may be mentioned that the word "*switch-spring*" has been substituted for the word "*jack*" by the Post Office. In the normal condition the switch-spring must maintain the connections as shown in Figure 59. The insertion of a peg must cut the circuit of the local battery and remove the indicator and main permanent current battery. It must also connect the trunk line itself to the peg. The switch-spring consists of seven insulated brass springs, in two sets of four and three springs, mounted upon a brass foundation. The lower four springs consist of two outer springs of different length and two inner springs making contact with them. The short spring comes into contact with the tip, and the long spring with the body, as shown in Figure 63. Thus the shoulder is connected to the B line and the tip to the A line. The central spring of the three springs at the top is moved upwards when the peg is inserted,

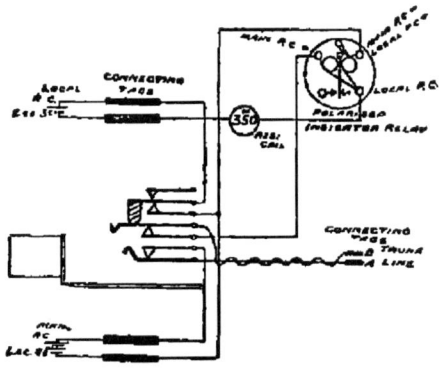

FIGURE 61.

thus breaking contact with the lower spring. This cuts the local permanent current circuit. The insertion of the peg also causes the two springs connected to the trunk to break contact with the inner springs, and this cuts the indicator and main permanent current battery out of the circuit.

The whole of the connections of the switch section terminate upon "connecting tags," which merely consist of thin brass stampings fixed edgewise into grooves in an ebonite block and secured by an ebonite cap. The ends of these brass stampings project beyond the ebonite, and have holes of sufficient size to take a No 16 wire at either side of the strip. Each strip, which is 6 in. × 1 in over all, holds twenty-four tags in four groups of six. These strips are screwed upon the inner parts of the side of the section. The left side (viewed from the front) is devoted exclusively to batteries, signalling wires, etc., whilst the other side contains the twisted speaking circuits. Each tag is numbered, and thus joining up is an ex-

Switch-Springs.

ceedingly simple matter. The manner in which the tags are appropriated in A, B, and C sections will be found in Appendix C.

The switch springs used by the Post Office are of two forms, the one having four and the other seven springs, the former being illustrated in Figure 62. The body or foundation of the switch-spring is of brass,

FIGURE 62.

one-eighth of an inch in thickness, the four springs fitting into straight nicks made in two thick ebonite washers, which are held together by screws. The shape of the body of the switch-spring is shown in Figure 62, and the circular brass tube fits into the ebonite foundations of the switch. When a peg is inserted, it passes through this tube and pushes the two outer springs open, and when pushed home is connected, as shown in Figure 63 It will be seen that the ball of the peg rests upon the

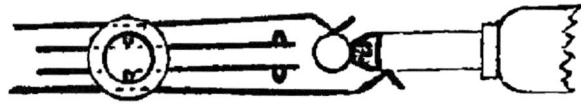

FIGURE 63

curved end of the shorter spring, and the long spring rests upon the back part of the brass peg. This raises the two outer springs off the inner springs, thus leaving the inner springs disconnected. In Figure 62 it will be seen that the long spring is in contact with the nearer inner spring, and the short spring is in contact with the other inner spring. These switch-springs are termed "*five-point switch-springs*," the fifth point being the body of the switch-spring, which is occasionally employed and serves to connect the body of the switch-spring to the long spring.

Switch-Springs.

The other form of switch-spring is the "*eight=point switch-spring*," which consists of seven springs. The three additional springs B, C, D are placed above the four springs, but at right angles to them (Figure 64).

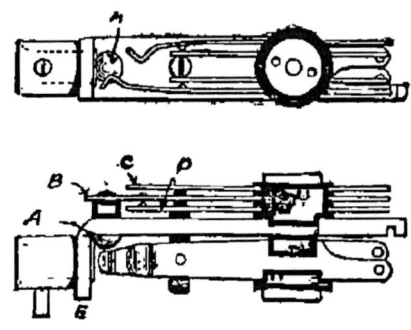

FIGURE 64.

The central spring carries an ebonite projection with a steel ball—resting in the body of the switch-spring. The insertion of a peg raises the ball, thus lifting the central spring from the lower to the upper spring.

CHAPTER XII.

Auxiliary Apparatus.

It has already been stated that two indicators—viz., the self-restoring indicator and the telephone exchange galvanometer—are bridged across the cords in order to register the ring-off signals The telephone exchange galvanometer (Figure 65) consists of two coils of wire mounted upon brass frames placed side by side, in the centre of which hangs a soft iron needle rendered magnetic by induction from the permanent magnet. The axle of the indicator passes through the permanent magnet at either end,

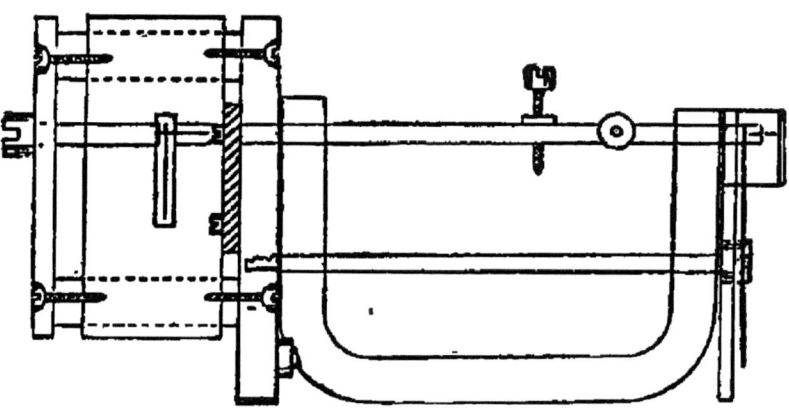

FIGURE 65.

terminating in pivots, one of which is secured in the removable pivot box fixed to the end of the magnet and the other at the back of the coils The axle is partly brass and partly steel. The portion passing from the left hand pole of the permanent magnet to the small forked soft iron needle is of steel. The remaining portion between the two poles is of brass. The coils of the instrument are wound upon two rectangular brass bobbins, which are removable from the brass base of the instrument. It will thus be seen that we have here a galvanometer with an induced needle. A light aluminium needle is attached to the other end of the pivot, serving as a pointer It will be noticed that we have both the pointer and the needle depending from the axle, and as this weight would render the instrument unsensitive, small balancing weights are provided. The first consists of a thin brass rod passing through the axle of the instrument, with round brass washers on either side Should the needle not hang vertically, compensating adjustments can be made by screwing the rod through the axle and clamping by the brass nuts. The second balancing system consists of a long thin brass screw, which passes through the axle in a straight line with the needles By raising or lowering the head of this needle, the weight of the aluminium and iron needles is to some extent balanced. The most sensitive condition of the instrument is when the arrangement is dead beat, this is to say, if, when momentarily deflected, the needle slowly returns to the central position without swinging from side to side. If the top screw is too high the weight of the screw will hold the needles over, even when there is no current flowing through the coils The coils terminate in four insulated collars, through which four brass screws are passed, thus serving to secure the instrument to the ebonite strip and also to connect it to the terminals at the back of the strip with which the screws are in contact. The resistance of each coil of the instrument is 500ω, as the coils have a very large number of turns in order that the very small current may produce a sensible magnetic effect. The coils of the indicators are always joined in parallel, thus offering a resistance of 250ω. In order that the black needle may be clearly visible, a circular green celluloid disc is fixed between it and the permanent magnet by means of two small brass pillars carrying screws.

In order to render the indications of the telephone exchange galvanometers more conspicuous, and at the same time increase the sensitiveness and reliability, it is in contemplation to provide a black disc in place of the present green one and to paint the needle white A strip of blackened brass of the same width as the needle will normally cover it. Stop-pins, limiting the deflection of the needle, will be provided, thus the small deflection will produce a conspicuous signal, inasmuch as a white needle will appear upon a black background. Signals, when they do not indicate a call, should be as unobtrusive as possible, and this object appears to be attained

It has been previously stated that a self-restoring indicator is joined in series with the exchange galvanometer This indicator (Figure 66) consists of two separate electro-magnets, each of which is iron-clad. The back electro-magnet is nearly three times as long as the front one, and before it is pivoted a heavy soft-iron armature held away from it by the weight of a long brass lever This lever is so shaped as to catch the armature placed before the front electro-magnet. The armature is of soft iron, pivoted at its lower extremity, and tilted slightly outwards, so that when the lever is raised it falls forward. A very light aluminium disc is suspended in front of this armature, and when it (the armature) falls forward the shutter is thrown forward by it, thus indicating a call. When the long coil attracts its armature the lever is raised, and the front armature being released throws the shutter forward. In order to restore the normal state of affairs a current is passed through the short coil, and this attracts the front armature, bringing it beneath the lever, where it is caught. The long coil is placed across the lines; thus any current passing along the lines leaks through this coil and drops the shutter. The shutter is restored by completing the circuit of a battery through the short coil by means of the speaking key when in the speaking position. It will be obvious that the indicator is not required to be down when speaking on the circuit to which it is attached.

The object of surrounding the electro-magnets with an iron sleeve is to concentrate the lines of force, thus preventing them from passing through contiguous indicators connected to other circuits. Were this precaution

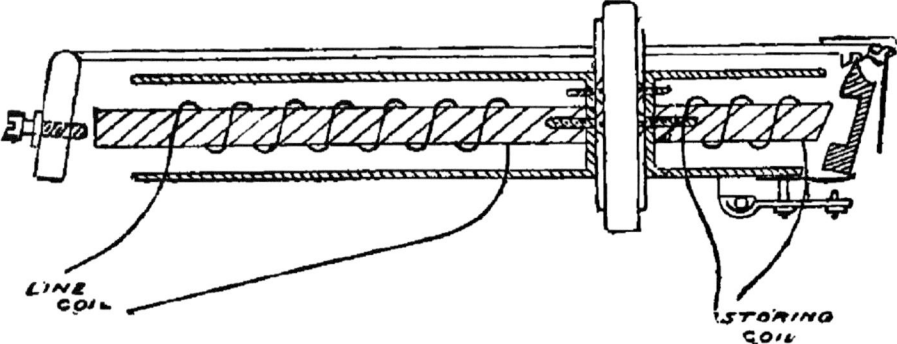

FIGURE 66.

not taken the lines of force would pass through the contiguous indicators, thus inducing currents which would reproduce the conversation upon the first circuit. A very little consideration shews that two contiguous unclad indicators are equivalent to an induction coil. Besides preventing overhearing, the iron sheathing also makes the magnetic circuit almost wholly of iron, thus rendering the indicator more sensitive. It also completely separates the two electro-magnets, so that there is little or no magnetic leakage from the line to restoring coil. The path of the lines is along the core into the iron disc at the junction of the coils along the sleeve through the air into the armature, and back through the air to the core. The line coil has a resistance of 1000ω and the restoring coil of 450ω. The former, when carefully adjusted, requires 5 milliamperes to actuate it, and the latter from 20 to 25 milliamperes. The local contacts consist of a very small light spring connected to the body of the instrument and placed beneath the bottom of the restoring armature. When this latter is thrown forward the spring is brought into contact with a small screw passing through an insulated brass projection. The body of the instrument and this projection thus form the local contact. The two electromagnets are fixed upon either side of an iron strip, which is secured at either end to the woodwork of the switch section.

These indicators, which are bridged across the cords, do not sensibly diminish the speaking currents, as their resistance is practically infinite to currents of such high frequency. The high self-induction is, of course, responsible for this state of affairs. (Vide Chapter XXIV.)

CHAPTER XIII.

OPERATING CONNECTIONS.

It is necessary to provide a means of ringing National subscribers. This is effected by means of a ringing key, which cuts off the black peg and joins a generator to the red one. The current passes over the junction to the subscriber, thus ringing his bell. Similarly, a battery is provided for the purpose of ringing Post Office subscribers, and also in order to assist the distant main permanent current in the event of its not being

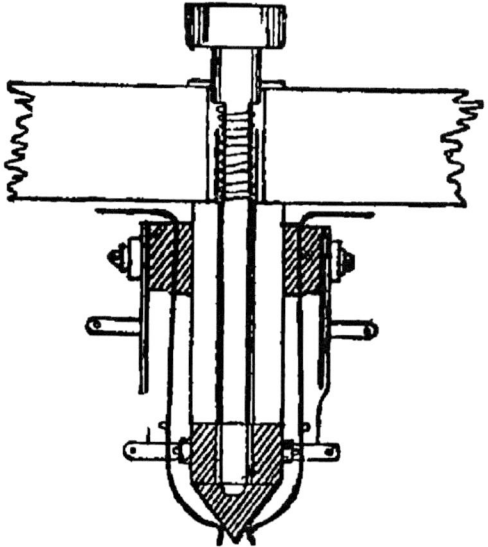

FIGURE 67.

sufficiently strong to both reverse the deflection and close the local circuit.

The ringing keys (Figure 67) consist of a brass block carrying four insulated springs and two insulated contact studs. The two inner springs normally make contact with the studs, and project beyond the brass block. These springs are curved inwards in such a manner that when the key is depressed the triangular-shaped piece of ebonite which is attached to the rod of the key pushes them outwards, where they come into contact with the outer or generator springs. The long inner springs are connected to the tip and shoulder of the red peg respectively. The studs are connected to the corresponding studs of the black ringing key, whose inner springs are connected to the tip and shoulder of the black peg. The outer springs of the black peg are connected to the ringing battery.

The connections of a pair of cords and ringing keys are shown in Figure 68. Depression of the black key connects the battery springs to the peg springs; thus the negative pole of the battery is connected to the tip of the peg which comes into contact with the A line. The positive is connected to the B line; thus it will be seen that the ringing battery is joined in series with the distant main permanent current. Similarly,

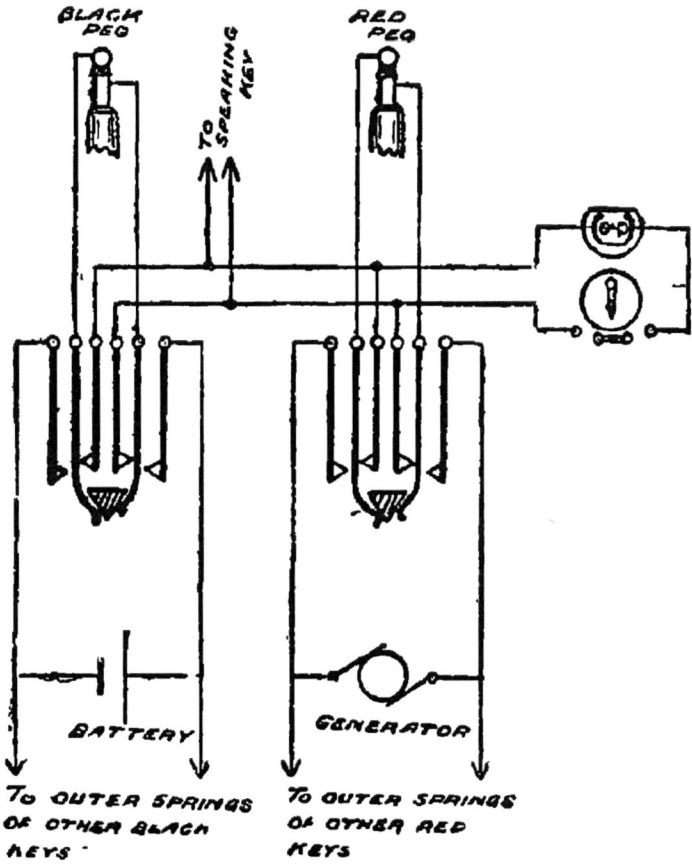

FIGURE 68.

depression of the red peg connects the generator to the tip and shoulder. In the normal condition the tip of the black peg is connected to the tip of the red peg, and shoulder to shoulder. The connection between the inner studs is also joined to the ring-off indicators and to the speaking key. The battery is teed along to all the outer springs of the black keys, and the generator is similarly connected to the outer springs of all the red keys.

A key is attached to each pair of cords which, when thrown forward, puts the operator's speaking set across the cords at the point indicated

Complete Operating Connections. 81

in Figure 68. The general form of the key consists of six springs and four studs; in fact, is very similar to two ringing keys placed side by side, but operated by one lever. The triangular piece of ebonite used to push apart the springs is twice as long as that used in a ringing key. On the left there are two springs, which rest upon insulated studs at the front

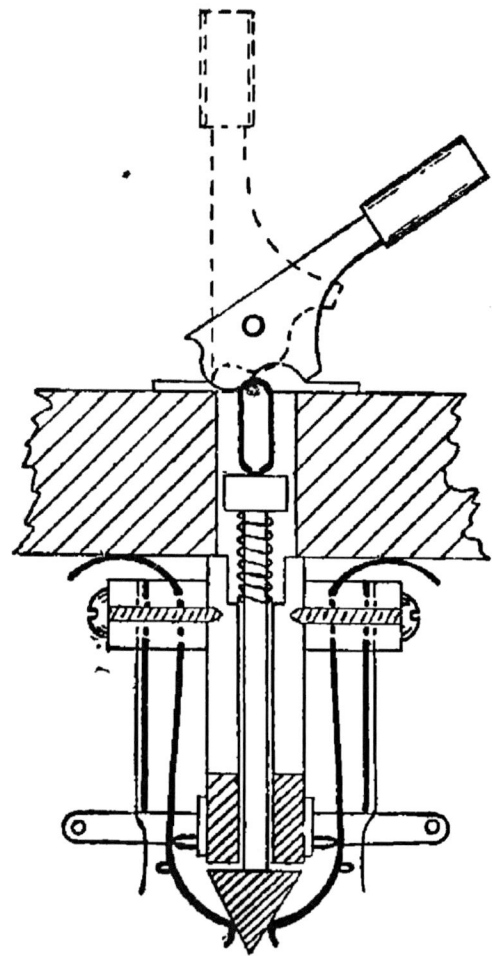

FIGURE 69.

and back of the key respectively. Similarly upon the right, two springs rest upon contact studs, but in this case two springs are placed outside these, so that when the ebonite block descends the studs are left disconnected, and the inner springs make contact with the outer This is the state of affairs when the key is in the normal or upright position (see Figure 69).

G

These outer springs are disconnected, not at present being in use The two inner springs upon the right are connected to the operator's secondary receiver, and may therefore be termed the "receiver springs." The corresponding studs are joined to the connection between the ringing keys— *i e.*, practically across the cords. Upon the left the front spring and stud are used to complete the primary circuit of the operator's speaking set. This prevents the battery being worked when the operator is not actually speaking. The back spring and contact are used to restore the indicator attached to the particular cord When the indicator drops, the operator goes in circuit by throwing the speaking forward, thus at once bringing in the speaking apparatus and restoring the indicator to its normal position.

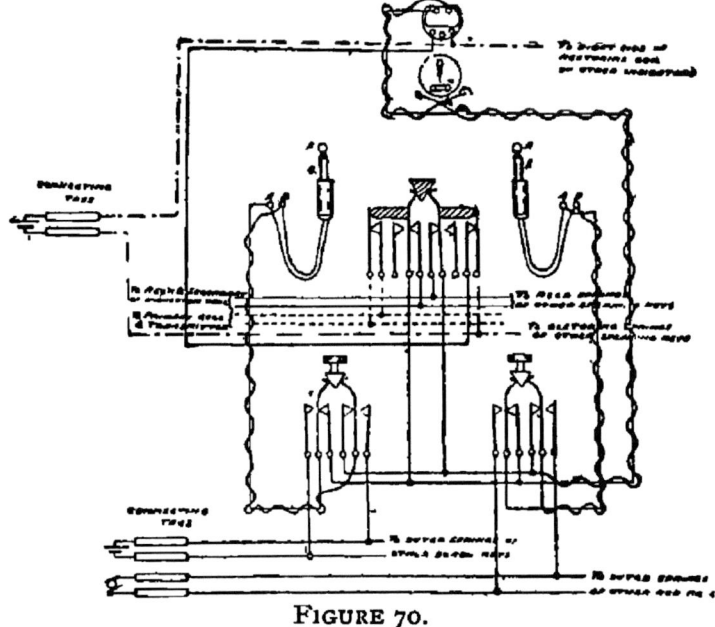

FIGURE 70.

We are now prepared to consider the whole of the operating connections, and these are indicated in Figure 70 It will be seen that each pair of cords has a self-restoring indicator and a galvanometer bridged permanently across it, and that the two ringing keys merely cut off the other side and join the generator or the battery to the cords as the case may be The generator is connected to the outer or generator springs of all the ringing keys, and the battery is similarly connected to all the battery springs. The connection between the ringing keys is joined to the back and front right hand studs of the corresponding speaking key. The front receiver springs are all connected together to one side of the secondary and receiver of the operator's speaking set, the back receiver springs being connected to the other side. The transmitter springs are all connected together and go to one side of the transmitter, battery, and primary of the induction coil. The transmitter studs are all similarly connected to the other side of the primary circuit. The left hand back or restoring springs are all connected together to the negative pole of the 10-cell Leclanché battery used to actuate the front coil of the self-restoring indicator. The right hand side of all these coils are connected together to the positive pole of the battery. The restoring studs are each connected to the left hand side of the corresponding indicator, and it will thus be seen that throwing forward the speaking key restores the corresponding indicator. The speaking key is shown conventionally in Figure 70. The receiver springs and studs are in the centre, with the two disconnected springs outside them. The receiver springs are shown with an insulated projection, which, when in the speaking position, allow the transmitter and restoring springs to make their respective circuits. When in the normal position all the contacts are severed.

The only point in regard to the operating connections still remaining to be considered is the connections of the operator's telephone itself. Provision has been made so that in the event of the failure of one of the speaking batteries a second one can immediately be substituted. In fact, the majority of the apparatus is in duplicate. The transmitter and receiver are connected to ordinary circular pegs and fit into switch-springs. There are four switch-springs—two for the transmitter and two for the receiver. Each set of two switch-springs is joined up with a battery, and thus changing from the one set to the other introduces another battery. Formerly two induction coils were also provided, but this has been found to be unnecessary, and all sections have now only one. Spare transmitters and receivers are also provided, so that it is possible to change practically the whole of the speaking apparatus instantly. This prevents the existence of a fault in the speaking apparatus from stopping the section. The switch telephone connector, as this set of switch-springs is termed, is one-and-a-half inches square, and is placed beneath the desk of the section. The front appearance of the connector is indicated at A in Figure 71. The right hand side and the bottom is of brass and forms a protection to the springs, the other sides being closed by the woodwork of the section. The pegs must always be inserted diagonally—*i.e.*, the receiver in R_1 and the transmitter in T_1, or R_2 and T_2. The switch-springs each have four springs, but only the outer ones are actually used. When the peg is in the position shown the second battery is in use. The path of the current is from the positive pole of No. 2 battery (joined to tags 62 and 63) through the primary of the induction coil to the outer transmitter springs of the speaking keys, thence, if a key be down, to the inner spring through short spring of T_2, through the ball of the peg, through the transmitter, back to the shoulder of the peg to the negative pole of the battery. The secondary circuit is from S, through the short receiver spring to the tip

84 *Connections of Switch Telephone Connector.*

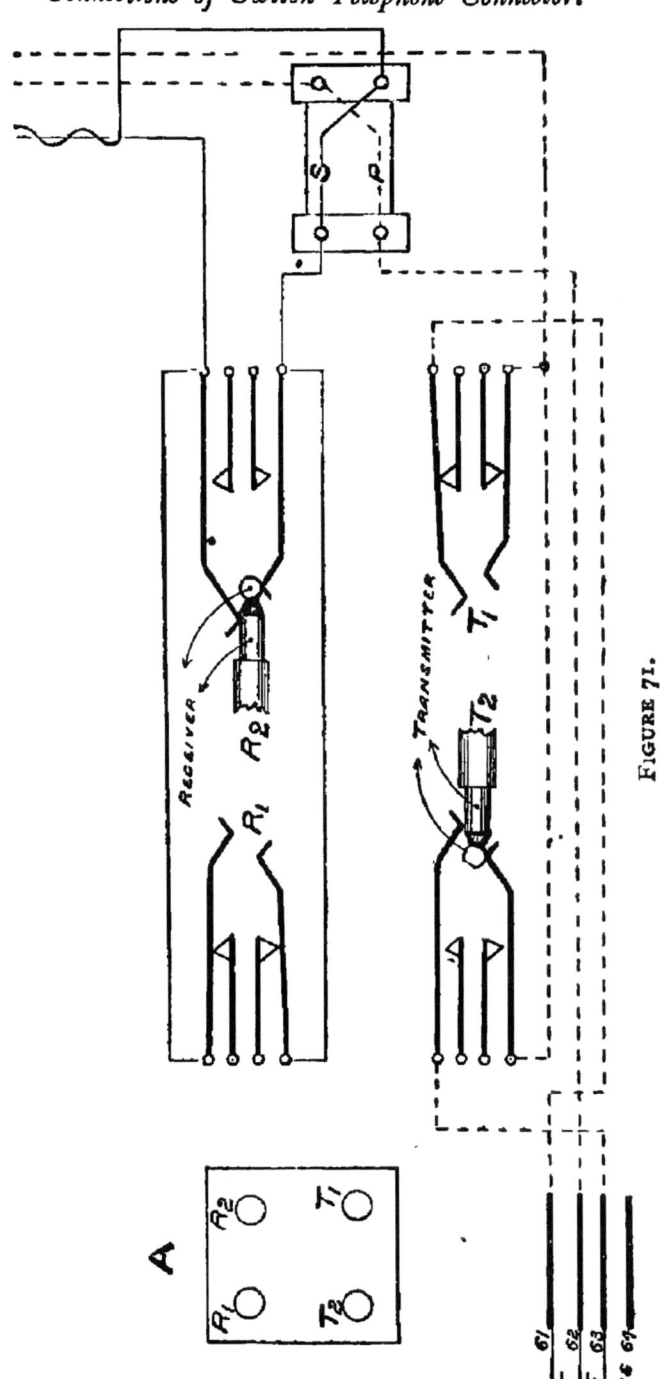

FIGURE 71.

Speaking Battery Circuit. 85

of the peg, through the receiver to the shoulder of the peg, to the long receiver spring, thence to the front receiver stud of the speaking key, through the front receiver spring to the tip of the pair of pegs, through the line connected to the peg to its shoulder, thence back *viâ* the back receiver spring and stud to S. This circuit, also, is only complete when a speaking key is down In brief, the speaking key attached to each pair of pegs and cords completes the primary circuit and tees the secondary

Figure 72.

Figure 73.

circuit across the pair of cords to which it is attached. It will be seen that putting the pegs in R_1 and T_1 brings in the first battery. In the case of small offices having only one section, the switch-board telephone previously illustrated is frequently used, but with circular pegs in place of the four-section peg In this case the two pegs are put into one cover, as shown in Figure 72. This prevents the possibility of the pegs being put into R_1 and T_2, or R_2 and T_1. Another form of hand telephone used is that made by the Western Electric Company, described under the heading of "solid back" transmitter The receiver is of the ordinary watch pattern, but the button placed upon the handle when depressed completes the primary circuit. This enables the operator to listen to a conversation without introducing the noise from the switch room upon the wire.

At the larger exchanges the transmitter and receiver are designed for attachment to the person of the operator in order that both hands may be left free for operating. The receiver is of the ordinary watch pattern, but with a steel band attached The other end of the band has a soft leather

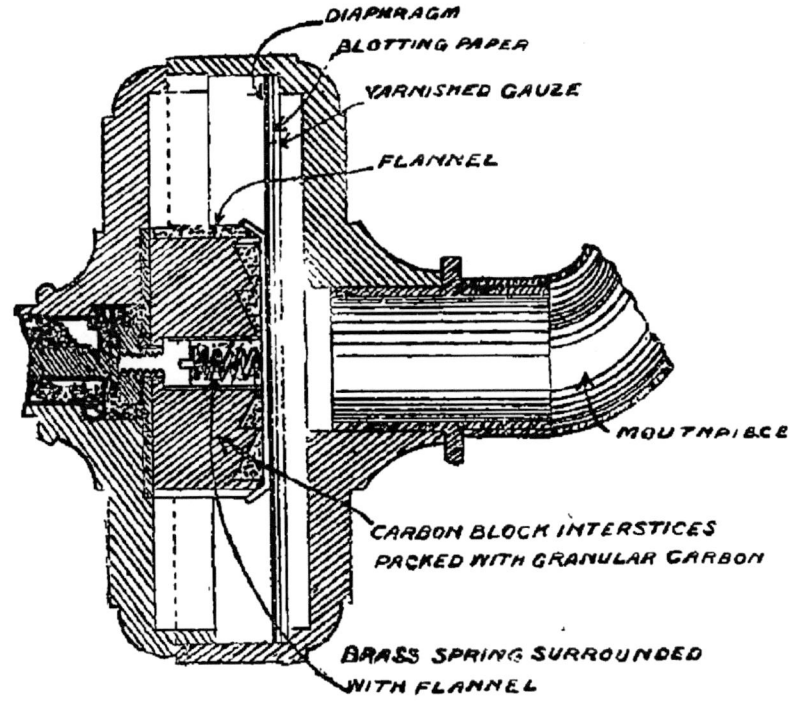

FIGURE 74

pad attached, which rests above the operator's right ear The connection is effected by means of a two-conductor flexible cord which terminates in a red-covered peg The general appearance of the apparatus is shown in Figure 73, but it should be noticed that the Post Office form of receiver has only one steel band. It has been found that many of the operators transferred from the Company prefer the receivers which are fixed to the head by means of elastic bands, and arrangements have been made to supply these when asked for, but it must be confessed they are scarcely so neat in appearance as the other form The transmitter is of the Ericsson pattern, and is shown in Figure 74. It is of the granular type. The ferrotype diaphragm forms one terminal, whilst the circular block of carbon forms the other. Two triangular grooves are cut in this block of carbon, which is covered with flannel, the edge of which lightly touches the diaphragm A round hole is also cut into the centre of the carbon block, and a light spiral spring in compression, also covered by flannel, is placed in this recess, thus putting a very slight tension upon the diaphragm. The space between the carbon and the diaphragm is filled with finely granulated carbon. A small circular brass disc is attached to the inside of the diaphragm, and this it is which is in contact with the granules A varnished silk diaphragm is placed in front of the diaphragm proper in order to prevent the access of moisture to the granules The whole arrangement is placed in an aluminium case, and may be rotated upon an axis at right angles to the diaphragm. The case forms one terminal, and an insulated spring, which rests upon the continuation of the insulated screw securing the carbon electrode, forms the other A key upon the transmitter permits of its disconnection, for the purpose already mentioned in the case of the switch board telephone. In some types of this instrument the switch is replaced by a spring and insulated contact upon the periphery of the case, so arranged that the circuit may be broken by rotating the transmitter by means of the mouthpiece

A transmitter of this pattern having an oiled silk diaphragm placed at the end of the mouthpiece in a small circular box at right angles to the tube is now being tried, with excellent results The diaphragm keeps the inside of the transmitter dry, and to clean it it is only necessary to remove the mouthpiece.

CHAPTER XIV.

THE "A" SWITCH SECTION.

Having now examined every part of the simpler switch section, it will be well to consider the section as a whole. At the very small offices, where there are less than three trunk lines, a section of the A type (Figure 75)

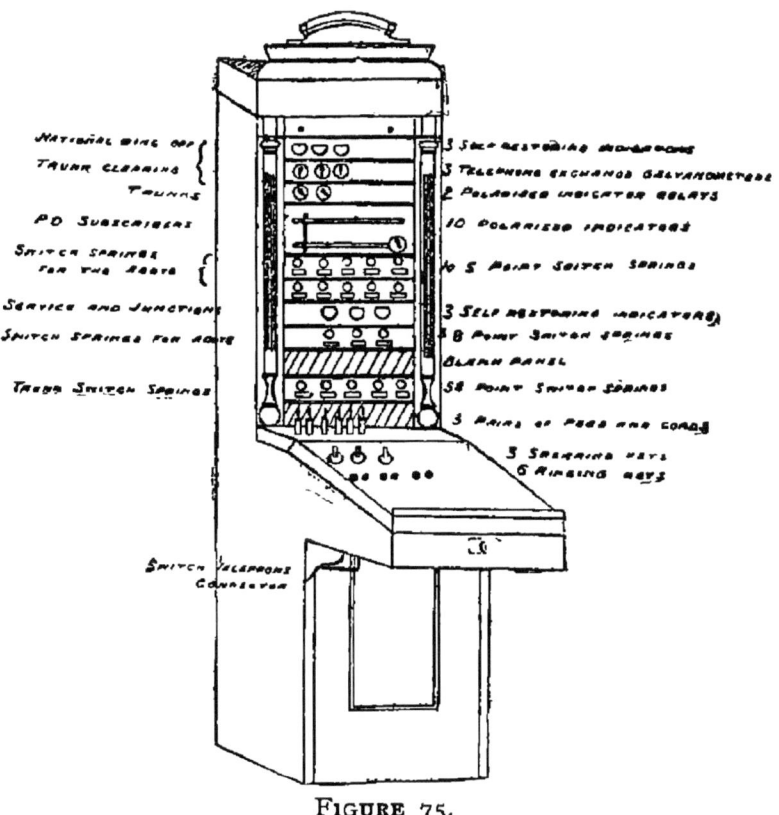

FIGURE 75.

is used. Upon an A switch section three pairs of pegs, with their corresponding three speaking keys, six ringing keys, and ring-off indicators, are fitted. The ring-off indicators are placed at the top of the section, the self-restoring indicators being placed uppermost. Beneath the exchange galvanometers come the polarised indicator relays corresponding to the trunks, the corresponding switch-springs for which are at the bottom of the board Next to the trunk relays comes a space for ten polarised drop indicators of the form previously described. Below these are ten five-point switch-springs, which are joined up as shown in Figure 76. The lines from the subscribers are connected to the outer springs, whilst the inner springs are joined to the indicator. The shutter is held up by the

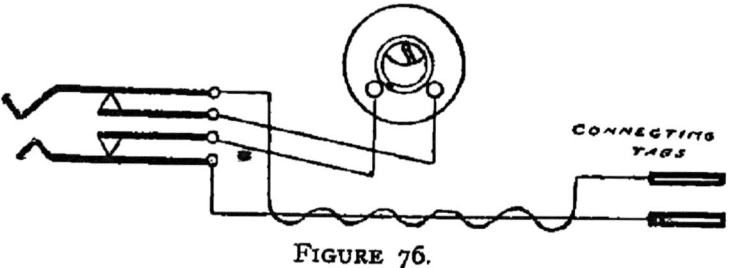

FIGURE 76.

permanent current, which also deflects the needle to the right When the permanent current is stopped by the removal of the receivers, the shutter drops, and calls the attention of the operator.

There are three self-restoring indicators attached to the three circuits between the switch and the National Company's Exchange. These are joined up as shown in Figure 77 It will be seen that the two lines from the

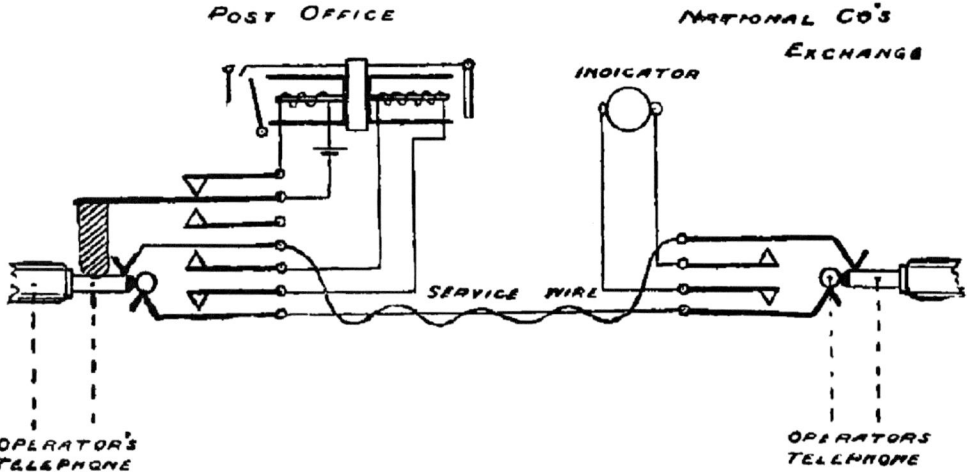

FIGURE 77.

National Company come to the two outer springs of an eight-point switch-spring. In the normal condition these two lines pass through the back or line coil of the self-restoring indicator by means of the inner springs (Figure 77). A ring from the National causes the shutter to fall forward

90   *Junction Arrangements.*

thus indicating a call. The insertion of a peg at the Post Office breaks the contacts of the inner springs, thus cutting out the line coil of the indicator and at the same time causes the two top springs to come into contact thus closing the circuit of a local battery and restoring the indicator to its normal condition.

The mode of proceedure is as follows:—Subscriber 1061 rings up, dropping the indicator in connection with his line at the National Exchange. The National operator inserts a peg into his switch-spring, and ascertains the nature of the service required by throwing forward the speaking key. If connection with a local subscriber is desired, the corresponding peg of the pair is inserted in the required subscriber's switch-spring, and he is rung up in the ordinary way, and the connection is

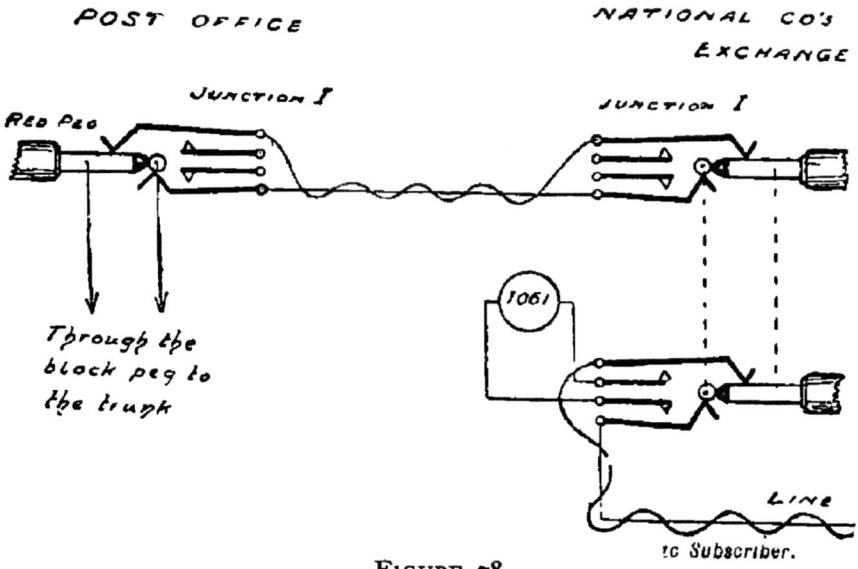

FIGURE 78.

complete. If a trunk connection is required, the operator takes particulars, removes the peg, and places it into the service wire switch-spring, and rings the Post Office, when the particulars are entered upon a numbered white ticket. When this subscriber's turn arrives for the use of the trunk line required, the Post Office operator rings up the Company on the service wire, and asks that the subscriber may be connected to one of the junction lines, and when this is done the connections are as indicated in Figure 78. The Post Office operator then rings up the subscriber with the red peg, and the connection is completed by the insertion of the black peg in the switch-spring of the required trunk.

The trunk ringing battery consists of ten No 1 Leclanché cells—*i e*, about 12 volts. The Company's subscribers have magneto bells so that

Generator Ringing. 91

when their attention is required for trunks alternating currents are necessary to ring them up. In the smaller exchanges, where there is only one switch section, a magneto generator is fixed on the right hand side of the switch section.

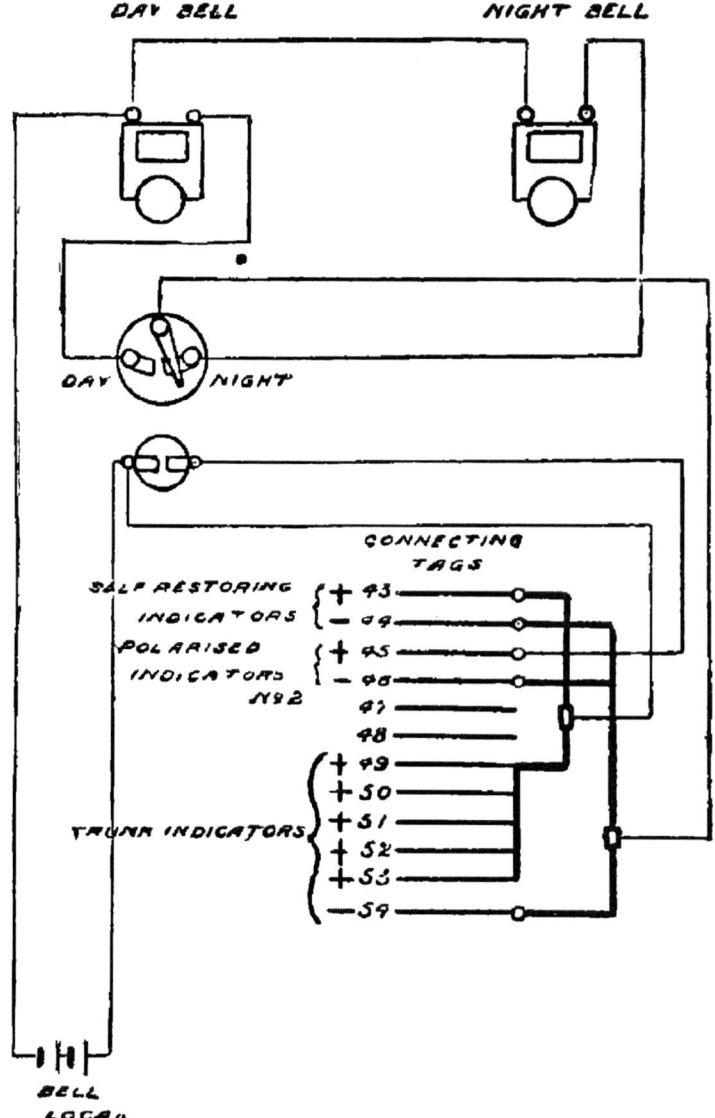

FIGURE 79.

This generator has three magnets, and has no cut-out switch upon the armature. In order to ring upon a junction, the handle is revolved, and the red button corresponding with the red peg in the junction switch-spring is depressed,

For periods of the day when constant attention at the switch is not necessary, a bell must be provided, in order to give an audible call. The complete external connections of the local contacts upon the self-restoring indicators, polarised indicators, and trunk indicator relays, together with the numbers of the connecting tags, are indicated in Fig. 79.

These connections appear somewhat complicated, but a very little consideration will show that, bearing in mind the general principle, they are remarkably simple. First let us suppose there is only one bell. The cell is joined in series with the bell and the two points of the local contacts. When the tongue touches the base of the self-restoring indicator the circuit is completed and the bell rings. In many cases a second bell has to be fixed in an upstairs room, in order that when no one is in the room attention may at once be called to the switch when a distant office calls. One side of each bell is joined together; the two other sides of the bells are connected to either side of a two-way switch. The centre of the two-way switch and the left hand side of the bells corresponds to the two terminals of one bell, but the position of the switch determines which bell shall be in circuit

The body of all the self-restoring indicators are connected together to tag 44, and the insulated screws are also teed together to tag 43. The trunk indicators are fixed upon a copper strip, which is connected to tag 54. The insulated screws of the five indicators are joined to tags 49, 50, 51, 52, and 53 respectively. If the drop indicators used for subscribers were joined up in precisely this way the bell would ring continuously while two subscribers were through In order to avoid this, a short-circuit piece is inserted in series with the two local contacts of the drop indicators This consists of two pieces of brass, so shaped that a brass plug may be inserted between them When the plug is inserted, the drop indicator local contacts are joined up precisely as the self-restoring indicator locals. Thus when any local contact is made, the circuit of the battery is made through either the day or the night bell, as the case may be.

CHAPTER XV.

THE "B" SWITCH SECTION.

Where there are from three to five trunks, one B switch section is used. The B section is of exactly the same size and shape as the A section previously described; but a strip of five five-point switch-springs is added to accomodate the additional junctions. In addition to this six pairs of cords, together with the necessary ringing and speaking keys, are furnished. In certain cases two visual indicators are added; but this is a matter which will be dealt with later

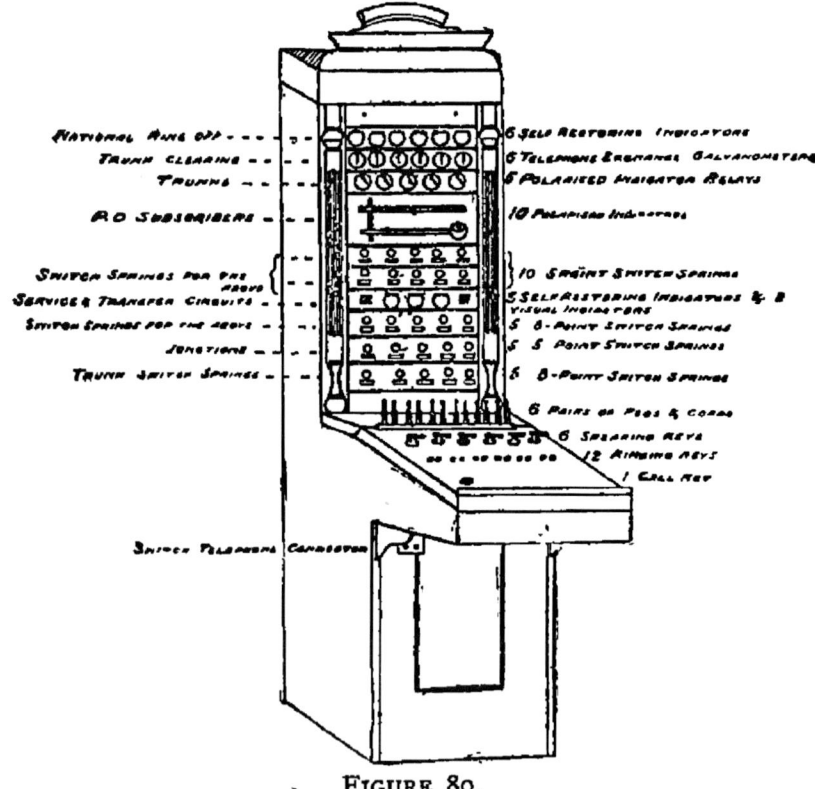

FIGURE 80.

The junctions all terminate upon five-point switch springs, and no indicators whatever are fitted upon them. The local contacts are precisely as described in the case of the A section. The arrangement of the apparatus upon the switch is shown in Figure 80, and requires no further remark, save that the service wire to the Company terminates in one of the self-restoring indicators. In the event of anything going wrong a junction may be used by leaving a peg in at either end, and thus leaving the ring-off indicators in circuit.

Upon a busy trunk switch section much time would be wasted in calling off each of the connections to the National. In order to avoid this the two inner contacts of the junction switch springs (Figure 81) are connected to an earthed battery, which, when the peg is withdrawn, sends a current along both lines to the National, where it passes through an indicator, and thus gives a disconnecting signal.

At the National end each junction terminates in a peg, the A and B lines being connected to the tip and body respectively. Across the lines

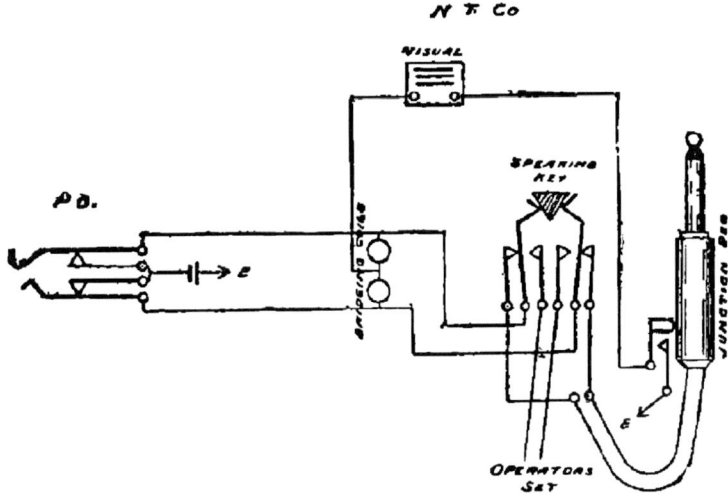

FIGURE 81

two bridging coils are joined in series. These coils are wound to 1000 ω each, and have a very high self-inductance. The coils are wound upon an iron core, and are surrounded by iron closed at both ends, thus forming a magnetic circuit wholly of iron. The self-inductance possessed by this arrangement is so high as to prevent any appreciable portion of the speaking current being drained away

The junction peg rests upon a spring and contact, which, when the peg is at rest—*i.e*, when the junction is not in use—breaks the circuit of the junction-clearing battery. When, however, the peg is in a subscriber's switch-spring the withdrawal of the peg at the Post Office joins up the junction-clearing battery, and the visual indicator (see page 97) shows white until the peg is removed and placed in its normal position at the Company's exchange.

Reed Ringers.

When an operator has a really busy section, containing five trunks, the ringing of subscribers by means of a hand generator would cause much delay. In order to avoid the necessity for this a special ringing apparatus, known as a reed ringer, is frequently employed. This apparatus provides an alternating current from primary batteries. Two sets are used, joined up in opposite directions, and are alternately connected to the line.

The apparatus is shown in the diagram (Figure 82). It consists of an electro-magnet with long flat steel armature, with a contact breaker similar to that of an electric bell. The steel reed is connected to one line, and the centre of the two sets of the batteries is connected to the other side of the ringing keys. Thus it will be seen that the left hand battery is joined up when the bar makes connection with the bottom stud, and the right hand battery when touching the top stud. These contacts consist of fine springs placed upon the reed in

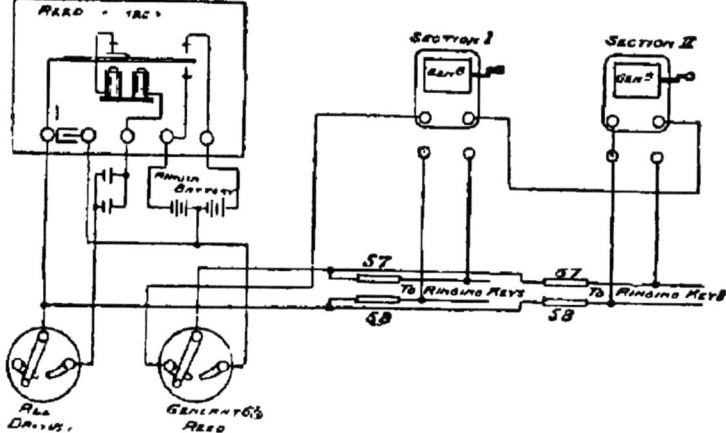

FIGURE 82.

order that the current may not be of too short duration. The reed is driven by a separate two five-cell Daniells joined in parallel. Across the whole arrangement a condenser of small capacity is inserted in order to slow down the rate at which the current strength rises in the circuits, in order that the disturbance caused to neighbouring circuits may be as small as possible. The ringing battery usually consists of two sets of from 30 to 35 Leclanché cells.

In towns where there is an electric lighting undertaking, current is obtained to work an electro-motor, which drives a generator of somewhat larger form than that used upon the switch sections. Unfortunately, where the current supply is alternating, this arrangement cannot be worked, as a reliable self-starting alternating current motor of $\frac{1}{8}$-horse power is not yet upon the market. The speed of alternation or periodicity of the lighting current is far too high for ringing bells.

At offices of the size of Manchester, Glasgow, and Liverpool, dynamotors run from the office lighting plant are supplied. These consist of an electro-motor with additional windings upon the armature. These conductors are dragged through the magnetic field, and thus provide alternating currents, which are utilised for ringing purposes.

Switches are provided for connecting either the reed-ringer or motor generator, as the case may be, or the hand generators. These hand generators have a cut-out upon the armature similar to that described in the earlier chapters The connections are indicated in Figure 82 It will be seen that the generators are all connected in series and that the tags 57 and 58 are respectively connected together upon each section. The two-way switches join up either the automatic or hand ringing apparatus as required. As the armatures of the generators are short-circuited, unless a generator is being turned, there is thus only one in circuit. During the evening, when the work is very light, the hand generators are used, and the automatic ringing apparatus cut out for economical reasons

It is frequently necessary to connect two trunk lines together, as, for instance, should Bolton have a call for Southport, Bolton would pass the call to Manchester, where the two trunk lines would be connected together. Where there are only two sections, the connection is made by means of a pair of cords upon one section, as the cords are made sufficiently long for this purpose

Where there are three sections, however, and it is desired to connect together a trunk upon the first section and one upon the third section, two courses are open to us: firstly to use a pair of cords upon the centre section, or secondly to provide a means of signalling and connection between the first and third sections In certain cases where it is considered that the sections are too busy to admit of the first remedy, the second is adopted, and with this object two indicators known as visuals are fitted (one upon either side of the three self-restoring indicators).

The visual indicator consists of an electro-magnet with a soft iron armature, attached to which is a thin flat piece of metal which is bent at right angles to its length over the end of the electro-magnet The disc is divided horizontally into six spaces alternately black and white. In front of this disc is placed a strip of metal with three slits. In the normal position black lines are opposite these openings, but when the armature is attracted the white lines cover the slits. The grid is painted black, thus rendering the signal very conspicuous.

These indicators (Figure 83) are usually mounted in s rips of five or ten, but a smaller form is made where twenty are mounted in a space of $11\frac{1}{2}$ in by $\frac{3}{4}$ in The front of the coil is screwed to a brass base strip and the play of the armature is regulated by means of two hexagonal

Visual Indicator.

washers upon a pin projecting upwards from this base. The cheeks of the electro-magnet are iron, thus improving the magnetic circuit.

The resistance of these indicators is 450ω and the current required is from thirty to forty milliamperes.

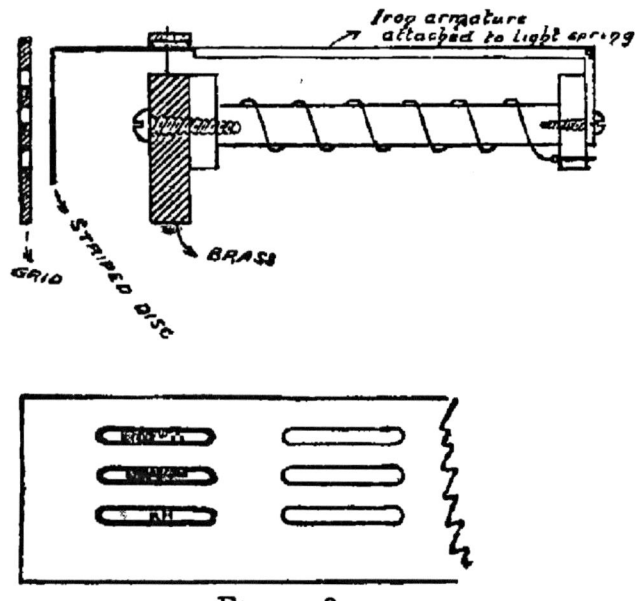

FIGURE 83.

Eight-point switch-springs are used for the junctions between sections 1 and 3. The loop upon which the trunk is extended is kept perfectly free from apparatus of any description, and is joined to the two line springs. The signalling is accomplished by means of the three upper springs, and is quite automatic, the mere insertion of a peg throwing the signals.

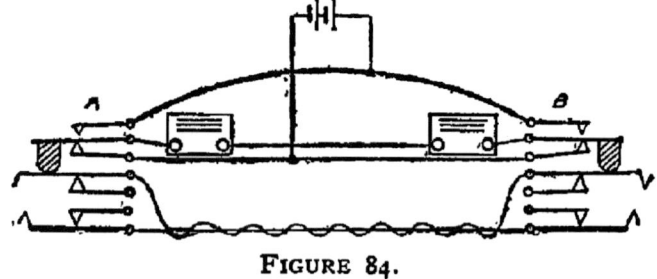

FIGURE 84.

The principle of the system is indicated in Figure 84, where a complete circuit is joined up in skeleton. The top and bottom springs of the two switch-springs are respectively connected to the positive and negative poles of the transfer battery. The two middle springs are connected together with the two visuals in series. In the normal condition the central springs at both ends are connected to the negative pole of the battery, and thus no current flows through the visuals. If now a peg is inserted at A the central spring is raised from the bottom to the top spring, where it is connected to the positive pole of the battery, and thus a current flows through both visuals. The path is from the positive pole of the battery to the top spring, to the centre spring and through both visuals to the lower spring at B (*via* the middle spring at B) and thence back to the battery. Thus both indicators show white. At A this indicates that there is no peg in at B—*i.e.*, the call has not been answered. At B the white visual indicates a call A peg is inserted at B in order to answer, and immediately both indicators go black, as it will be seen that the middle springs are now both connected to the positive pole of the battery. Upon the conclusion of the conversation A withdraws his peg and thus both indicators show white To B this indicates that the connection should be severed, and to A it indicates that B has not done this so long as the visual remains white In other words, we may say that the visuals are normally black when the circuits are either through or disengaged, but that white indicates that attention is required. Thus it will be seen that the insertion of a peg gives an automatic call, and its removal gives an automatic clearing signal. The long and short springs are the B and A lines respectively, and the insertion of a peg in each switch spring connects the two pegs together.

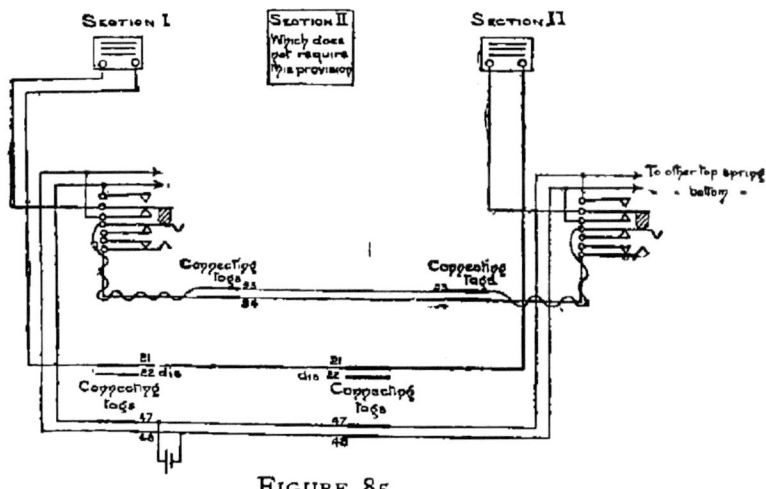

FIGURE 85

The actual connections are shown in Figure 85, in order to help in tracing faults Only one transfer battery of twenty-five Leclanché No 1 cells is used The top and bottom springs upon each section are respectively teed together, and pass to the battery tags. A visual signalling wire

Up and Down Service Circuits.

is required for each circuit, and this is upon tag 21 in the case of the first circuit, and upon 23 in the second.

When there are from five to ten trunks, two sections are necessary, and these are of the B form previously described. The only point which is worthy of special mention is in reference to the working of the service wires. In this case two are provided, one for up and the other for down calls. Where possible it is best to make one section fairly easy, in reference to traffic, by arranging the trunks upon that section, and to give this operator the work of taking all the up calls and making out all the tickets.

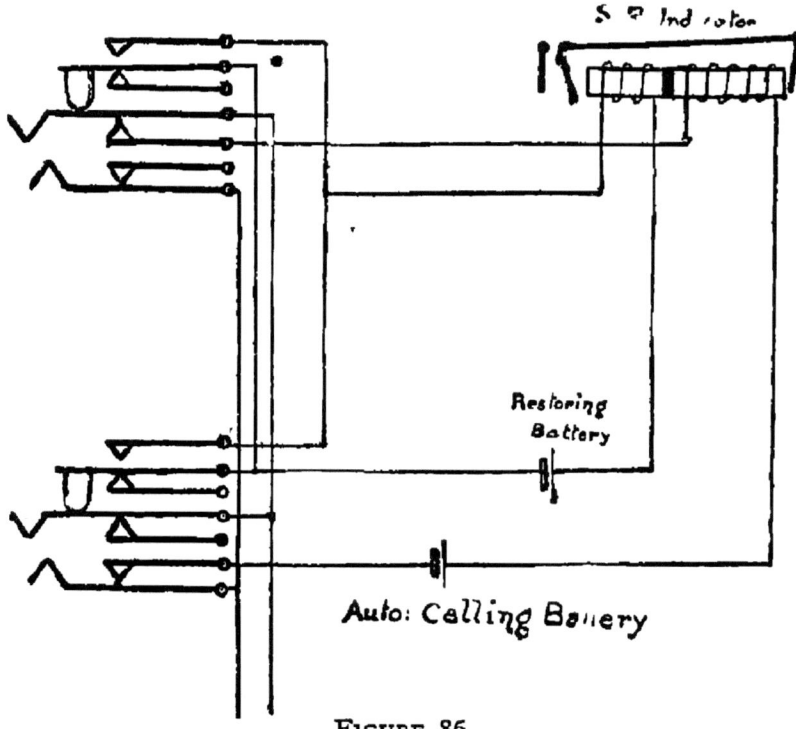

FIGURE 86.

Where, however, this is not possible the wire is multipled upon both sections, but the indicator in connection with it is placed upon the first section. It is necessary to be able to restore it from either section, and this is accomplished by tee-ing the self-restoring battery and indicator coil to the second switch-spring, as shown in Figure 86. As both operators require to obtain connections upon their junctions, it is necessary to multiple the down call wire upon both sections. This, however, is a perfectly simple and obvious matter, as the indicator is not required at the Post Office end, and thus all that is necessary is to tee the outer springs of the switch-springs set apart upon each section.

In some offices the two service wires are used indiscriminately, *i.e.*, each operator has a service wire, and it is used both to receive demands and to obtain connections; but this is scarcely so satisfactory.

In other cases a battery is joined in series with the line coil of the self-restoring indicator. At the Company's end the lines terminate upon a switch-spring without indicator. Normally the circuit is open, but when the Company's operator inserts a peg with her speaking telephone in circuit, the battery sends a current through the speaking apparatus and indicator, thus calling the Post Office operator The insertion of the Post Office operator's peg, of course, restores the indicator The down call wire is similarly equipped with an indicator and battery at the Company's end, and the insertion of a peg at the Post Office thus effects the call It should, however, be noticed that in order to accomplish this the self-restoring indicator at the Post Office must be removed.

Where there are from eleven to fifteen trunks, three B sections are sometimes provided. This, however, is only done where it is almost certain that development will be extremely slow, or where the number of trunks is in excess of requirements

Where eleven or more trunks have to be dealt with, it is not possible for the operators to make out the white tickets, and a special operator is therefore provided for this purpose. The up call wire, instead of being placed upon the sections, simply terminates in an operator's set connected to a special table known as a "*record table.*" The tickets made out by this operator are collected and handed to the respective switch section operators.

CHAPTER XVI.

Up and Down Call Wires.

In order to have a readier means of obtaining the Company's attention, each operator has upon her switch section a special press button termed a call wire key, which, when depressed, joins her speaking apparatus to

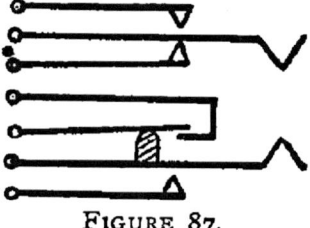

FIGURE 87.

the call wire. At both the Company's end and at our own the operators wear head-gear telephones, and thus are listening continuously for instructions. During the less busy parts of the day clearly this is not

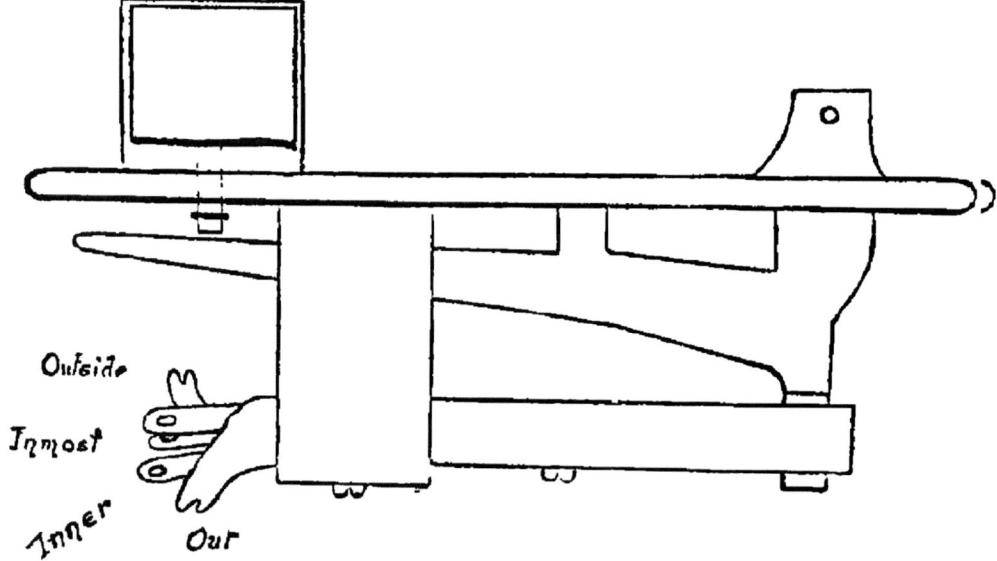

FIGURE 88

necessary, and in order to meet this the call wires at either end pass through switches, which put the call wires on to indicators At the Post Office this switch consists of six holes upon the test board The central pair of holes are connected to the call wire, the top and bottom pairs being connected to the record table or to the battery and indicator by means of U links. The up call wire terminates in one indicator, but there are three switch-springs in connection with it, so that any one of the operators may take calls from the Company At the Company's end the wire in connection with the Post Office call keys is switched through to a switch-spring and indicator with a battery in circuit

The call key consists of seven springs (Figure 87), which, when the key is depressed, are pushed outwards, thus connecting the two long springs to the two short ones, and so joining the call wire to the operator's speaking set The central springs come in contact, and thus complete the primary circuit of the speaking set The mechanical connections of the key are shown in Figure 88

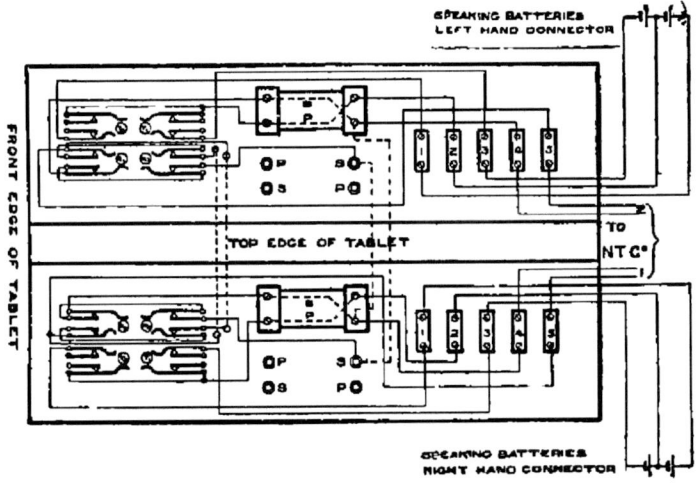

FIGURE 89

The record table tablet is joined up as shown in Figure 89. It will be seen that there is only one induction coil for each circuit, and that the reversal of the operator's pegs brings in a new battery. When only one operator's set is in circuit both call wires are thrown on to that operator's set The switch telephone connector is placed in the centre of the table and is covered by a small door which is cut to permit the cords to pass through it. These tables accommodate two operators, but this is only necessary in larger exchanges

In certain offices it was found expedient to fit record tables in exchanges where there were only two B sections It must always be remembered in dealing with telephone problems that absolute rigidity of practice is not always desirable, as in this instance

CHAPTER XVII.

THE "C" SWITCH SECTION.

At all the larger offices switch sections of the C type are fitted Where it is thought that the number of switch sections is likely to grow to four, *i e.*, sixteen or more trunks, it is not desirable to fix B sections, as to change a B into a C section is somewhat difficult and expensive. To take a case in point, a certain office at the time of the transfer had only some twelve or thirteen trunks; but here C sections were fitted, and the wisdom of this policy is shewn by the fact that an additional section has recently been fixed. In another case the number of trunks was about the same, but their growth was so improbable that B sections were fitted Thus it will be seen that fixed and immutable rules are not wise, and that each case should be taken upon its merits.

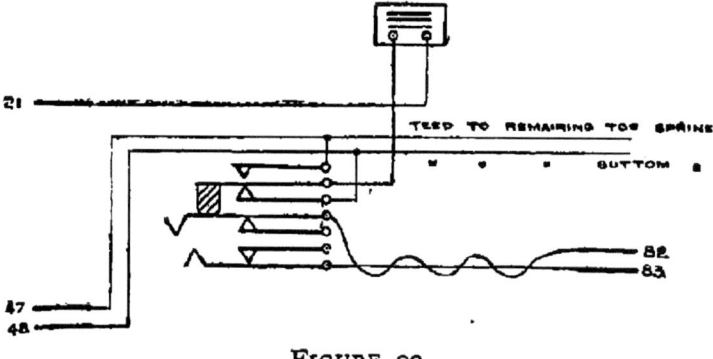

FIGURE 90.

The chief point of difference between a B section and a C section lies in the transfer circuit provision, indicators and switch-springs, for ten transfer circuits being fitted instead of two, as in the B sections. These are fitted in four strips The top strip consists of five visuals, underneath which is placed the strip of five switch-springs corresponding to them; then comes the second five visuals and switch-springs

Two transfer circuits are provided from Section 1 to Section 3 and two from 1 to 4 Section 2 can reach all save Section 4, between which two circuits are provided In the case of five sections two circuits between the following sections must be provided 1 and 3, 1 and 4, 1 and 5, 2 and 4, 2 and 5, 3 and 5. For six sections· 1 and 3, 1 and 4, 1 and 5, 1 and 6, 2 and 4, 2 and 5, 2 and 6, 3 and 5, 3 and 6, 4 and 6.

Where the number of sections exceeds this a special transfer switch is usually employed, but this will be described in Chapter XVIII.

The connections of the visuals and switch-springs to the tags is indicated in Figure 90 It will be seen that they are precisely as shown in the case of the B switch section, and that when joining up a transfer

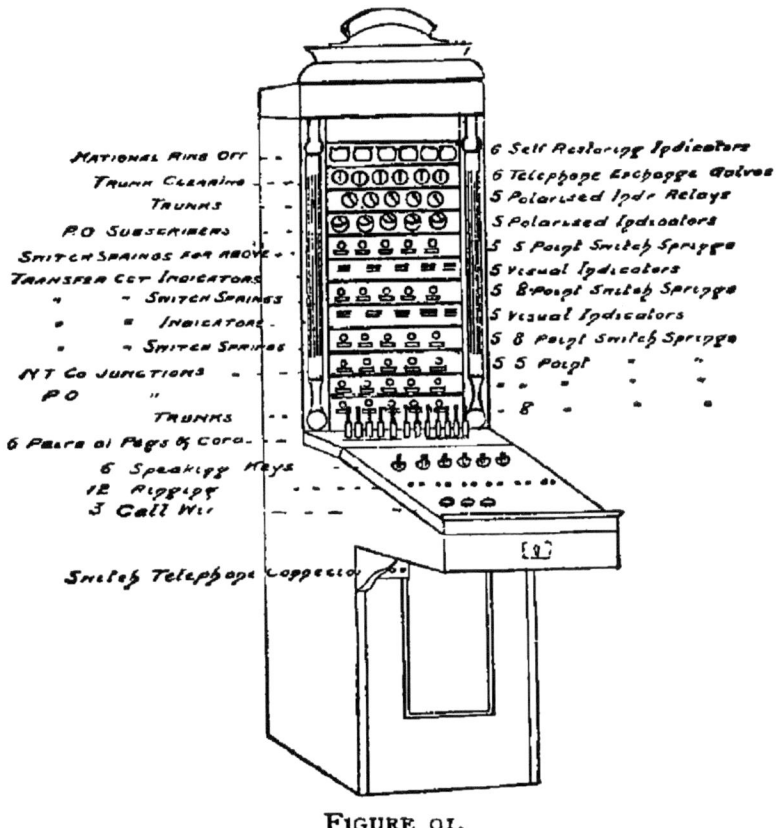

FIGURE 91.

circuit between sections 1 and 3, tag 21 goes to tag 21, and tag 23 to 23 of the other section. Similarly the ends of tags 47 and 48 are connected. The reason of this is obvious. Tags 47 and 48 are respectively connected to the positive and negative poles of the battery. Tag 47 is connected to the top springs of all the switch-springs teed together, and tag 48 is connected to the teed bottom springs. The visual signalling wires are connected to the respective circuits to which they are intended to work. The corresponding loops are 83 and 84 to 101 and 102.

Junctions to Post Office Local Switch.

Where there are more than three sections the tags 47 and 48 should be taken to the test board and there joined to the battery by means of U links. If this is not done very great difficulty will be experienced in tracing faults, owing to the multiplicity of teed connections. It should be noted that only one battery must be used for the whole exchange. If a single set of cells proves inadequate, other single sets joined in parallel must be added

The disposition of the apparatus is indicated in Figure 91. It will be seen that the space for Post Office subscribers is reduced from 10 to 5, as operators cannot attend to Post Office renters in addition to trunks; and, indeed, at all the larger offices a separate switch is provided for them. The transfer circuits have already received suitable notice

In the case of C sections, record tables are always provided, and hence we notice the disappearance of the three service self-restoring indicators.

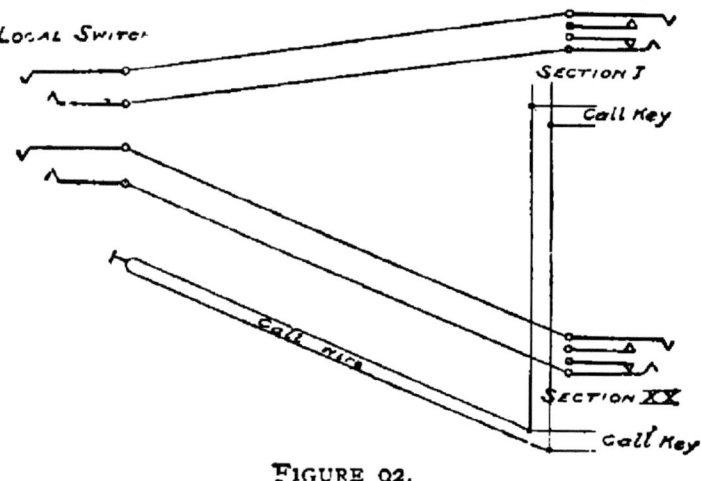

FIGURE 92.

A strip of five-point switch-springs is provided for junctions to the Post Office local switch. Where the renters are all accommodated upon slack sections, these junctions are, of course, not required; the switch-springs are, however, always fitted.

Two junctions are provided from each section to the local switch, where they terminate in switch-springs with two springs only. These latter are fitted in strips containing twenty switch-springs. No. 1 switch section's junctions are numbered 1 and 2; No. 3's, 5 and 6; No. 20's, 39 and 40, and so on. A call wire is provided to the local switch and this passes round all the sections, being connected to each call wire key The local operator listens continuously, and receives all instructions upon it. Thus, if Section 3 wants subscriber No. 20, she depresses the Post Office call wire key and says "20 on junction 5," or, if junction 5 is in use, on 6. The call wire arrangements are indicated in Figure 92.

From what has already been said, the arrangement of the down call wires will be obvious The Company's operators are allotted twenty-five junctions each, *i e*, the junctions of five switch sections, and the down call wire is therefore passed to each of the five sections where call wire keys are fitted as already explained.

The local contacts are quite the same as in the case of the A and B sections, and do not require any especial mention The vibrating sounder is substituted for bells, as the sound produced is such as not to cause interruption of service It has also been found that one sounder for four or five sections is quite adequate, but provision is made so that one, two, three, four, or five sections may be put on to it. The vibrating sounder consists of an electro-magnet with a trembler bell make and break contact. The armature is attached to a stiff steel spring, and thus the sounder merely makes a buzz. In order to prevent sparking at the contact, and for other reasons, a condenser is joined across it. This condenser is placed in the base of the sounder.

CHAPTER XVIII.

The Transfer Board

It will be quite obvious that where a large number of trunk switch sections have to be provided with transfer circuits, direct circuits from each section to every other section within the exchange would be utterly unfeasible. Where it is possible to adopt this system it is obviously desirable to do so, as it saves switching operations, which, however smartly performed, occupy time. It is somewhat difficult to say how many sections may be dealt with in this way, as conditions vary so much. For example, an office may have forty trunks, twelve of which go to one town. Again, by carefully considering the arrangement of the trunks upon the sections, the transfer work may be reduced to a minimum. Generally we may say that where the number of sections exceeds six or eight a transfer board will be essential.

The transfer board is the connecting link between the various sections. There are circuits from each section in the room to the transfer board, and means for connecting them together in any prescribed manner are provided. In order to render the working as rapid as possible the circuits between the sections and the transfer board are divided into two groups, known as A and B circuits. The A circuits are those upon which the section operator passes forward a call to the transfer board operator. The B circuits are those upon which the latter again passes forward the call to the required switch section. The A circuits then are used outwards from and the B circuits inwards to the sections. To each section there are allotted three A circuits and two B circuits—*i.e.*, the section operator can pass forward three calls and receive two simultaneously if necessary.

The A circuits are those upon which calls come inwards to the transfer board, and these are placed upon the slanting desk (Figure 93). The visuals in connection with these circuits are at the top of the slanting desk, and immediately below them come the *combination keys*, the object of which is to enable the transfer operator to speak and signal upon any circuit. The loop of each circuit terminates in a peg, and upon this circuit there is absolutely no apparatus. These pegs are to be seen above the desk. Each A circuit is provided with a peg, a visual indicator, and a combination key. It will be noticed that the board shown is only half fitted; but, it is, of course, a very simple matter to add more apparatus when required.

Trunk Line Transfer Board.

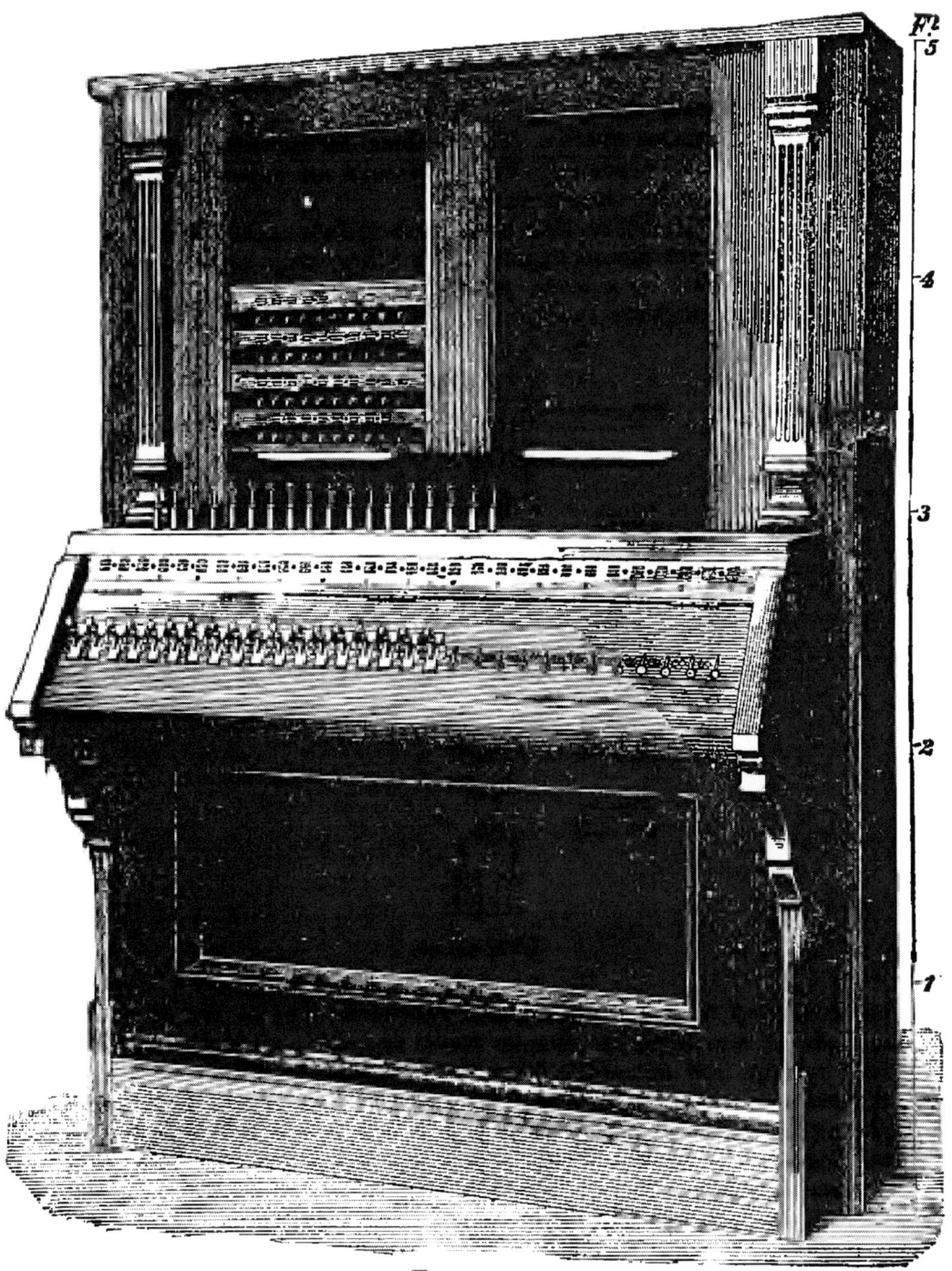

FIGURE 93.

Combination Key. 109

The insertion of a peg at the section drops the visuals at the section and transfer board. The operator depresses the combination key, thus connecting up her telephone. Having ascertained the nature of the service, the corresponding peg is taken up and inserted into a B circuit of the required section. The combination key is then raised, thus putting the visuals at normal. The B circuits are accommodated upon the upright part of the transfer board.

The combination key consists of thirteen springs arranged in two sets. These two sets are placed opposite each other, with a round piece of ebonite, controlled by a lever, playing between them. In the normal condition the springs are as shown in Figure 96. The upper long springs

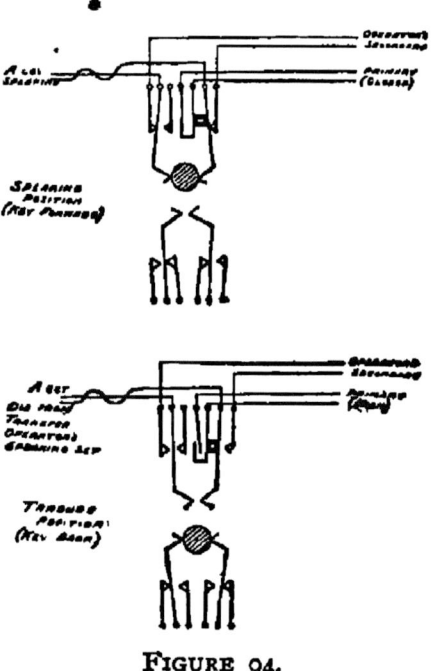

FIGURE 94.

are connected to the A circuit, and the outer ones to the operator's secondary; thus when the ebonite moves upwards and pushes apart the long springs, the operator's telephone is connected to the circuit. At the same time the central pair of springs make contact, thus completing the operator's primary circuit. This is shown in the upper part of Figure 94. The inner spring on the left is not used at all. The bottom springs are arranged exactly like a ringing key, and when the ebonite descends, forcing the long springs apart, they leave the inner springs and make contact with the outer ones. Of these six springs only the right hand three are utilised. The effect of depressing the key is indicated in the lower part of Figure 94 The mechanical design of the key is illustrated in Figure 95.

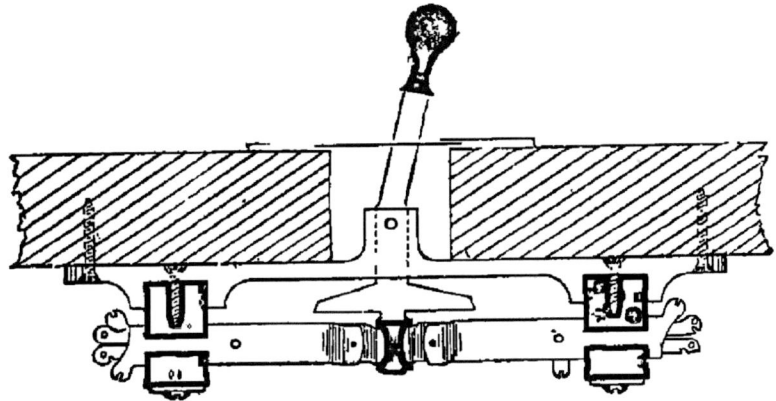

FIGURE 95.

The connections of an A circuit are shown in Figure 96. It will be seen that the speaking circuit passes from the line switch-springs to the peg at the transfer board, whence it is teed off to the long springs of the combination key. This provides a method of connecting the operator's telephone to the circuit Only when the key is depressed is the operator's telephone in connection with the circuit. These are the whole of the speaking connections.

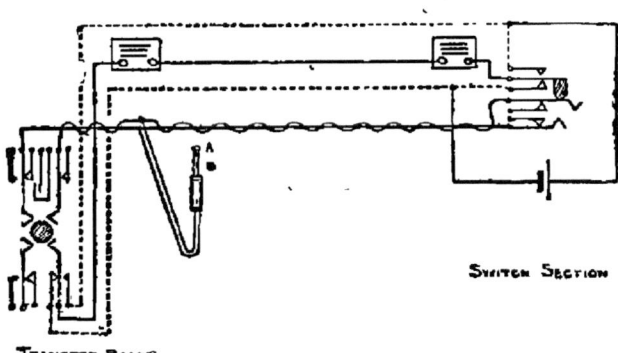

FIGURE 96.

It has previously been explained how visual signalling from section to section is accomplished (page 104). It is for this purpose that the three lower right hand springs are used The long spring corresponds to the central spring of the eight-point switch-spring, the inner spring to the lower, and the outer to the top. This long spring passes through the

Method of Working.

visual indicator, along the signalling wire, through the section visual, to the middle spring. The top and outer springs and the lower and inner springs are connected together to the positive and negative poles of the signalling battery respectively

When a peg is inserted at the section, the central spring and the upper spring make contact, thus throwing both visuals. The transfer operator, seeing the signal thrown, pulls forward the lever of the corresponding

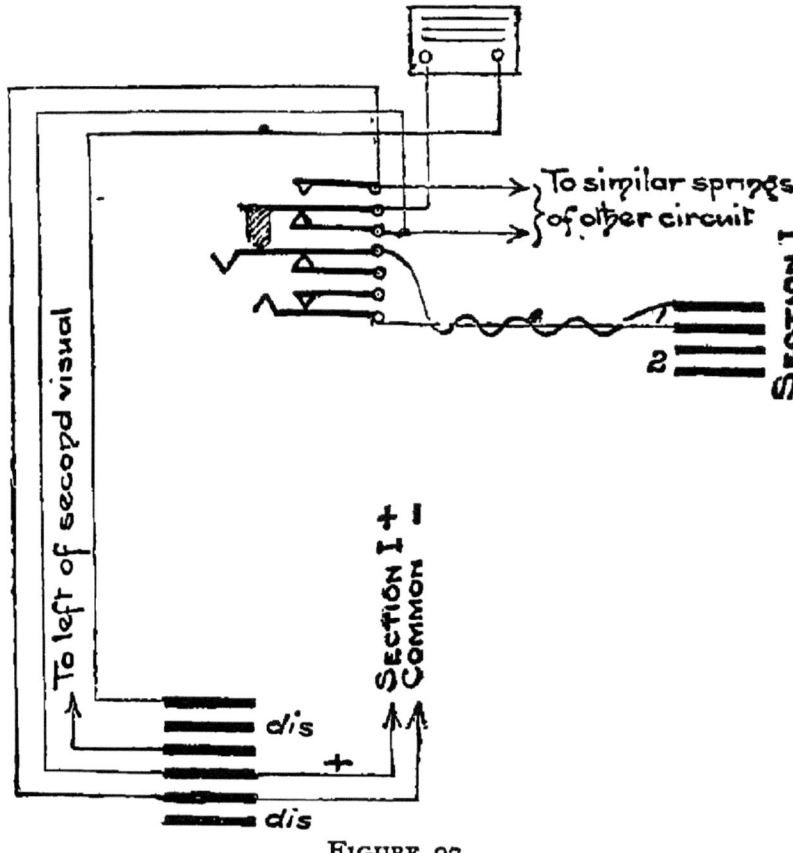

FIGURE 97.

combination key, thus putting her speaking apparatus across the circuit. The section operator states the town required, and the transfer operator then puts the peg in connection with the circuit into a B circuit in connection with the section upon which the required trunk line is to be found. Having done this the combination key is pushed upwards, thus connecting the lower long and outside springs. This causes both visuals to go black again. Having finished, the section operator removes the peg, and both visuals are again thrown. The transfer operator removes the connection and returns the key to the central or normal position Everything is again normal.

In order to pass forward the calls received at the transfer board, B circuits are provided as already explained. The B circuits are each equipped with an eight-point switch-spring and a visual indicator. These circuits are joined up in precisely the same way as the pair of circuits shown in skeleton in Figure 84. There is no apparatus upon the loop, and the whole of the signalling is done upon the separate wire. These B circuits with their corresponding visuals appear above the A circuits upon the vertical portion of the board. The lowest row consists of two strips of five eight-point switch springs, which correspond to the second visual of the first ten sections. Next come the B circuits of Sections XI. to XX., and above this, XXI to XXX. By putting two strips of ten visual and switch springs (as in Figure 93) in place of strips of five, it will be seen that we may go on to sixty sections, and this course was pursued at Manchester.

The actual connections are shown in Figure 97. The principle of the connections needs no comment, since it is precisely the same as that indicated upon page 98. The insertion of a peg automatically calls the wanted section, and the transfer operator sees when the call is answered by the visual going black.

As in the case of trunk switch sections, the cross-connection strips upon the left accommodate the signalling and those upon the right the speaking circuits By left and right are meant left and right looking at the section from the front.

Every transfer board is fitted with fifteen cross-connection strips, each containing four groups of six tags, placed upon either side, thus providing accommodation for sixty sections As the boards were originally designed for a different method of signalling, half the tags are not now required, and are left disconnected. In future boards this will, of course, not happen. Each set of six tags accommodates three A or two B circuits, and are marked with the number of the section to which they correspond. An accurate A circuit diagram is given in Figure 98.

The first two rows of B circuits upon the transfer board are those corresponding to Sections I. to X, and the tags accommodating these circuits appear opposite a label marked "Row I." From XI to XX is marked "Row II," and so on Each set of tags is marked by the side in white, with the number of the section to which it corresponds

The ten A circuits appear beneath a label marked "Vis ccts. A," and occupy two-and-a-half cross-connection strips. The remaining twelve tags are in use for the one negative and the ten positive leads coming from the ten A circuits. These ten tags are, of course, all teed together.

The speaking batteries are to be found upon the last set of tags upon the central bottom cross-connection strip.

Actual Connections. 113

The tags which are left disconnected will readily be seen from a very brief consideration of Figure 96 The speaking circuits are similarly arranged and marked. The call wire occupies the same relative position as the first two A circuit positive lead tags. Thus it will be seen how easy it is to trace the tags corresponding to any particular circuit.

A single battery must be used to work the whole exchange, but the battery leads to each section should pass through U links upon the test board, so that a short-circuit upon one of the switch-springs may be readily localised. Where secondary cells are in use, the leads pass through fuses,

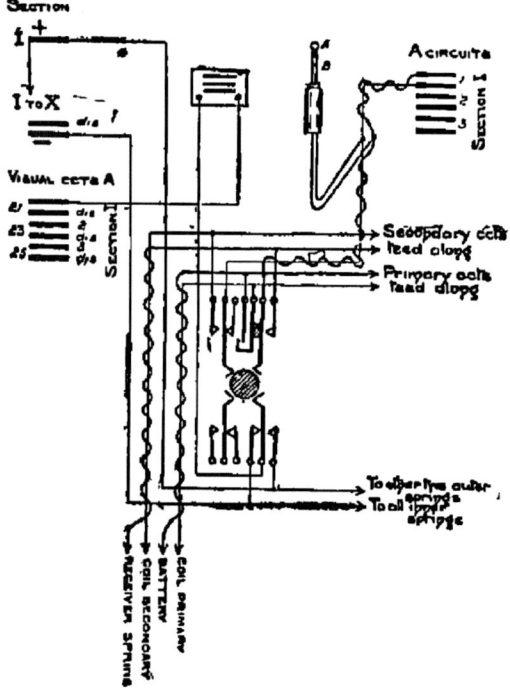

FIGURE 98.

which are blown in the event of a fault. This fuse indicates upon what section or transfer board the fault lies. In the case of transfer boards the A and B circuits are frequently divided into groups, so that the position of the fault may the more readily be ascertained The top spring is connected to the positive and the bottom spring to the negative pole of the battery, so that if the top spring touches the central spring in the normal condition the battery is short-circuited. Upon a switch section this fault blows the section's fuse. The fuse is then replaced by a glow lamp and a peg inserted into each switch-spring in turn until the fault disappears,

I

due to the contact being broken with the bottom spring. A short-circuit, which occurs immediately the peg is inserted, due to a faulty bottom spring, may similarly be proved. As a rule, this is instantly discovered by the operator.

Now, at the transfer board a precisely similar proceedure may be followed. It should be remarked that owing to the formation of a derived circuit all the circuits which are through—*i.e*., indicator black—have their indicators thrown. The faulty circuit does not drop its indicator. The A circuits may be dealt with by manipulating the combination keys.

The transfer boards now in use are, as a rule, of far larger dimensions than is necessary, and it is probable that in future designs the size will be considerably reduced. Space for two operators was provided, but only one is required. The combination key might be replaced by a speaking key of the plug pattern and the signalling accomplished by means of a socket contact, exactly as described in the case of the R.C.J circuits (page 120). Of course, the present signalling wire would replace the bridging coils.

It may be mentioned that a key for connecting two transfer boards together is added. This key merely connects the two speaking circuits together so that an operator may answer calls upon the second board without removing her telephone.

CHAPTER XIX.

Record Table Switch Sections

When the trunk lines were in the hands of the Company, subscribers who desired trunk connections were at the larger exchanges put through to a special table where tickets were made out. At the smaller Post Office trunk exchanges the Company's operators repeat demands to the Post Office record table operators, but as the Company's operators also have to attend to local requirements, there is some chance of error. Accordingly, at the larger offices, the subscribers who ask for a trunk are put straight through to the record table, where they repeat their demand. Having taken their demand, the Post Office operator gives instructions for their disconnection by pulling forward a plug, which lights a little lamp placed by the side of the ticket wire which has been utilised. This is the Company's signal to disconnect

Each record table switch section accomodates ten or twenty ticket wires (officially designated "*record table circuits*"), according to requirements One such circuit is shown in Figure 99 The speaking

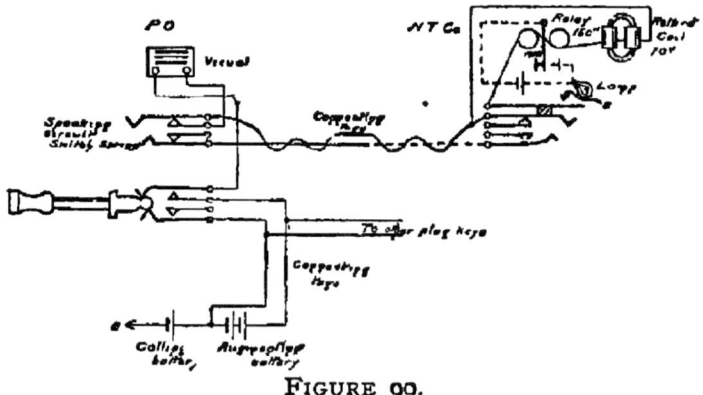

FIGURE 99.

circuit or loop passes from the short spring of a five-point switch-spring to the short spring of the Company's switch-spring, and from long spring to long spring. It will thus be seen that any subscriber connected at the Company's end will be through to the Post Office. The Post Office record table operator is provided with a pair of pegs. One of these pegs is placed in a switch-spring in connection with the ordinary record table tablet, to which the operator joins her telephone. Thus it will be seen that the record table operator is able to speak to any subscriber connected to this circuit by means of the other peg of the pair mentioned. It will at once be apparent that if a subscriber who calls up has merely to say "Trunk," and is put through to the record table, where he is immediately attended to, the system will involve but little delay.

The fact of the insertion of the peg, connecting the subscriber at the Company's end, drops the visual indicator in connection with the circuit. This is accomplished by using the B line of the loop as signalling wire also. Normally, a battery of about sixteen volts is connected through a visual indicator to the B line at the Post Office. The insertion of a peg at the Company's end earths the B line through a relay, which is, however, biassed against this current. The visual at the Post Office shows white, and the record operator pegs on to the loop. A white ticket is then made

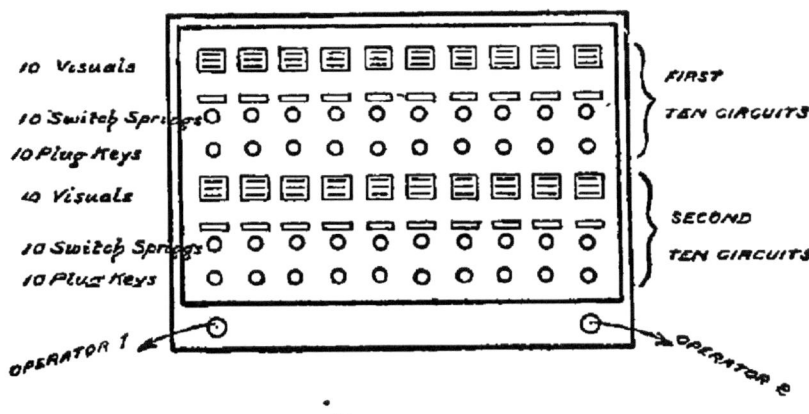

FIGURE 100.

out, and the operator withdraws her speaking peg, at the same time pulling forward a plug-key, which increases the voltage of the battery to about thirty, the current due to which overcomes the bias upon the Company's relay, thus lighting the small lamp attached to its local circuit. The visual at the Post Office also shows white. The lighting of this lamp is the Company's clearing or disconnecting instruction. The subscriber's peg is withdrawn, thus removing the earth from the B line, the lamp goes out, and the visual at the Post Office goes black, since there is no path for the battery. The Post Office operator sees this, and pushes the plug-key back, thus putting on the smaller battery, and everything is in *status quo ante*.

The switch-spring at the Post Office end consists of four springs, as shown. The plug-key consists of a similar switch-spring, but with the outer springs of the same length. A brass plug is fixed to the front of the section so, that when pushed home, as shown in the figure, the outer springs are joined together through it. When pulled outwards the outer springs make contact with the inner. At the company's end a switch-spring with five springs is employed. The insertion of a peg there causes the top sp ing to touch the contact, which is joined to earth; thus a current flows from the smaller battery to the bottom plug-key spring, through the brass plug to the outer spring, through the visual to top inner spring of the loop switch-spring, and thence along the B line to the Company. It there passes through the retard coil and relay through the top spring to earth. This causes the Post Office visual to show white, but the Company's relay is not affected The insertion of a peg at the Post Office end cuts out all the signalling apparatus by disconnecting the top inner spring and visual. The visual now shews black. Having taken the demand the plug-key is pulled forward and the speaking peg withdrawn, thus a current from the whole battery leaves *via* the top inner and top outer springs of the plug-key through the visual and line to the Company's relay, which is to earth The relay is now actuated and the lamp lights. The Company disconnect and the Post Office indicator goes black. The plug-key is pushed back, and everything resumes its normal condition.

The object of the retard coil is to minimise overhearing between the several circuits when at normal

It will be seen that the battery connections are teed along, and this is done by means of bare copper wire in the actual apparatus

The disposition of the apparatus is shown in Figure 100

To receive calls at night a relay is placed in the positive lead of the calling battery, and the local contacts are connected to a vibrating sounder and battery In the daytime this relay is short-circuited by means of a two-way switch. The arrangement is similar to that described in Chapter XX.

CHAPTER XX.

Direct Junction Circuits.

In the suburbs and outlying districts, instead of bringing the subscribers' lines into the central exchange, the Company sometimes establish sub-exchanges. If a subscriber at one of these exchanges desires to be connected to a trunk line, he would ordinarily have to go through the central exchange to the Post Office. Where there is a considerable amount of trunk traffic to any particular sub-exchange, direct junctions from the sub-exchange to the Post Office are provided exclusively for this traffic.

These junctions are dealt with in three ways at the Post Office. Where there is no record table, or where there are only two or three sections, the circuits are placed upon the least busy section, or upon the central section in the latter case. Where, however, there are several sections, a special switch, in size comparable with a record table switch section, is used. This is placed upon the record table, and is attended to by one of the record table operators. Where the number of junctions to be dealt with exceeds ten, a junction transfer section has to be employed.

All these devices are worked upon the same principle, and having described the simplest form, it will be but a step to the more complicated arrangements.

Since only two wires are provided for each circuit, the signalling has to be done over the circuit itself. It is not practicable to do this by sending currents round the loop, and therefore the earth has to be requisitioned as a return wire. In Chapter XXII. it is explained to what trouble an earth upon one side of a loop gives rise. In order to avoid this difficulty bridging coils are used. These coils are merely electro-magnets with their magnetic circuit permanently closed. A coil of wire is wound around an iron core. An outer iron sheath is next passed over the whole, and both ends are closed by discs of iron touching the core. Two soldering tags project through holes in one end of this disc. The resistance of these coils is usually either 600ω or 1000ω. If now we join two of these coils in series and tee them across a telephone loop, we may put an earth upon the central point of the two coils, as we shall thereby treat both lines alike, and thus shall not disturb the balance of our circuit. The object of using these magnetically short-circuited electro-magnets in preference to resistance coils lies in the fact that the former possess a large amount of self-induction, and thus their resistance to a speaking current is enormously enhanced, and the speaking volume of sound, therefore, is not sensibly diminished by their application.

If now bridging coils are placed at either end of our circuit, we may perform whatever signalling we choose over the centre of the loop without interfering with the speaking round the loop. It is, of course, assumed that the circuit is not faulty.

One R.C.J. (*Record Call Junction*) circuit terminated upon a switch section is illustrated in Figure 101. It will be seen that the loop passes to the long and short springs of an eight point switch-spring, the three top springs of which are used for signalling, as in the case of the ordinary transfer circuits. Across the loop is placed the bridging coils, the centre of which passes through a visual indicator to the middle spring At the Company's end the circuit terminates upon a five-point switch-spring, the inner springs of

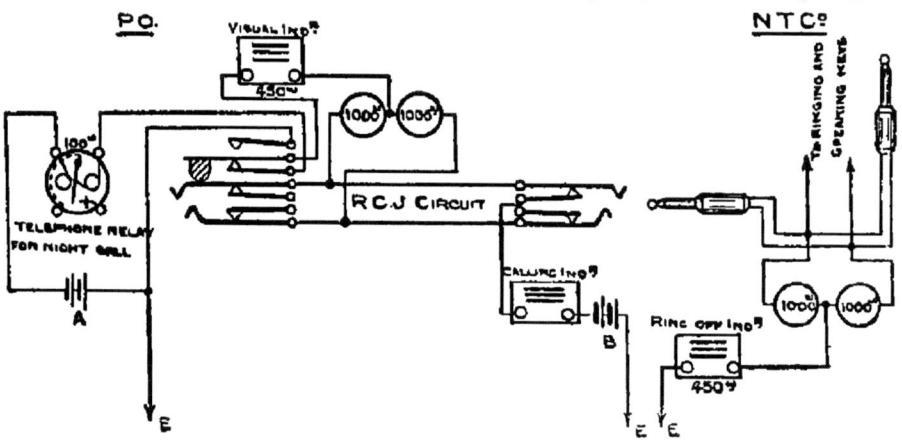

FIGURE 101.

which are connected together to a visual indicator, having an earthed battery joined to it. In the normal state of affairs, the negative pole of the battery A at the Post Office passes through the relay, bottom and central springs through the visual and along both lines in parallel. The battery B is exactly equal to the A, and as both have their negative poles to line, no current whatever flows through the indicators. At the Company's end a special pair of cords having bridging coils with an earthed visual indicator across them is used for connecting subscribers to the R.C J circuit. Immediately a peg is inserted at the Company's end the inner springs no longer make contact with the line springs, and in place of this the lines are connected to the ring-off visual across the cords, and thus the circuit of the battery A is completed. This drops the Post Office visual also, and the operator's attention is thereby called. A peg is inserted at the Post Office in order to answer the call. This disconnects the battery A and substitutes an earth in its place; thus both indicators go black, showing the Company that the subscriber is receiving attention.

The withdrawal of the peg at the Post Office again drops both visuals. The Company clear the line by withdrawing the peg, and the opposing battery B is again inserted. The signals are now normal

The insertion of a peg at the Post Office removes the battery A, and the battery B drops both the calling and the Post Office visual. When the Company insert a peg to answer, the battery B and the calling indicators are cut out, and the Post Office visual goes black, thus showing that the Company have attended. The withdrawal of the Post Office peg gives the clearing signal.

It will thus be seen that the whole arrangement is entirely automatic, the insertion or removal of the pegs giving all the requisite signals. It

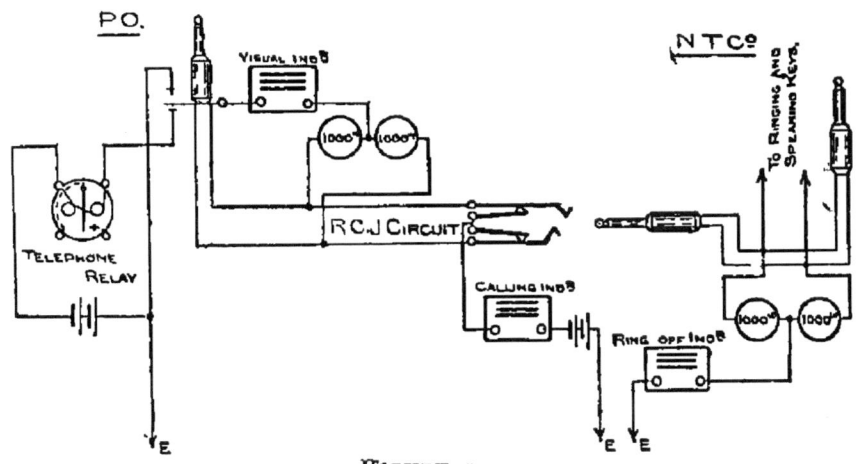

FIGURE 102.

may be well, however, to trace the ordinary procedure. A subscriber calls up and asks for a trunk connection. He is then connected to the R.C.J. circuit by means of the special pair of cords. This act calls the Post Office, who answers him and takes particulars of his request. The peg is withdrawn, and the Company receive a clearing signal upon the ring-off indicator, which is instantly obeyed When this subscriber's turn comes for the use of the trunk the Post Office operator inserts a peg in the R.C.J. circuit, thus calling the Company. This subscriber is asked for, and is then connected to the R.C J circuit He is rung up by the Post Office, and after having been put through, is cleared by the withdrawal of the peg at the Post Office

The use of the relay at the Post Office end is the only point which has not been dealt with Its object is to provide an audible signal at times of the day or night when continuous attention is not given. It will be seen that whenever the Post Office visual is actuated a current flows through this relay, closing the local circuit, which is joined to the vibrating sounder of the section upon which the circuit is placed.

Upon a B section five circuits may be placed by the addition of a strip of five visuals and one of five eight-point switch-springs Ten circuits may similarly be accommodated by using strips of ten indicators and switch-springs. It will be obvious that this can only be done where the section is not a very busy one. If these circuits are placed upon the central section of three sections, the central operator will make out all the tickets. The

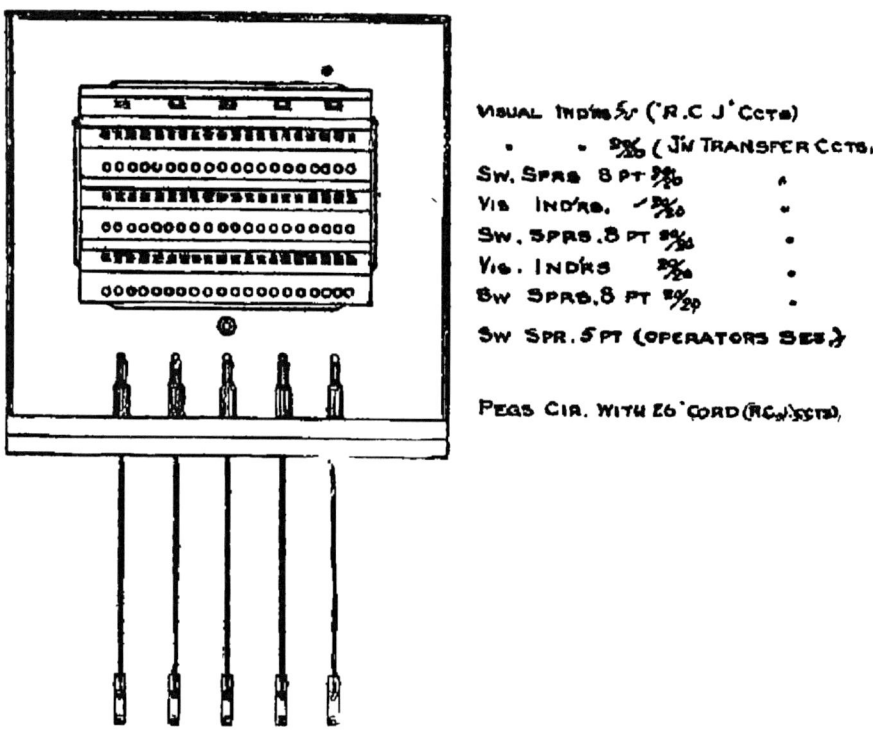

FIGURE 103.

outer operators will easily be able to reach the circuits when they want sub-exchange subscribers.

Where there are a large number of sections such a system would be quite impossible, owing to the delay in getting through the transfer boards. Let us suppose that there are three of these circuits to A, B and C sub-exchanges to be dealt with at an office having twenty sections. In order to avoid the necessity of the section operator speaking to the R C.J. operator, one of the visual indicators upon each section is marked A, another B, and a third C   At the R.C.J. switch the ten circuits marked A at the sections are placed beneath a label marked A. These circuits are equipped with visuals and eight-point switch-springs, and are joined up and worked exactly as explained in the case of ordinary transfer circuits The ten circuits marked B are collected under a heading B, and the circuits are similarly dealt with Suppose now an operator wants B sub-exchange. A peg is inserted in the transfer switch-spring marked B, thus dropping the indicator in connection with this circuit at the R.C.J. switch. As this indicator appears below the heading B, the operator at once knows that B is wanted here. If the circuit is disengaged the required connection is made by the insertion of a peg, and both indicators go black When the section operator has done with B, she removes her peg, and thus the visuals both show white until the R.C.J. operator disconnects (which this signal instructs her to do)

It now only remains to show what modifications it is necessary to make in the apparatus for this purpose. Firstly, then, there are these circuits to the sections These are accommodated upon strips of twenty visuals and twenty switch-springs, there being space for three such sets of strips. Above these come the five visuals in connection with the circuits terminated upon the sections. At the base (Figure 103) are five pegs in place of the switch-springs used when the circuits were terminated upon the sections These pegs are furnished with a socket-contact, which takes the place of the three top springs in the switch-springs The peg (Figure 102) rests upon a lever, which, normally, it holds on to the lower or battery contact. Raising the peg allows the lever to rise to the earth stop, thus calling the Company automatically. The remainder of the signalling is precisely as explained before, the replacement of the peg giving the clearing signal upon the ring-off indicator.

Upon seeing a signal under C drop, the operator takes up the C peg and puts it into the switch-spring of the calling circuit The act of raising the peg calls the Company, and the operator at the section sees she is connected by her visual going black A peg connected to the operator's speaking set is provided for answering calls from the sub-exchanges, and also for informing the operators that the lines are engaged.

The sections are placed upon the record tables, and accommodate five circuits. Occasionally, however, ten circuits are put upon one switch by the addition of five more pegs and visuals

Where the number of sub-exchanges is large a section of a larger type is used This stands separately, and accommodates thirty circuits, but in principle it is precisely the same as the record table transfer section just described

In London, where there are several exchanges, this system is adopted, as obviously it would be out of the question to give to every section five junctions to each of London's ten or twelve exchanges

CHAPTER XXI.

CALL OFFICE CIRCUITS.

At all Post Office trunk exchanges a silence cabinet is provided, in order that the public may be able to use the trunk lines. These cabinets contain a telephone, and are made sound proof, in order to ensure privacy of conversation. At the counter a switch is provided, so that the clerk

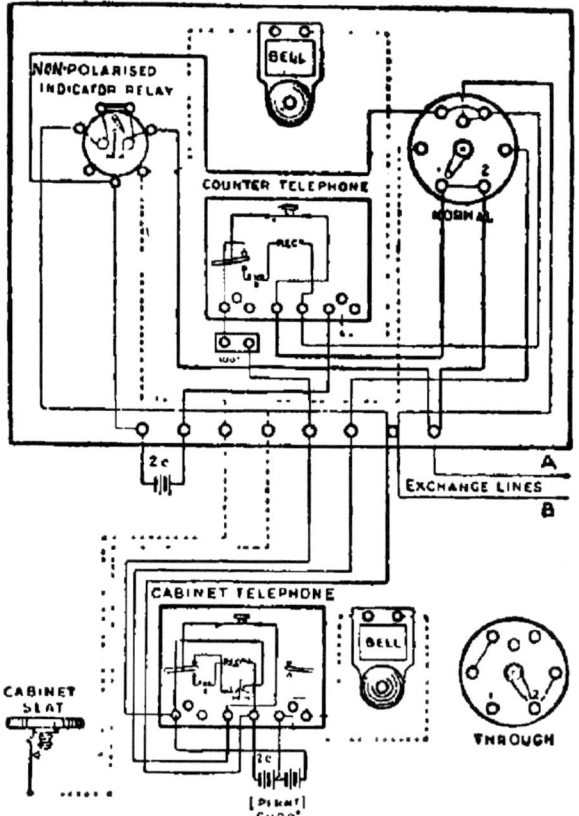

FIGURE 104.

may speak to the exchange or to the cabinet, also that the cabinet may be put through to the exchange. Further, an automatic arrangement is made use of, which rings an electric bell immediately the speaker rises.

It is the duty of the counter clerk to ascertain from each applicant for the use of a silence cabinet the details of the service required, and to communicate these details by telephone to the trunk exchange operator in charge of the counter circuit

A four-cell battery is joined to the cabinet telephone, and this sends a permanent current to the exchange, where it holds up a shutter, as previously explained in the case of local subscribers This battery also serves for the counter telephone speaking to the exchange.

The arrangement is depicted in Figure 104 A bell, relay, switch, and telephone are mounted upon a wallboard at the counter. This is known as the "*counter communication switch*" The current flows from the positive pole of the silence cabinet four-cell battery to the fifth terminal of the counter switch, where it passes through a 100ω resistance coil through the telephone to the seven-terminal switch In the normal position the battery goes on through the switch to the A line, thence back along the B line to the negative pole of the battery. The two last terminals of the counter communications switch are used for the lines, and it will be seen that they are also connected to the non-polarised indicator relay The indicator relay is thus bridged permanently across the exchange lines and will be deflected to the right when the permanent current is flowing When the counter clerk depresses the button upon his telephone or removes the receivers, the permanent current is stopped and the exchange is thus called. The counter is called by ringing from the exchange by means of a battery which acts in the same direction as the permanent current battery, and it is therefore necessary to have resistance in circuit with it, so that it (the permanent current battery) may not short-circuit the relay and thus prevent the receipt of the ring The local circuit of the relay is from the positive pole of the two-cell battery attached to the switch to terminal 6 of the telephone, thence through the bell to the right hand contact of the indicator to the tongue, and thence back to the negative pole of the battery

When the clerk speaks from the counter switch the two-cell battery is again used. It passes to terminal 6 through the primary circuit to terminal 5, and back through top right and left terminal of the 7-terminal switch back to the negative pole of the battery. The secondary circuit is from terminal 4 through the lower two terminals of the switch to the A line, back along the B line to the top centre terminal of the switch, back to terminal 5 of the telephone. This provides for all the operations from the counter.

In order to put the cabinet through to the exchange, the switch is turned to position 2, and the connections are altered so that the cabinet telephone is joined to the exchange lines. Terminal 5 of the cabinet telephone is permanently connected to the B line, and terminal 4 passes through the two lower terminals upon the right of the switch to the A line. Thus the secondary circuit is completed, and when the conversation is finished the battery sends a current along these lines, thus giving the clearing signal. The primary circuit is completed through the instrument in the usual way by means of the agglomerate cells in the cabinet. The caller is able to speak to any place to which he is extended by the switch room. It will be noticed that when the switch is at position 2 the permanent current passes through the cabinet relay, and thus ringing currents from the exchange will ring the bell in the silence cabinet when necessary.

When the caller rises, the contact which is placed upon the cabinet seat is made, and the circuit of the two-cell battery is completed from the positive pole of the battery, through the bell, etc., through the seat contact, back through the 7-terminal switch to the negative pole of the battery. The bell rings until the switch is put back to the normal position. This is the counter clerk's clearing signal, and by turning the switch the local circuit is broken. The cabinet battery gives the clearing signal to the exchange as explained.

Where it is necessary to provide more than one silence cabinet a special switch is used which will accommodate five cabinets. The lines to the exchange terminate upon polarised drop indicators upon the switch sections or upon indicators upon the local switch. At the counter these lines terminate upon the long and short springs of a five-point switch-spring. The inner springs of this switch spring are connected to batteries to supply a permanent current, and in series with the battery, resistance coils of 200ω are inserted in order that ringing currents sent from the exchange may not be short-circuited by this small battery. Non-polarised indicator relays are, of course, connected across the loop, and it is upon these indicators that calls are received. Normally, then, the indicator is deflected to the right by the permanent current sent from the counter. When the line is connected the permanent current battery joined to the inner springs is cut out and the needle hangs vertical. Ringing currents from the exchange deflect the needle to the left and at the same time close the local circuit attached to the armature, thus ringing a bell. A diagram of these arrangements is given in Figure 105.

The lines from the cabinets to the counter switch terminate upon eight-point switch-springs (Figure 106). It will thus be seen that any cabinet line may be joined to the exchange lines by means of a pair of plain cords—*i.e.*, a pair of pegs connected together by two-conductor cord without any apparatus connected across: in fact, cords such as are used upon the record table switch sections previously described. At the cabinet a speaking battery only is employed, and no permanent currents are sent. In order that the counter clerk may speak to the exchange or to any cabinet, a telephone connected to the outer springs of a five-point switch-spring is provided, and this may be connected to any line by means of a pair of pegs. In order to actuate the cabinet bell, a ringing battery is also added to the counter telephone In the case of the exchange the insertion of the peg cuts off the permanent current, and thus automatically registers a call at the exchange by allowing the shutter to drop.

The only point which now remains to be dealt with is in reference to the automatic ring-off given when the caller rises from the seat. This is accomplished by the speaking battery and a non-polarised drop indicator at the counter The B line of the pair of wires between the counter and the cabinet is connected to the negative pole of the speaking battery at the cabinet as terminal 5 serves for one pole of the speaking battery and also for the B line. The positive pole of this speaking battery

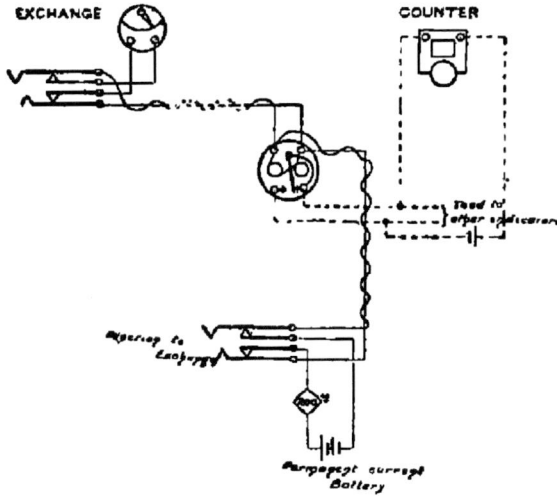

FIGURE 105.

passes through the contacts of the cabinet seat to the counter, and thence through the non-polarised indicator in connection with the cabinet on to the top spring of the eight-point switch-spring. The central spring of this switch-spring is connected to the B line of the circuit to the cabinet, and thus when a peg is inserted in this switch-spring the speaking battery from the cabinet sends a current along the seat wire and through the indicator, thus attracting its armature and dropping the shutter. This closes the circuit of the local battery and rings the bell, thus calling the attention of the counter clerk. In the normal state of affairs (as shown in Figure 106) the circuit is broken at the switch-spring, but when a caller is speaking the circuit is broken at the cabinet seat. When, however, he rises the circuit is completed, and the indicator falls For five cabinets, we should require five lines to the exchange, each connected with an indicator relay and a five-point switch-spring, and five lines to the cabinets, each connected to an eight-point switch-spring. The seat wires (one from each cabinet) would each have to be provided with a non-polarised indicator. One bell and one local battery would serve for the whole board, but separate permanent current battery resistance coils would have to be provided for each exchange line. One operating telephone and half a dozen pairs of pegs and cords would also be required.

At the base of the board containing this switch there are two rows of twenty terminals, which are appropriated as follows:—

Row 1.—Five loops (ten wires) to the exchange, and five loops (ten wires) to the cabinets.

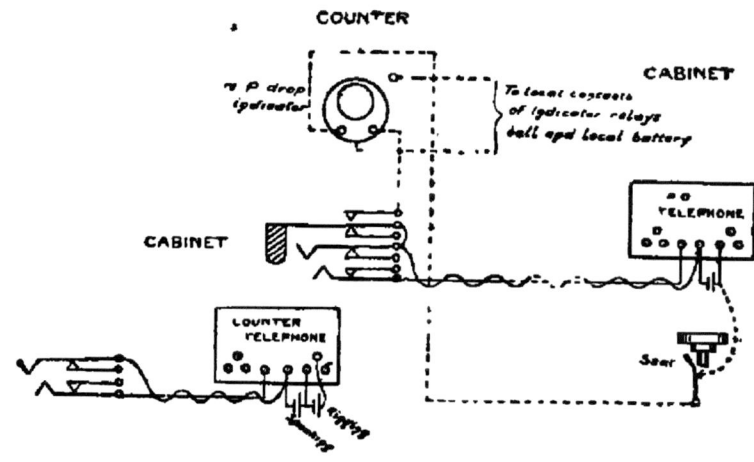

FIGURE 106.

Row 2.—Ten wires to accommodate the five permanent current batteries; three wires to take the speaking and ringing batteries for the operating telephone; two wires for the bell local, and five seat wires.

The arrangement of the apparatus upon the switch is now the only point which requires consideration. At the top are placed the five indicator relays in connection with the exchange. Below this are placed the five non-polarised indicators, and then come the strip of five-point switch-springs, and below this the eight-point switch-springs. Beneath all this the operating telephone, 200ω resistance coils and terminals are placed. The bell surmounts the whole arrangement.

At the Stock Exchange a very rapid system of working is in vogue. It is of first importance to members of the Stock Exchange to be able to get through upon trunk lines without having to return to their offices. Now the amount of traffic justifies the use of an operator at the Stock Exchange, and a most rapid system has been designed.

The member gives to the operator his number (*i.e.*, his number upon the Company's local system) together with the town and number of his correspondent. This is repeated to the record operator at the Post Office upon an up call wire, and a ticket is there made out. Since the call is booked to the subscriber's number no money transaction has to be entered into by the operator.

The whole of the cabinets at the Stock Exchange are multipled on to every switch section in the central exchange. A call wire is provided running round all the sections to the Stock Exchange operator. This operator specifies the cabinet to which any call shall be put through, and, therefore, the fact that every cabinet appears upon every section does not lead to confusion or the design of engaged tests.

When the call matures, the section operator enters the down call wire to the Stock Exchange by depressing her call-key, and asks where to connect the subscriber. The Stock operator replies by mentioning the subscriber's number and that of a disengaged cabinet. The section operator forthwith makes the necessary connection. An attendant stands by the Stock Exchange operator and hears the information given to the section operator, which he repeats by shouting. This is the method in which the subscriber is called. An incoming call is dealt with in precisely the same manner. In reply to the section operator's request for a cabinet for the required number, the Stock operator gives the number and that of the cabinet, which is loudly repeated by the attendant, and thus the wanted subscriber is advised if he is in the exchange.

Now, in order that the Stock Exchange operator may know which cabinets are engaged, a current is normally sent from the Post Office over the loop through bridging coils and an earthed galvanometer. When a peg is inserted at any switch section, this current is stopped, thus indicating cabinet engaged. At the switch sections, the cabinets are connected to eight-point switch-springs. The cabinet lines are, of course, teed on to the respective line springs of all the switch sections. The indicating or clearing battery for each circuit passes through the lower and central springs of each switch-spring on to the inner springs of the last switch-spring, thus the insertion of a peg at any switch section stops the current, and thus serves as a reminder to the Stock Exchange operator that that particular cabinet has been engaged. In the busiest part of the day, the operator can always see which cabinets are vacant by glancing at the galvanometers.

The silence cabinets are joined up similarly to those shown on page 123, save that the seat contact is omitted and no counter switch provided.

The permanent current is restored when the speaker puts back the receivers. This actuates the section operator's exchange galvanometer, and the peg is withdrawn, thus restoring the indicating current, and thereby showing the Stock Exchange operator that the cabinet may now be used again.

It may be mentioned that the cabinet lines each pass through two five-point switch-springs, in order to provide a means of cross-connecting lines and cabinets when necessary. Such a necessity would arise if two circuits were faulty, one in the cabinet and one in the line or Post Office switch-springs. One good circuit could be made up from the two faulty ones.

CHAPTER XXII.

INDUCTIVE DISTURBANCES.

Unless special precautions are taken it is impossible to obtain a silent telephone circuit. Neighbouring wires act inductively upon the circuit, thereby introducing currents which cause disturbance. The telephone receiver is so extremely sensitive that these currents produce effects which very often render speech impossible. In order that we may clearly apprehend the way in which these induced currents are produced, it may, perhaps, be desirable to consider one or two very simple cases of induction.

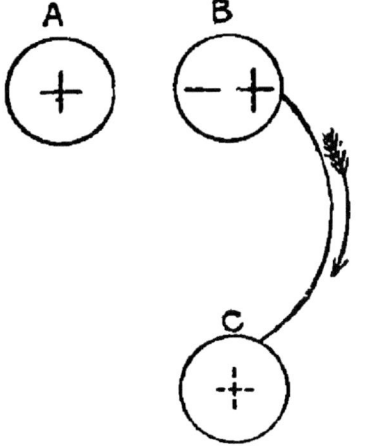

FIGURE 107.

Consider three insulated brass balls, A, B, and C (Figure 107). A and B are close together, and C is at some distance from both, but is joined to B by a copper wire. If now the positive pole of an earthed battery be joined to A, it (A) will become positively charged. This will attract a negative charge in B, which it will hold bound, the positive being repelled. This positive charge will flow along the wire to the ball C, which will receive a positive charge. In other words, charging A will cause a current to flow from B to C. It will be noticed that the effect of A upon C has been neglected; its effect is merely to reduce the quantity of electricity flowing from B to C; in fact, we may say that A exercises precisely the same influence upon B and C, but that owing to the greater proximity of B the charge induced in B is correspondingly greater. Since, then, the two spheres are at different potentials, a flow of electricity takes place

Let us now consider what happens when A is discharged. The bound negative charge upon B is set free, and is neutralised by the free positive formerly existing upon B, and *by the positive upon* C. In order that the positive upon C may get to B, it has to flow along the wire, so that a current in the opposite direction to the first current flows along this wire. Thus we may say that any change in the electrical condition of A produces currents in the wire between B and C, a positive increment in charge producing a current from B to C, and a decrement of charge producing a current from C to B. If these balls were sufficiently large, a conversation could be held between A and B by placing a telephone in the wire between B and C, and one between A and earth. This is a typical example of electro-static induction.

Now to apply this knowledge to the case of a circuit, imagine a metallic circuit B C, beween X and Y, with telephones at either end (Figure 108).

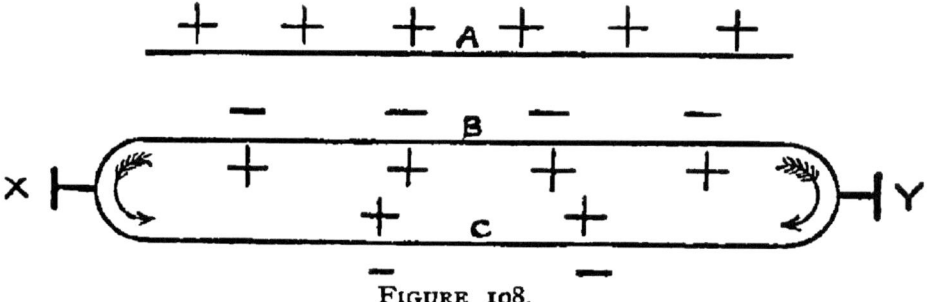

FIGURE 108.

The wire A is the disturbing wire, and is much nearer to B than to C. In the normal condition there are equal quantities of positive and negative upon B and upon C. Now, immediately A is positively charged, the negative electricity in B is attracted and the positive repelled to C, since the repelled positive charge upon C is so much smaller than that upon B. Obviously this can only take place by currents flowing through X and Y. If the charge upon A be still further increased, then a further current flows from B to C. If now the charge upon A be reduced, some of the bound negative upon B is released and flows to C through X and Y. A negative charge passing from B to C is obviously the same thing as a positive current flowing from C to B; therefore we see that every variation in the charge upon A causes corresponding currents through the telephones at X and Y.

The connection of the positive pole of an earthed battery to A at either end charges it positively. If the wire is disconnected at the distant end

Dynamic Induction.

the potential is the same at both ends, but if the distant end be earthed the potential at the battery end will be that of the battery, but will be zero at the other; hence the charge upon an earthed wire is half that upon the same wire disconnected, or, what comes to the same thing, we may say the capacity of the line is half that in the former case. Any change in the value of the current flowing along A will induce currents in X and Y, and conversations taking place along A will be heard at X and Y; and, similarly, conversations taking place between X and Y will be overheard in A. This is static induction. If the circuits did not possess capacity, obviously charges could not be induced upon them, and thus overhearing due to this cause could not take place.

There is yet another kind of induction, viz., electro-magnetic or dynamic, and this is due to the magnetic lines of force due to a current cutting conductors. Let us consider the circuits A and B C (Figure 109). Let us

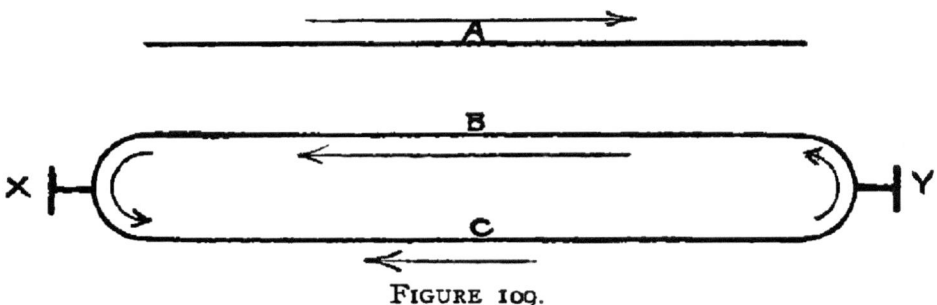

FIGURE 109.

suppose that a current is suddenly started in A in the direction shown. The lines of force from A cut through B and C, thus inducing currents in them flowing in the opposite direction to the originating current in A. Since B is nearer to A than is C, the magnetic field is greater at B, consequently a higher E M F. is induced in B than in C, and this E M F. overpowers that in C, thus causing a current to flow round the loop as indicated by the arrow heads. Thus, any changes in the value of the current flowing along A will produce corresponding currents in X and Y. This is a typical case of dynamic induction.

Both static and dynamic induction take place at the same time in the cases shown where one wire of a loop is nearer to any disturbing source than is the other. Referring to and comparing Figures 108 and 109 it will be seen that a current as shown in Figure 109 will charge the wire A positively, hence we shall have currents induced in B C due to static induction as shown in Figure 108, and at the same time currents due to dynamic induction, as shown in Figure 109. At X these currents add together, since they are flowing in the same direction, but at Y they are flowing in opposite directions and oppose each other. Here we see an explanation of the curious phenomenon that whilst one end of a circuit may be quite silent the other may be very noisy indeed. At the silent end the static and dynamic induction is equal and opposite, whilst at the other they add together. This state of affairs is somewhat rare, but there are certain faults which will bring about this result.

If now the disturbing wire were as near to B as to C, the inductive effects upon the two wires would be the same, and no effect would be produced (Figure 110.) Static induction would rot affect X and Y, since

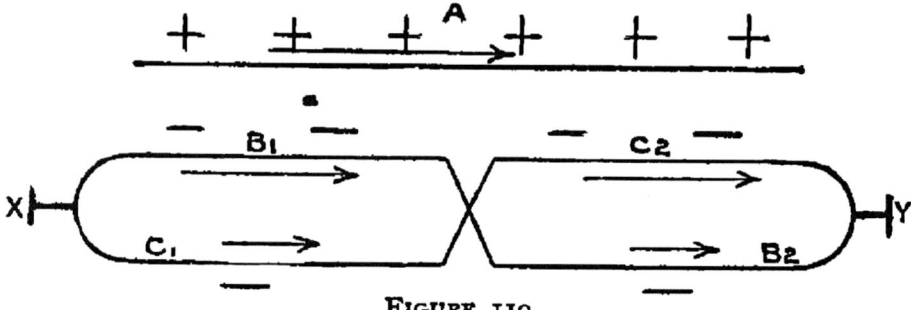

FIGURE 110.

the repelled positive charges upon B and C would be equal. Dynamic induction could not produce any effect upon X and Y, since the currents induced in each wire would be equal, and none could flow from one wire to the other.

In order to overcome the trouble due to induction from neighbouring circuits, two courses are open to us. The currents induced upon each wire must be made equal, and then, since they would tend to flow round the loop in opposite directions, no effect would be produced. Prof. Hughes solved this problem by his suggestion of symmetrically twisting each

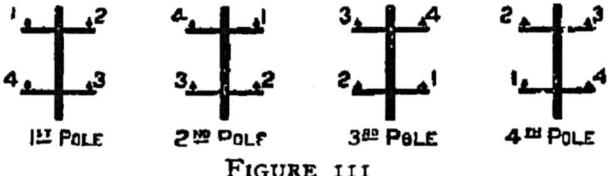

FIGURE 111

pair of wires. The other alternative is to cross the A and B lines; but these crosses become exceedingly complex where a large number of wires have to be dealt with, and though the system is much used in America it is unquestionably inferior to the symmetrical twist as carried out by the British Post Office.

The wires are twisted in fours, each wire forming the meeting-point of two sides of a twelve-inch square. The diagonal wires each form a loop. The four wires perform a complete revolution every four poles. The positions taken by two pairs of wires are shown in Figure 111. Nos 1 and 3 are the A and B lines of the first circuit, and Nos. 2 and 4 those of the second circuit. By following the changes of No 1 it will be seen that in turn it occupies each one of the insulator positions, but with No. 3 always diagonally opposite to it. Nos. 2 and 4 similarly revolve between Nos. 1 and 3 At the fifth pole the wires assume the position shown for the first pole The distance from No. 1 to No. 4 is twelve inches, as also is the distance from No. 1 to No. 3 Similarly the distances from 4 to 1 and to 3 are equal, thus the currents induced will be equal. Now let us consider the effect of bad regulation of the wires. Suppose at the first pole No. 2 dips far more than do the others, No. 2 will then be closer to No 3 than No 1, hence induction will take place. Again, the canting of the arms will bring about a similar result. In fact, anything which tends to destroy the square will give rise to inductive disturbances. Lack of uniformity in the spans may sometimes cause trouble owing to local circumstances, such as the presence of trees This increases the capacity of the nearer wires more than the more distant ones by bringing the earth

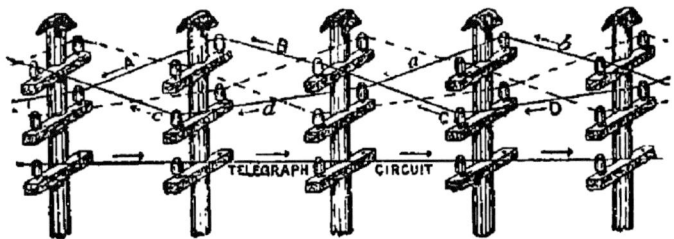

FIGURE 112.

up nearer to the wires. All these difficulties are to a very large extent overcome by symmetrical twisting and careful maintenance

When through any fault more current passes along one wire of a telephone circuit than the other, manifestly this is equivalent to a single telephone circuit If now we indicate a telegraph circuit upon the same poles as telephone loops, we shall see that it will have no effect upon the perfect and symmetrically twisted telephone circuits (Figure 112).

The dotted wires form one loop, and the full lines the other It will be seen that A, B, C, and D balance a, b, c, and d. The effects produced are equal and opposite the two wires of each loop

Let us now see what happens in the case of telephone lines which are not perfectly insulated. Where the lines are equally and uniformly insulated the insulation resistance of the lines is equivalent to a fault at the centre of each line equal to the insulation resistance of the lines. Where the insulation resistance of the two lines of a loop is equal, no effect will be produced upon the circuit provided it is uniformly twisted.

It will be seen (Figure 113) that each earth fault clears half of each line's charge. The neutral point is at each telephone, and therefore no discharge passes through the telephones. Where the insulation of one line is lower than that of the other, the lower resistance fault clears some portions of the other line, and, in order that this may occur, current must pass

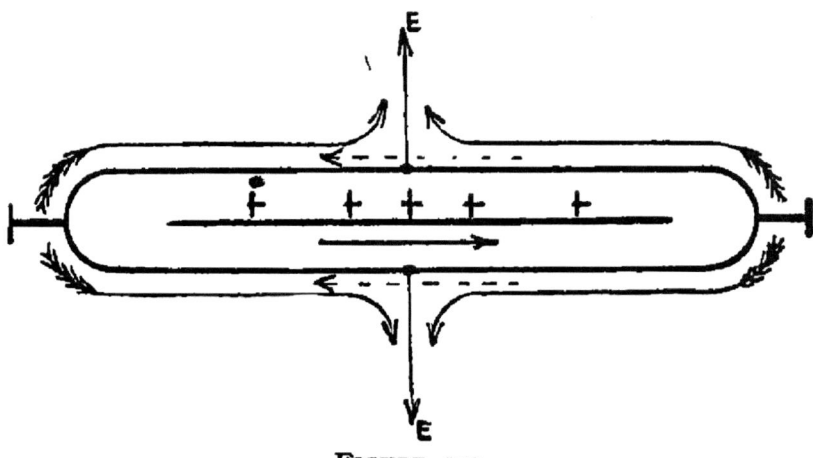

FIGURE 113.

through the telephone. Where the capacity or resistance of the lines of the loop are unequal, the neutral point of the discharges is altered, and thus more or less current flows through the telephone and we have noise from neighbouring circuits. Where a definite fault upon one line exists, the neutral point would be moved, as shown in Figure 114. Here we see that currents pass through the telephone, but it should be noted that all these troubles are due to *static* induction. In only one case in twenty can inductive disturbances be traced, even in part, to *dynamic* induction, and then the majority of the trouble is due to static induction. Again, it is somewhat difficult to separate dynamic and static induction and direct leakage from circuit to circuit.

It should be noted that under no circumstances should circuits be twisted with the pole between them, as shown in Figure 112. Forty-eight-inch arms are used and four wires upon either side of the pole fill two arms. To maintain the insulation as perfect as possible, Cordeaux's double shed white insulators are employed. This is necessary with even the shortest trunk lines, as they are liable to be connected to long lines. From a consideration of the principles enunciated previously it will be seen that a small fault upon a short circuit may not cause any disturbance upon that circuit, yet when connected to a long trunk in perfect condition the disturbances caused will be sufficiently pronounced to prevent speech. A full earth upon a junction line or subscribers' line may not be observed till it is connected to a trunk line having a large capacity. In fact, the conditions of Figure 114 will be reproduced. Thus we see the cause of the phenomenon that two circuits

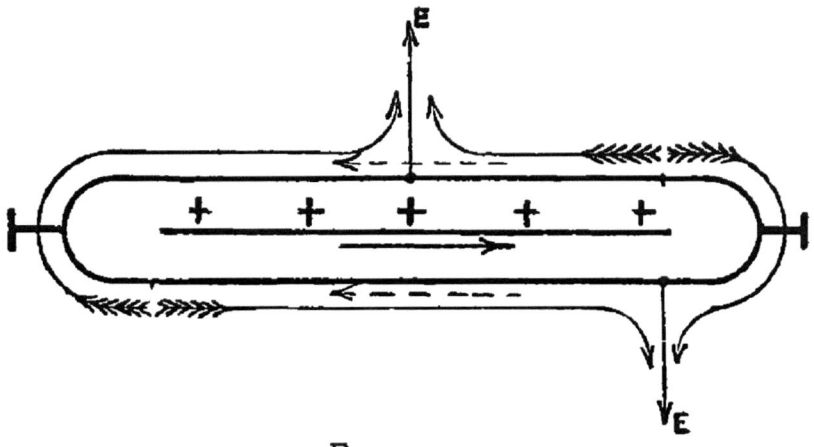

FIGURE 114.

apart may each be silent, yet when connected together are excessively noisy

It may be mentioned that the wires in cables are always symmetrically twisted either in pairs or in fours In the latter case the diagonal wires should always be chosen for forming each loop.

CHAPTER XXIII.

Superimposed Circuits.

It has been found possible to obtain three circuits where only two pairs of wires existed between two points. The third circuit is termed a superimposed circuit, since the principle of its application consists in using the first trunk as an A line and the second as the B line, bunching together the two lines of each trunk for this purpose.

In order to accomplish this, four transformers are used. These transformers are in reality specially designed induction coils. The primary coil is wound upon a bundle of thin iron wires, the ends of which project far beyond the windings. Over this is wound the secondary coil, consisting of twice the number of windings, but with the centre of the coil specially connected to a separate wire, known as the tap or centre of the secondary. The iron wires are now bent over the coils from either end, carefully covering each other, so as to form a closed magnetic circuit. The instrument is indicated in Figure 115 as made by Messrs. Ericsson.

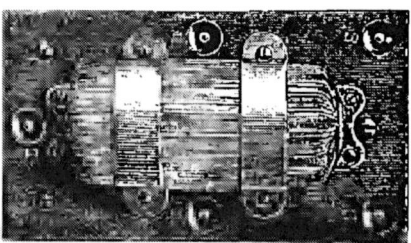

Figure 115.

The two terminals marked S are the ends of the secondary, the single terminal the centre of the secondary, and the central terminals the ends of the primary. The iron wires from the left hand side extend to the outer margin of the right hand brass band, and those from the right to the outer margin of the left hand side.

When a current is stopped, started, or altered in strength, the strength of the magnetic field flowing through the iron wires is altered in value, and E.M Fs are thus generated in the secondary in exact accordance with the variations in the primary Thus it will be seen that if telephones be connected to the primary and secondary terminals of the transformer, it will be possible to speak from the one to the other just as though a metallic connection existed between the two circuits. Similarly generator currents will be reproduced by the secondary, and will drop an indicator or ring a bell as the case may be.

Two trunks with a "+ 1" circuit superimposed upon them are shown in Fig. 116. The thick windings terminating upon switch-springs, marked Nos 1 and 2, at A and B are the primary circuits of four transformers. The trunk lines are connected to the secondary windings. If now two subscribers are connected to No. 1 switch-springs at A and B, they will be able to converse with ease The A subscriber's currents will pass through the primary of transformer 1, thus inducing currents in its

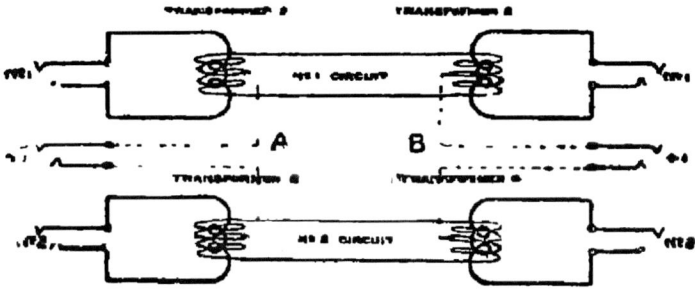

FIGURE 116

secondary which pass along the trunk line through the secondary of transformer 3, thence back along the trunk line to the secondary of transformer 1 The currents passing through the secondary of transformer 3 alter the value of the magnetic field circulating round the iron wires and thus currents exactly corresponding to the original ones are induced in the primary of transformer 3 at B. These currents circulate through the apparatus of the subscriber connected to No. 1 switch-spring at B. Similarly, B subscriber speaks to A subscriber through the two transformers No 2 circuit is arranged in a precisely similar manner and subscribers connected to this circuit may similarly converse If now two subscribers are connected to the superimposed circuits they will be able to converse without producing any effect upon the circuits No. 1 and 2, and without those circuits producing any effect upon them The path of the current is from the long spring to the centre or tap of the secondary of transformer 1, where the current splits equally through the two windings, passing in the same direction along the A and B lines of the trunk to the ends of the secondary at B, at the centre of which the currents re-unite and flow through the subscriber's apparatus connected to B to the centre of transformer 4, where it again splits, equally flowing along both lines of the trunk to the centre of transformer 2, where the two portions unite and flow back to the subscriber at A. Thus, it will be seen that the subscribers connected to the + 1 circuit are able to converse. No effect will be produced upon circuits 1 and 2, since equal currents flow through each half of the secondaries, but in opposite directions. In the case of No. 1 circuit it will be seen that the currents flowing from that circuit pass through the primary, thus inducing currents flowing from end to end of the secondary in the same direction throughout, whereas the currents from No. 1 circuit would, in the one case, be in the same direction, and, in the other case, in precisely the opposite direction to this current; and, since currents circulating in the two halves of the secondary are equal, no effect is produced, since the magnetic fields would be in opposite directions This has the further beneficial effect of annulling the self-induction of the coil for the + 1 circuit, the winding being, so far as this circuit is concerned, exactly like that of a resistance coil, where the wire is doubled back upon itself Since the + 1 circuit is connected to the centres of No 1 and No 2 circuits, there is no current flowing through the + 1 circuit from Nos. 1 and 2 Thus it will be seen that all three circuits may be speaking at once without interference the one with the other

Two perfect circuits have been postulated in this case, but as these are things which exist only in imagination it will be well to consider what happens with ordinary circuits. Upon each circuit there will be a certain amount of leakage, owing to the insulation resistance of the circuits not being perfect. In the case of circuits in good order, we may imagine this insulation leakage as due to single faults at the centre of each line. In the case where the insulation resistances are all equal no trouble is caused, but in the event of unequal insulation derived circuits from one circuit to another are formed. If the two lines of circuit No. 1 differ in insulation resistance, conductor resistance, or capacity, the current splits unequally from the superimposed circuit, thus causing overhearing

The conditions for obtaining a satisfactory circuit are —

    The circuit shall not exceed 50 miles in length.

    The two circuits must form the diagonals upon two arms throughout, and must be carefully twisted and regulated.

    The circuits must not differ in conductor resistance, insulation resistance, or capacity.

These conditions will be rendered more apparent by a re-perusal of the last chapter.

It will be apparent from a consideration of Figure 116 that it will not be possible to employ the permanent current system upon circuits No. 1 and

No. 2, since the primary circuit is not in direct connection with the trunk line Thus it is necessary to ring through by means of a generator. Only the two line springs with their inner springs are used to join up the indicators The inner springs are connected to the indicators Upon the superimposed circuit it is possible to work with permanent current, since circuit at either end is connected directly to each other, *via* the trunk lines. This is accordingly done.

The form of indicator used upon circuits upon which a circuit is superimposed is known as the non-polarised indicator relay (Figure 117) It differs but little from the polarised form used upon trunk lines for

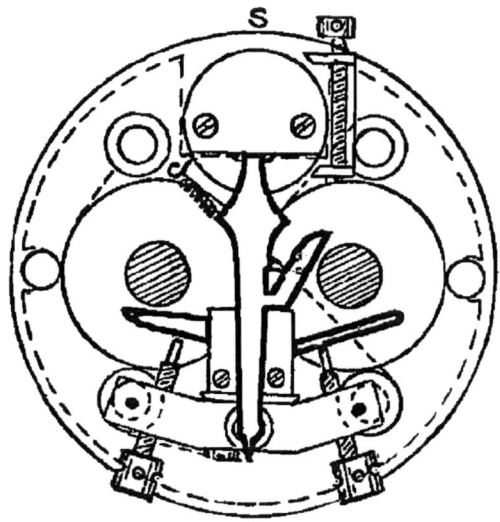

REAL SIZE.

FIGURE 117.

permanent current working The chief point of difference consists in the absence of the permanent magnet which magnetises the armature in the case of the polarised form The armature of the non-polarised relay is of soft iron, and passes over the projecting core of the right hand core and under the left hand one, therefore a current in either direction attracts the armature and thus closes the local circuit An alternating current will therefore permanently attract the armature The needle is, however, rendered magnetic by the permanent magnet upon which the soft-iron needle is pivoted. An alternating current, such as is furnished by a generator, therefore causes the needle to oscillate, and at the same time closes the local circuit.

Actual Connections. 141

The complete connections for a superimposed circuit at the test board and section are shown in Figure 118. It will be seen that five sets of four test holes are taken up at the line test box (see Chapter XXIV.). The two circuits upon which a + 1 circuit is superimposed are marked circuits 1 and 2 Circuit No. 1 passes through the top pair of U links, through the secondary of the first transformer; the primary passes through the second set of U links on to the line springs of the trunk switch-spring It

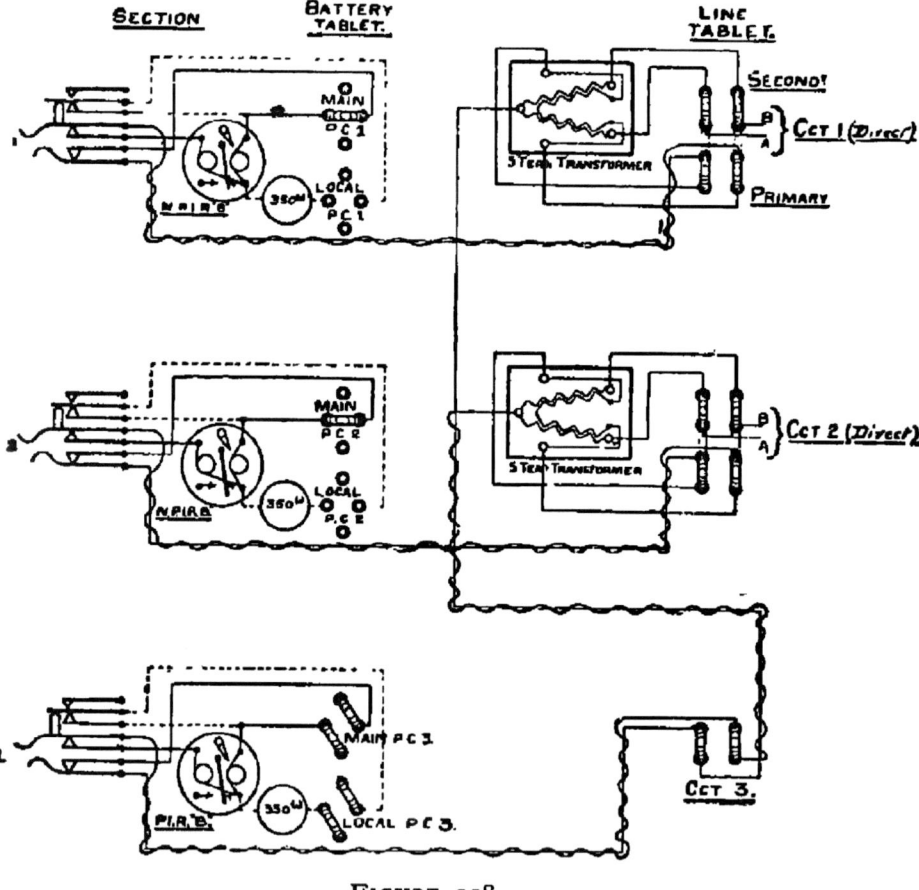

FIGURE 118.

will at once be obvious that ringing will have to be done by means of the generator, since there is no direct connection between the switch-spring and the circuit. A non-polarised indicator relay is substituted for the usual polarised relay, and the batteries which would be necessary for permanent current working are cut out The connections at the sections are not in any way altered. At the battery tablet the main permanent current leads to the section are connected together by the insertion of a U link horizontally. This puts the relay directly on to the inner springs without any other connection. The local permanent current battery is not required, and therefore the U links are removed altogether. It will thus be seen that the top three springs are not used at all upon circuits 1 and 2. Circuit 2 is precisely the same as circuit 1.

The centres of the secondaries of the two transformers go to the lower pair of the fifth set of test holes, and thence through the U links to the line springs of the trunk switch-spring. Since this circuit is in metallic connection with lines at both ends, the ordinary permanent current system is employed. The top and bottom holes upon the battery group are respectively the positive and negative poles of the battery, and it will thus be seen that the main permanent current battery is joined up in series with the polarised indicator relay, and the whole arrangement connected to the inner trunk springs. The local permanent current is bridged across the right hand coil of the relay, with 350ω in its circuit. These circuits are, of course, broken when a peg is inserted.

The needles of circuits 1 and 2 hang vertically, whilst that of + 1 is deflected to the right in the normal condition. It has previously been pointed out that the generator must be employed for ringing upon circuits 1 and 2, and in order to emphasise this distinction the lower half of the indicator relays are painted black. As the generator is here required both to ring the trunk and to ring upon the junction, the two pairs of cords opposite circuits 1 and 2 are both connected to the generator. The black peg is fitted with a red cord, and the ringing key in connection therewith has a black ring round it. Half of the black peg is also coloured red.

The circuits upon which a + 1 circuit is formed are termed the " transformer circuits " on account of the transformers included in their circuit. Such circuits should not be used for long through calls.

Occasionally, owing to climatic conditions or to faults upon circuits 1 and 2, it is not possible to work a superimposed circuit, and it then becomes desirable to cut it off. At the same time the transformers which are in the line circuit are not necessary. By removing all the U links and inserting four links in the dotted positions the two circuits are connected to the trunk switch-springs direct. Where there is a slight fault upon say No. 1 we shall be able to use it, and of course No 2, but if the + 1 circuit were also connected up we should only be able to use one circuit, as faults cause what is said upon any circuit to be overheard upon the remainder. In actual practice it is not found possible to obtain a satisfactory + 1 circuit upon circuits exceeding fifty miles in length.

Before a superimposed circuit is pronounced satisfactory it should be subjected to the following tests. Ring with the generator upon circuits 1, 2, and + 1 in turn, listening upon the remaining circuits. If the generator can be heard the circuit should be abandoned. The cause of this should be traced, and measurements taken of the conductor and insulation resistance of each wire. Dry joints are fatal to superimposing. Next, the circuits should be carefully listened upon for overhearing from other circuits upon the same set of poles If this is observed, then crosses should be made upon the line till the overhearing vanishes, unless, of course, it is due to bad regulation of the wires. The behaviour of the circuits should then be watched for a week or two, noting how often it is necessary to suspend the superimposed circuit.

CHAPTER XXIV.

Test Room Appliances.

In order that faults upon trunk lines, etc, may be rapidly localised and remedied, the provision of a suitable test board at once becomes essential. At the smaller offices where a single section only is necessary a very simple form of *test case* is employed This accommodates the trunks, junctions, and other circuits, but no provision is made for batteries, the leads being taken direct from the battery rack to the switch section. Each circuit passes to two test holes which are connected to the two similar test holes in connection with the switch section by means of U links. Each circuit has then four test holes allotted to it In order that the apparatus upon the switch sections may not be damaged by lightning, protectors are fixed, but upon the instrument or switch section test holes. The object gained is that by no crosses is it possible to leave an unprotected circuit connected to the switch section. If a through wire is terminated upon the section the protector is upon the section, and thus no damage can be done.

At the larger offices test boards are employed, and here provision for batteries is included. First, however, it will be well to consider the design of the test holes. These test holes are made of brass chemically tinned for the sake of appearance. They consist of a brass tube a secured to an ebonite base b by means of a nut and washer d A hole e is drilled through the tube, and through this the connecting wire is passed. It is bent over the tube and securely soldered, thus making an excellent joint. Into the end of the test hole is screwed a brass plate, carrying a carbon disc f, which is one of the pairs of plates of the lightning protector The mica disc has three small circular holes cut into it, through which discharges may take place from the plate f to h, which latter plate is connected to earth by means of the clamping spring g, which is used to mechanically hold the plates together. Thus it will be seen that the two plates are separated only by a small air gap. The distance between the centres of these test holes is one inch, and therefore it is necessary to make the test pillars of different lengths in order to accommodate the two protectors required for the A and B lines. This will be amply apparent from the lower part of Figure 119.

Lightning Protectors.

The action of all lightning protectors is very much the same. When dealing with lightning we confront quite a new aspect of our subject. The currents are of an exceedingly sudden character, hence protection which will suffice for slow heavy currents will be useless in the case of lightning. If an explosive such as gun-cotton is laid upon a stone in the open air and is ignited with a match nothing beyond a "fizz" will take place, but if fired with enormous rapidity by means of a detonator, the air above it, possessing inertia, will not move instantaneously with sufficient rapidity, *i.e.*, it will offer an enormous amount of inertia resistance, with

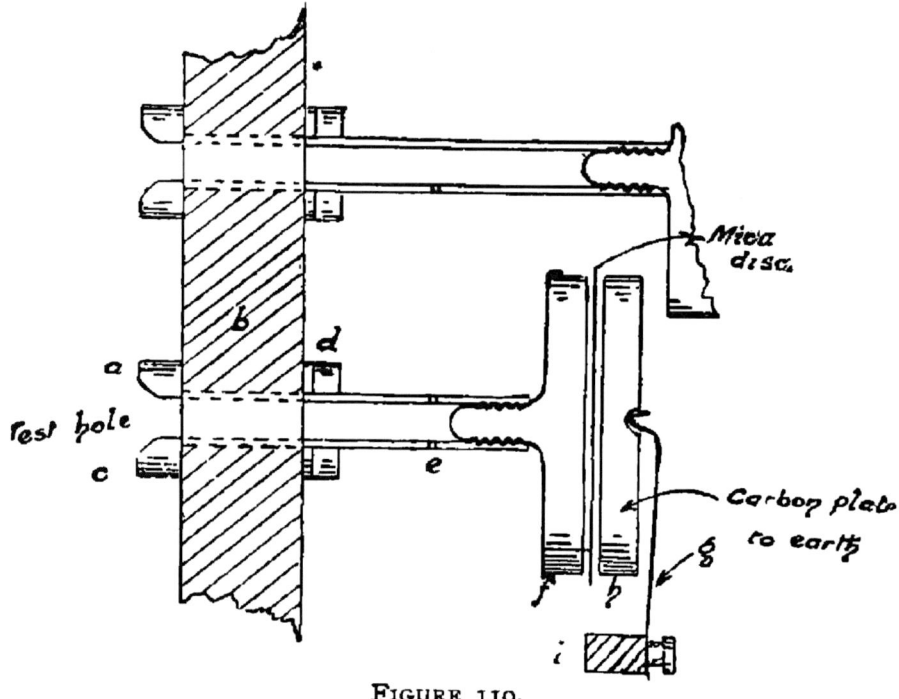

FIGURE 119.

the result that the stone will be blown to pieces. Lightning behaves in an analogous manner to the gun-cotton fired by a detonator. The electro-magnetic inertia resistance offered by a coil of wire to a lightning discharge is enormous, and, if given a chance to rebound and avoid traversing the coil by cracking through a small air gap, it will naturally do so as a path of lesser resistance. This means that a current cannot reach a finite value in an infinitely short time, and the reason of this lies in the self-induction of the apparatus. Wherever a current exists there is a magnetic field in existence. Now this magnetic field is the result of the current, and, in coming into existence, cuts through the current-conveying conductors to which it owes its origin; and we have seen that

L

wherever a magnetic field cuts a conductor an E M F is generated. This E.M.F opposes the current to which it owes its origin. The more suddenly the current is applied the greater is the opposing E.M.F., or, in other words, the greater is the resistance offered. This resistance, which differs from the ordinary ohmic resistance, is frequently termed impedance.

The test board for two sections consists of two tablets of roughly the same size and shape, having respectively twenty-five and thirty-two sets of four test holes. The upper tablet is arranged in five rows of five sets of

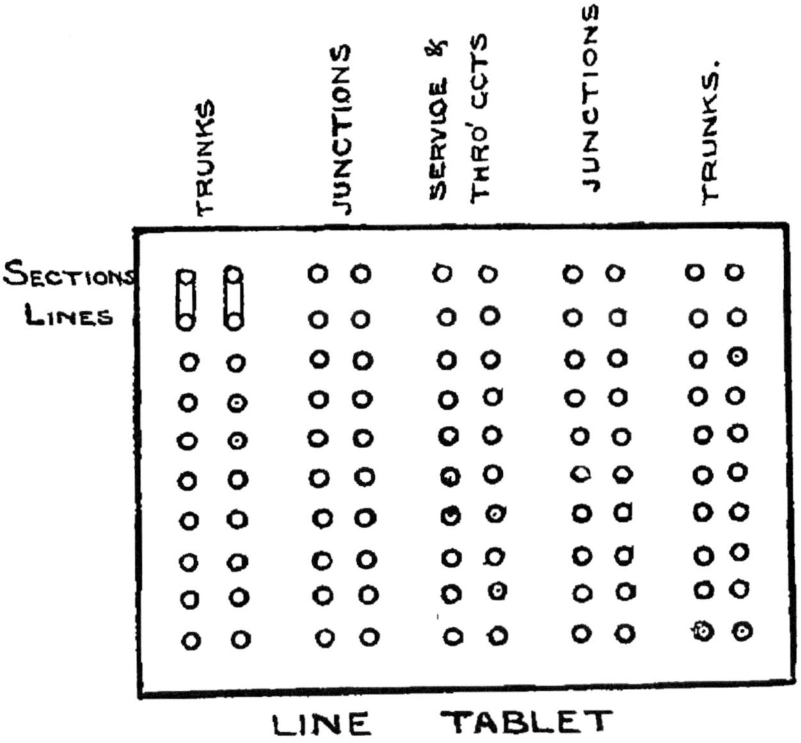

FIGURE 120.

four holes to accommodate the lines The upper pairs of each set of four holes carry protectors, and are utilised for the lines from the test board to the switch section The lower holes are the trunk or junction lines coming into the exchange from the roof or underground cellar, as the case may be. The A line is on the left and the B line on the right.

To each switch section are brought five trunks and five junctions, together with service circuits and, perhaps, a Post Office subscriber or two, but the number of these is distinctly limited, and at the majority of the smaller exchanges there are none. The five rows are appropriated as indicated in Figure 120, the centre row being appropriated to the up and

Battery Test Tablets.

147

down service circuits, the silence cabinet circuit, telegram circuit, and perhaps a through trunk. Where the number of through circuits is large a larger tablet is usually provided

The battery tablet (Figure 121) is appropriated to ten main and ten local permanent current batteries, together with the two batteries used to work the visual and self-restoring indicators upon the two switch sections. In addition there are other batteries which are required, as the bell local, reed ringing and driving, junction clearing batteries, etc.

The top and bottom holes are respectively the positive and negative of the batteries, and it will be observed that it is impossible to short-circuit the batteries by the insertion of a U link in any position. The links are inserted top to right and bottom to left.

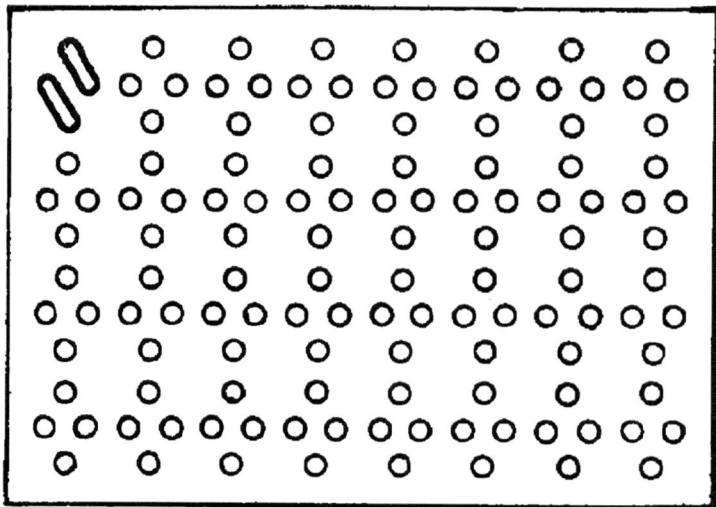

BATTERY TABLET.

Figure 121.

These test holes, both line and battery tablet, are connected to cross-connection tags at the base of the test board, to which the trunk lines, batteries, etc., and the lines from the switch sections are joined. These cross-connection strips each consist of five groups of four tags. The tags are merely thin strips of brass fitted into ebonite blocks and clamped thereinto by means of a thinner strip of ebonite secured by screws. Into the end of each tag a hole is bored at right angles to its length. For the line tablet ten strips are employed. The wires from the test-holes pass to one of the tags. This first set of tags is connected to its fellow by means of tinned copper wire (Figure 122). The object of this arrangement will be dealt with subsequently

L 2

The battery tablet is only accommodated with one set of four tags for each set of test holes. Eight strips are provided, and thus the four lower tags are not required.

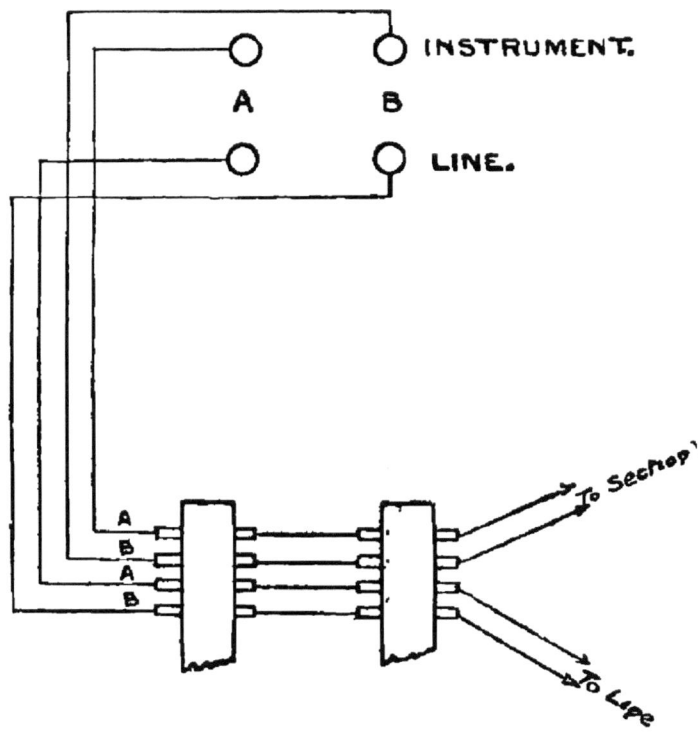

FIGURE 122.

The general arrangement of the cross-connection strips is shown in Figure 123

Here it may be mentioned that by the use of protectors in separate cases, or by the use of a smaller form of protector directly affixed to the cross-connection strips, it is possible to place eight sets of five groups of four test holes—*i.e*, forty circuits—upon a line test tablet of the present dimensions. By this means, the size of the test board can be greatly reduced.

The protectors are of similar design to those already described, but differ in dimensions Two small oblong carbon blocks ($1'' \times \frac{1}{2}''$) are separated by perforated paper, and held together by a spring which forms the line terminal. The other block rests upon a strip of brass, which is earth-connected, and upon the other side of which two similar protector blocks are fitted

Later Forms of Test Board.

A test board of a totally different character is now being tried. This consists of nothing more nor less than rows of ten five-point switch-springs The trunk line is connected to the left hand switch-spring, and the switch section side of that trunk is connected to the right hand switch-spring The inner springs are connected across. Thus in the normal state of affairs the trunk line passes from the line springs to the inner springs, thence to the section inner springs, and to the long and short springs, which are in turn connected to the section. Thus every two switch springs correspond to a set of four holes upon an ordinary test board. Now it is possible to get twelve of these strips into the space of a line tablet—*i.e.*, 60 lines instead of 25 or 40 In order to perform crosses, etc., circular pegs and cords are used. To loop wires, a

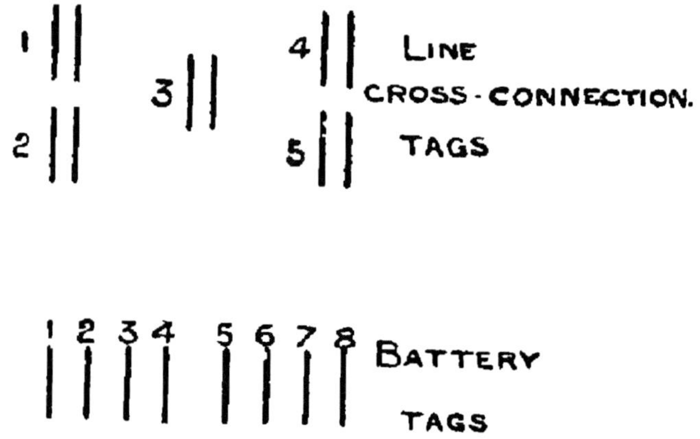

FIGURE 123

brass peg is provided All the testing apparatus is so arranged that tests may be made with facility by the insertion of suitably connected pegs It will of course be quite obvious that, by plugging into the left switch-spring of a pair, the trunk line side is connected, and by plugging the right the section is obtained Through wires take up two holes, one for each side

In a large exchange considerable trouble would be caused if the trunk lines appeared upon the test board in the order in which they appear upon the sections For instance, three trunks to the same town might follow three different routes In tracing, say, a contact, it would be necessary to traverse the board from end to end in order to pick out the wires following the same route as the faulty wire. In all large offices the lines are arranged in the order of the routes which they follow It would not be desirable to place the lines upon the sections in this order, and even if it were so the removal of a trunk from one section to another would be a very awkward matter.

It is, then, necessary to have the wires both in geographical and in the section order. In order to accomplish this object the double row of line tags is utilised The right hand set of tags contains the whole of the trunks in the exchange, and the left hand set of tags contain the whole of the positions upon the switch sections. As five trunks are placed upon each section we see that each strip corresponds to a section It has already been pointed out that the central set of five holes upon the test board are used for through wires, counter-cabinet, and such-like circuits. The junctions and service wires take up two rows, and thus there are only ten positions left for the trunks (*i.e.*, the equipment of two sections). The extreme left hand and extreme right hand strips are therefore devoted to trunk lines. Upon the left side of each of these strips are the trunks and sections in geographical order, and upon the right side in the section order. The right strip then accommodates the wires from section I. The

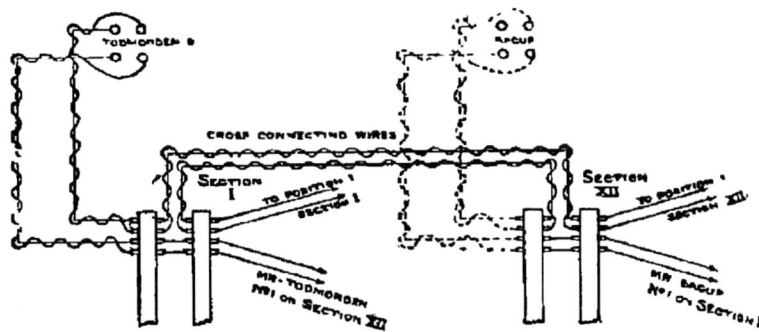

FIGURE 124.

right strip at the right hand side accommodates the wires from section II. If there are forty sections to be accommodated, then the extreme right and left strips of each test tablet will be marked consecutively, section I to XL

To take a case in point, let us suppose that we have to deal with two trunks, Todmorden and Bacup, coming into our office by different routes, the former being No 1 on section I and the latter No 1 on section XII. The Todmorden lines come in upon the right hand tags and are joined through to the left ones by means of bare wire, thence they pass to their position upon the test board. Here they are linked through to the switch section—*i e*, the top set of holes must be joined to the first position on section XII. This is accomplished by taking a pair of wires from the right hand side of the left tags to the right hand side of the first position on section XII. Similarly, Bacup section side is cross-connected to its proper position.

The ten wires accommodating the five trunks upon section I. are all taken to one strip; in fact, the right of the left sides of the trunk strips are the positions upon which all the sections terminate. This enables us to use a six-wire and a four-wire cable to take the whole of the trunks upon a section. Had the trunks upon a section to go to different places, five separate pairs of wires would be necessary. The same remarks apply with equal force to the incoming trunks. Since the wires following the same routes are put together, cabling is again possible.

In order to remove trunks to different places upon the sections, it is only necessary to alter the pairs of wires used for cross-connecting purposes. Suppose that it is necessary to place Todmorden upon the third position of section XXXVI., that the trunk occupying that position is to go to position 1, section I., and that Bacup is to go to position 5 on section V. (unoccupied at present). A pair of wires is soldered in the place of the present pair upon the instrument tags of the route side of Todmorden. These wires are then taken to the left side of the row of tags accommodating section XXXVI., and are soldered to the third position. The wire taken off in order to perform this last operation is taken to the left side of section I., position 1 tags, and the wire removed from there is taken to the fifth pair of tags on the strip appropriated to section V.

All this appears complicated, but in practice it is the simplest imaginable matter. The crossing of a few trunks or their removal to other positions is readily dealt with without incurring either joints in the conductors or a large expenditure of wire.

Where there are only a few trunks these cross-connection strips are not always utilised, but in a large exchange they are essential.

At Manchester, owing to want of space, trunk lines only are placed upon the line tablets. The junctions are accommodated upon a special set of tablets placed above the ordinary line tablets. The record table circuits, etc., are placed upon the battery tablets, and the batteries are temporarily taken direct to the sections. Accumulators will subsequently be used for the permanent currents, and these will be accommodated upon the fuse tablet.

CHAPTER XXV.

The Universal Battery System.

The universal battery system consists in employing a single set of cells to provide power for several circuits. Its object is to provide the necessary electrical energy as cheaply as is possible. The maintenance of a large number of primary batteries, both as regards stores and attention, is most costly. At the larger exchanges where a great number of batteries would be required, accumulators are employed, thus saving not only money but also space.

In order to illustrate the principle of the system let us imagine that we have a battery whose E M F is 20 volts, and whose internal resistance is absolutely nothing. Through a resistance of 1000ω this battery would send a current of 20 milliamperes. If, now, a second circuit of 1000ω be added, a current of 40 milliamperes will be sent out, owing to the total resistance of the circuit now being half its former value—$i.e.$, there will be 20 milliamperes flowing through each of the 1000ω circuits. Thus the application of the second circuit does not alter the value of the current flowing through the first. Similarly it may be shown that the application of circuits of any resistance whatever will not alter the 20 milliamperes flowing through the first circuit. If, however, our battery has a large amount of internal resistance, the application of other circuits will largely alter the value of the current flowing through the first circuit. This will mean that the values of the current through the various circuits will largely depend upon how many circuits are closed at the time, or, in other words, the current will greatly fluctuate. Now this must not occur if the working is to be reliable, and thus it will be seen that batteries whose internal resistance is very low can only be employed.

The batteries employed must also be capable of supplying large currents for a considerable time. Now, the accumulator or secondary cell fulfils all these conditions. The smallest size of accumulator is more than sufficient for the drain of even the largest exchanges. As regards internal resistance, this may for all practical purposes be considered as negligible. The type employed are the E.P.S. K_7 cells, having a capacity of about 100 ampere hours.

Since the internal resistance of the cells is negligible, the calculation of voltages necessary for any particular purpose is remarkably simple, it being merely necessary to multiply the current required by the resistance of the circuit.

Speaking Fuse Tablets.

For working the operator's telephones a single cell, *i.e.*, two volts, suffices About fifteen transmitters are worked from each cell. The positive and negative leads from the cell pass through a system of switches to the speaking fuse tablet, which consists of four sets of brass bars carrying fuse terminals These fuse terminals (Figure 125) consist of a tinned brass screw with a long stem having a washer held firmly against its inner surface by means of the spring (in compression). The general arrangement of a single set of bars is shown in Figure 125 One lead from the cell passes to the top bar and the other lead to the bottom bar. Between these two bars are placed a set of fuse pillars corresponding exactly with those upon the bars. The inner pillars are connected to tags

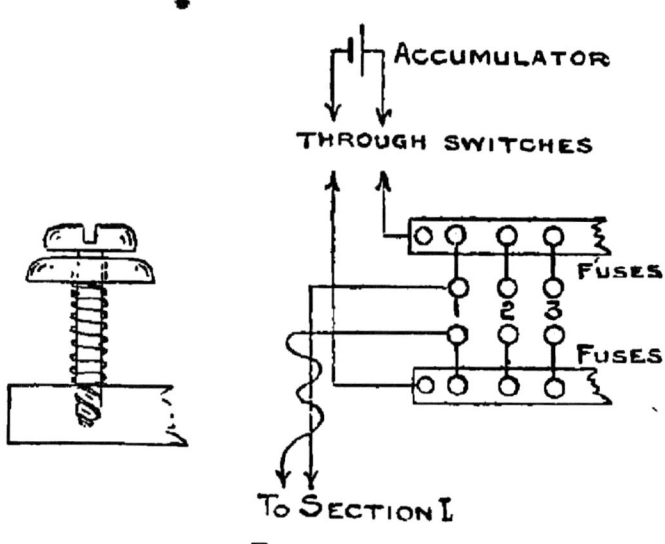

FIGURE 125.

61 and 62 of the respective sections, and thus by placing pieces of fuse wire, as indicated in the above figure, the cell is joined up to the sections which it supplies with current. Tags 61 and 63 are connected together.

The use of secondary cells renders fuses essential, since the maximum current which they will supply is very large—in fact, sufficiently large to burn up the conducting wires, and thus run a great risk of fire as well as injury to the cells. Normally, of course, the currents supplied are very small, owing to the resistance of the circuits, but in the event of a fault which causes a short-circuit a very large current may be supplied In order to avoid this, thin platinoid wires are placed in the circuit, and when the strength of the current reaches one ampere the thin wire is fused and the circuit broken, thus avoiding all risk of fire. It will be quite obvious that it is not possible to insert a fuse between the cells and the point of distribution, owing to the necessity for keeping down the resistance. The speaking fuse tablet is placed inside the case containing the charging switches in order that the length of wire between the cells and the point of distribution may be as short as possible.

Usually two sets of four cells are provided for speaking purposes. This enables sixty operators' speaking circuits to be dealt with without difficulty The speaking tablet, arranged in four rows, also accommodates sixty circuits.

It is absolutely necessary that the resistance of the cells and leads, together with the necessary contacts up to the bars, shall be very low—in

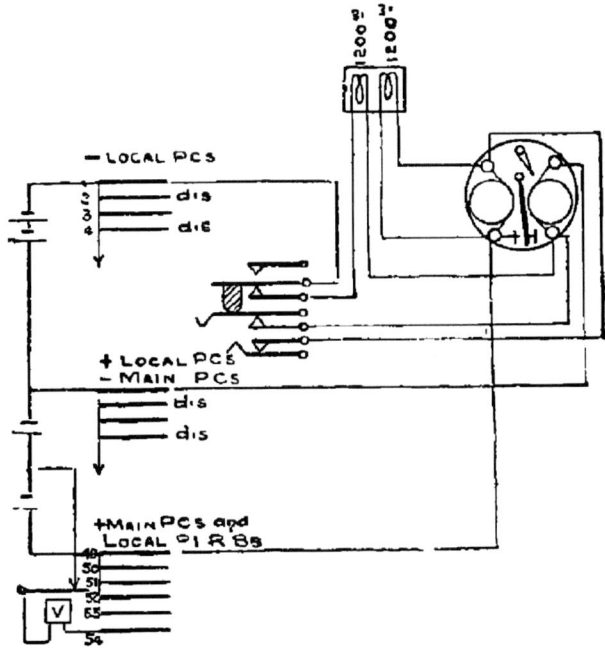

FIGURE 126.

fact, under one-tenth of an ohm. Let us suppose that there are fifteen transmitters joined up to these bars. If now the resistance before the point of distribution is large, then speaking upon any one circuit will be heard upon all the remainder. The working of a telephone depends upon the transmitter varying the current flowing through its primary circuit. If now these variations in current alter the value of the current flowing through other circuits then clearly overhearing takes place It is only where the resistance of the cells, etc , to the point of distribution is exceedingly low that overhearing does not take place There is always a slight amount of overhearing present, but under normal conditions it is not discernible unless the room is perfectly silent and the speaking is carried on in a different room to the listening. The leads between the cells and the bars are usually of seven-sixteens stranded copper. The points where the resistance comes in is, of course, in the various contacts and connections, which are, on account perhaps of the acid-laden air, more or less liable to rapid deterioration.

In order to work the main and local permanent currents from the signalling accumulators, several modifications have to be made. Let us suppose that all the permanent current leads were grouped, just as they are, on to a set of accumulators. We should now find that all the circuits were noisy until a peg was inserted which cut off the signalling circuits. This noise is due to lack of symmetry, since the A lines of all the circuits not in use are directly joined together, whereas the B lines have to pass through the trunk relay to become connected. This ill-balanced circuit would cause trouble by overhearing. An operator at say Bury, listening upon a disengaged Manchester-Bury circuit, might hear an operator at Carlisle calling out upon a disengaged Manchester-Carlisle circuit, due to the fact that the Manchester-Bury and Manchester-Carlisle trunks were put in contact through the lead of the main permanent current battery.

All difficulty may be avoided by placing the main permanent current battery in the centre of the coils of the relay, instead of at one side. This necessitates the changes in the connections of the apparatus indicated in figure.

In the first place the coils of the relay have to be divided so as to place the main permanent current battery in the middle of the coils. The point formerly used for the local contact is appropriated for the end of the left coil. The local contact is joined to the end of the left coil, which is connected to the battery. Now in order that the local permanent current may not cause trouble, a resistance coil of 1200ω is used in place of the 350ω coil and a larger voltage is therefore required. In order to preserve the balance as regards the main permanent current the right hand coil is permanently shunted by 1200ω—*i.e.*, by the same resistance used for the local permanent current. Eight volts is required for the main and also for the local—*i.e.*, 16 volts for both. Now, in order to avoid adding fresh terminals to the relays, the bell local contact is connected to the left hand coil, which is in turn joined to the positive pole of the main permanent current battery—*i.e.*, to the 16-volt lead. The 12-volt lead is connected to one side of the day bell, and thus when the local circuit is completed the 12-volt and 16-volt leads are connected to either side of the bell, thus giving a ring due to four volts. Here, then, we have 0, 8, 12, and 16-volt leads carried to each section. Now 12 volts is used for trunk ringing, and 16 volts for the self-restoring indicators. One other lead is also required—viz., for the transfer circuits and for the junction clearing—

for which 32 volts are used. The generator has also to be provided for. This occupies another two wires. Thus if two 4-wire cables are run to each section we can provide all the signalling power necessary.

In the test room, near the test boards, a fuse table is placed. This fuse tablet consists of rows of brass bars and fuse terminals arranged in a fashion very similar to that described in the case of the speaking fuse tablet Each row, with the exception of the last two, has forty-five fuse terminals, and there are six rows of pairs of bars. They are usually appropriated thus:—

Row 1 —Transfer circuits. Sections 1 to 45.

Row 2 —Generator. Sections 1 to 45

Row 3 —+ Main P.C , + S.R. indicators, + Local. Sections 1 to 45,
+ Trunk ringing   Sections 1 to 45

Row 4 — — Main P.C , + Local P.C. Sections 1 to 45.
— Trunk ringing — S.R indicators — Local P C. Sections 1 to 45.

Row 5.—Transfer circuits, transfer board, record table, transfer sections, and odd voltages (30 circuits).

Row 6.—Junction clearing, sections 1 to 25.   Odd voltages, 10 fuses.
Junction clearing, sections 26 to 50   Odd voltages, 10 fuses.

Thus there is a fuse in every signalling lead to every section Now on row 5 are placed the transfer board leads, the record tables (calling 16 volts, clearing 32 volts), the motor generator (30 volts provided as a stand-by in case of necessary shutting down of electric light plant), the electric clocks, etc , and, in fact, any odd voltages required for special purposes. There is further space at the end of the sixth row for ten circuits.

In order to prevent the fuses being blown every time a faulty circuit is connected to a switch section, a 200^w coil is placed at each section in the generator leads and a 30^w coil in the trunk ringing lead for a like purpose.

At the end of the fuse tablet, rows 5 and 6, is placed a tablet containing switches for crossing the dynamotors. The sections are divided into groups of fifteen, and four switches are provided, thus permitting the number to grow to sixty without any alteration being necessary The switches are remarkably simple, merely consisting of six test holes arranged in circular form with a test hole placed in the centre. This central test hole carries a U link which is capable of connecting the central hole to any one of the six outside holes Now there are eight of these arrangements in four rows The top central hole is connected to the top fuse tablet bar for the first fifteen sections, and the bottom central hole to the lower first fifteen section bars Similarly, the other three sets of two switches are connected to sections 16 to 30, 31 to 45, and 46 to 60 respectively

One pole of the first dynamotor is joined to No 1 test hole upon each of the four upper sets, and the other pole to No. 1 test hole upon each of the four lower sets. No 2 dynamotor is connected to test holes No. 2, top and bottom, and the motor generator to No 3. Thus we can put any particular fifteen sections on to any particular generator by means of this switch The three spare holes are provided in case they should at any future time be required.

The only point which remains to be dealt with is the accumulator switches. These are placed in a special case in the same room as the cells In this case are the speaking and signalling switches, together with the speaking fuse tablet already described It will, perhaps, be most convenient to deal with the speaking battery switches first. Two sets of four cells are employed. One switch, practically consisting of a series of specially designed two-way switches, is used for connecting up either set No. 1 or set No. 2 to the speaking fuse tablet bars. A second switch in one position connects the cells not in use to the charging leads usually taken from the office lighting plant. In the second position the set of cells not in use is insulated. An ammeter for observing the charging current (10 to 15 amperes) and a switch for inserting resistance to vary it are also interpolated in the charging circuit An automatic switch is also inserted, so that should any fault occur the cells may not discharge through it.

The signalling battery usually consists of two sets of sixteen cells, tapped off as follows:—0, 8, 12, 16, 20, 24, 28 and 32 volts The local permanent currents put very much more work upon the cells than the main permanent currents, and therefore it is necessary to carefully group the cells so as to avoid having half the cells completely discharged whilst the other half are practically fresh In order to do this the sections are divided into three groups:—

From 0 to 8 takes Local P Cs , Group 1.
,, 8 ,, 16 ,, Main P.Cs., Group 1 ; also Local P.Cs., Group 2.
,, 16 ,, 24 ,, Main P.Cs., Group 2 ; also Local P.Cs., Group 3.
,, 24 ,, 32 ,, Main P.Cs., Group 3.

It will be obvious that the sixteen volts taken to each section is taken in three leads—*e.g.*, Group II., 8, 16, 20 and 24 volts leads are utilised 8-16 local P.C., 8-20 trunk ringing, 16-24 main P.C., 20-24 bell local. 0 and 32 are taken to each section for transfer circuits. The junction clearing is taken from the telegraph accumulators at offices where these exist, or from primary batteries where they do not. This is due to the objection to having any earth connection upon the signalling accumulators.

Charging Switches.

The object of the switches provided is precisely the same as in the case of the speaking circuits. In one position No. 1 set, together with all its taps, is connected to the signalling fuse tablet in the test room, and in the second position No 2 set is similarly connected. The charging switch insulates or charges the set of cells not in use. It is, of course, needless to say that all leads to the points of distribution, viz, to the fuse tablets, are of heavy wire, usually seven-sixteens stranded copper insulated with vulcanised rubber. Fuses are inserted in all the leads from the cells before they pass to the charging and controlling switches. In the case of the signalling leads the slight resistance inserted is not of such vital consequence. A fault at a switch section blows the small fuse on the fuse tablet, but a fault between the fuse tablet and the cells blows the fuse in the leads of the cells affected.

It has been found possible to considerably reduce the number of primary batteries in use at the various exchanges by suitably grouping the various

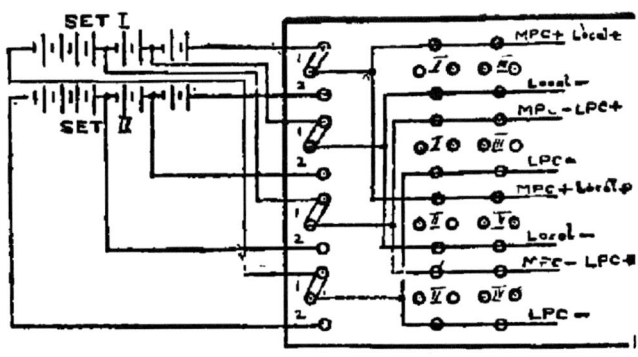

FIGURE 127.

circuits on to a single set of batteries. The whole of the permanent currents are arranged precisely as described in the case of accumulator working, but as no fuse tablet is necessary the batteries are grouped upon the battery tablet as shewn in Figure 127. Two sets of batteries are used, one being a stand-by in case of failure. The left central holes upon the first row of test holes are used for the leads from the sections. The top holes are the leads from set 1, and the bottom ones from set 2, so that it will be seen that, by reversing the U links from the top holes to the bottom ones, set No. 2 will be joined up in place of set No 1 (as shewn)

The local and main permanent current tags are teed at the sections as already indicated. Each section occupies two sets of test holes, so that one battery tablet will accommodate the permanent current leads for twelve sections.

The trunk ringing, self restoring, and bell local may also be worked from this battery precisely as indicated in the case of accumulators. This leaves four sets of holes for junction clearing and any other powers, such as reed ringing or generator, as may be required.

The contacts upon the speaking keys for closing the self-restoring indicators have been modified, so that the current only flows momentarily upon raising or depressing the speaking key. This has been accomplished by rounding off the side of the plunger which works the self-restoring contact. The contact is only made when the key is half way up or down. This improvement has greatly reduced the work upon the self-restoring battery, and it has now become possible to group it upon the common primary battery.

At all the larger exchanges one or more sets of bichromate batteries in parallel will be used.

It has been pointed out that one battery tablet will now serve for twelve sections. At an office of this size a six-panel test board having six line and six battery tablets would at present be required. Now under this arrangement five battery tablet spaces would be left idle, and by filling these up with line tablets the size of the board could be reduced to four panels.

A form of lightning protector has been designed which will fit on to the cross-connection strips of the test boards. These protectors consist of small rectangular carbon blocks insulated by perforated paper. Now by dispensing with protectors upon the test holes it is possible to get forty sets of four holes into an ordinary tablet—*i.e.*, one of twenty-five holes. By replacing the present tablets an exchange of twelve sections could be accommodated upon a test board of three panels—*i.e.*, five line tablets and one battery tablet. Thus, the size of the test board may be reduced to about half its present dimensions in this case. With a switch-spring test board a still further reduction is possible. This is a most important development in view of the value of space in Post Offices.

It will, of course, be obvious that it is not possible to work more than one operator's telephone from a primary battery owing to the latter's internal resistance.

Post Office telephones cannot be worked from the secondary cells owing to the primary and secondary circuits being in unsymmetrical contact, and hence telegram telephones are always worked by primary batteries. Similarly the primary and secondary circuits of switch-board telephones have to be separated.

CHAPTER XXVI.

SMALL LOCAL EXCHANGES.

The system adopted by the Company for dealing with their subscribers varies very considerably with the requirements. Where the number of lines is under 200, separate switch-boards, each accommodating 50 subscribers, are employed.

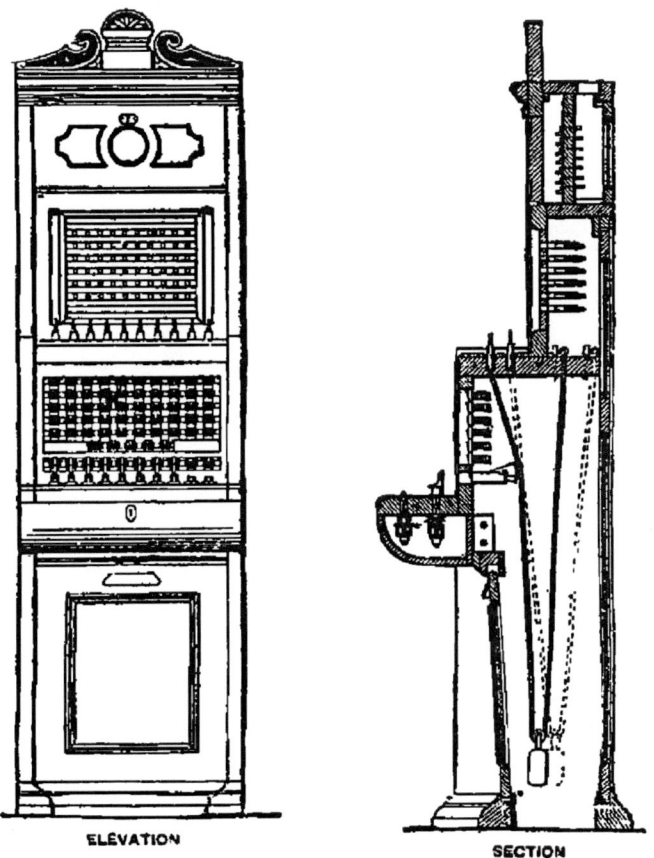

FIGURE 128.

The general appearance of the switch-board and a sectional drawing are shewn in Figure 128. Each subscriber's line terminates upon a switch-spring and an indicator. The switch-springs are acommodated at the top of the board, and it will be observed that there are six rows of ten. These ten extra switch-springs are provided for various junction circuits, should they be necessary. Similarly the five indicators below the fifty subscribers' indicators are provided for similar purposes. The pairs of cords are placed upon a small shelf above the indicators and below the switch-springs, the object being to avoid the cords crossing in front of and thus obscuring the view of the indicators. The last row of ten indicators are for the ring-off signals, and upon the shelf below these indicators are placed the ringing and speaking keys.

The subscribers' lines terminate upon five-point switch-springs, the inner springs of which are connected to low resistance (100 ω) indicators, the form of which is indicated in Figure 129. It consists of an electro-magnet

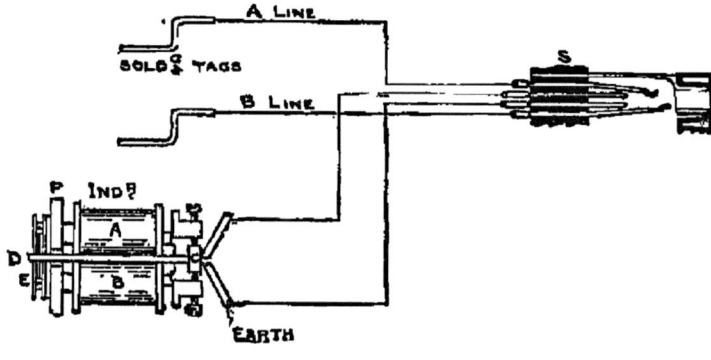

FIGURE 129.

A B with a small iron armature C carrying a lever D pivoted in front of it. The lever catches the pivoted shutter E, which falls forward when the armature C is attracted. Upon a brass disc, normally covered by the shutter, the subscriber's number is painted in black figures. It may be mentioned that these indicators occupy about one square inch each. Thus, the subscriber turning the crank, discloses his number at the exchange

The ring-off indicators, which are in circuit whilst subscribers are conversing, are of the tubular form, very similar to the back coil of the self-restoring indicator, but much smaller and more compact. Of these there are ten, one for each pair of cords. The indicators are covered with an outer iron sheathing to prevent overhearing from one circuit to another *via* the contiguous indicators. The low resistance line indicators are not in circuit during conversations, and therefore do not need this provision.

The pegs are of precisely the same construction as those used by the Post Office and need no comment.

Only one pair of ringing keys is provided for the whole ten pairs of pegs and speaking keys, and thus it becomes necessary to put these ringing keys in with the operator's telephone—*i e.*, the speaking keys switch the particular pair of cords through the ringing keys to the operator's telephone. In order to accomplish this, a speaking or, as it is usually called, a listening key of more complicated structure is required The ringing keys are of the same type as those used by the Post Office, but the mechanical design is slightly different.

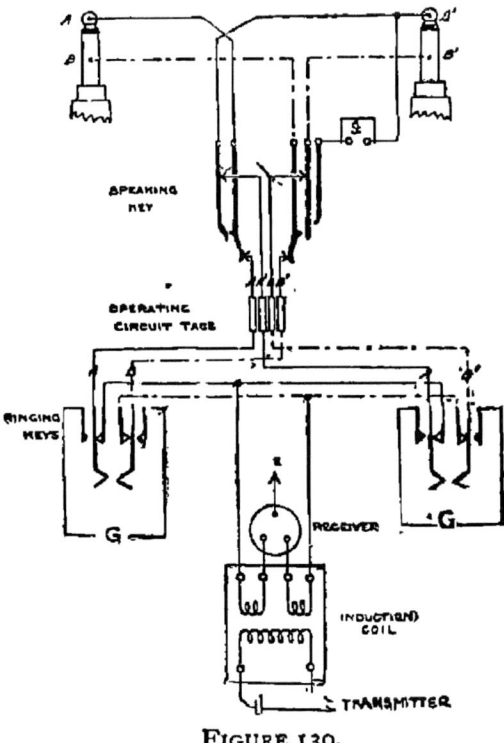

FIGURE 130.

The complete connections of a pair of cords, speaking key, and the operating connections are shewn in Figure 130 The five springs of the speaking key are furnished with four contact stops, upon which they rest when in the speaking position shewn.

In order that we may ring upon either pair of cords, both lines have to pass through the ringing keys; hence each speaking key, when in the speaking position, passes the A and B lines of each peg to the four bars. The four lines A B A^1 B^1 of the two pegs then pass to the long springs of the ringing keys, whose inner springs are connected together. Teed across this connection comes the induction coil and operator's receiver. The B line of the pegs is dotted throughout the diagram in order to facilitate tracing. Depression of the left key rings on to A and B, and depression of the right key rings $A^1 B^1$. The depression of either key cuts off the other one as in the case of the Post Office trunk system. It will be obvious that the four bars marked "operating circuit tags" are common to the ten speaking keys

The ring-off indicator is permanently teed to the A lines, but is only joined up to the B lines when the key is in the normal position, in which case the two left springs are in contact, thus connecting the A lines of the two pegs, and disconnecting them from the operating circuit bars. The B lines are similarly connected by the corresponding springs on the right hand side, but in addition to this the outer spring also makes contact, thus joining up the ring-off indicator in bridge across the cords

It will be seen that the induction coil has six terminals and that the secondary coil is thus divided into two half-coils, the operator's receiver being placed between them instead of at one side as is the case in the Post Office system The object of this will be seen later when the multiple board is considered, but suffice it to say that in this case such arrangement is quite unnecessary and has only been utilised for the sake of uniformity of connections.

The subscribers' lines are all brought to soldering tags and lightning protectors placed in the space above the switch-springs The protectors merely consist of a series of serrated brass plates placed very close to an earth-connected bar.

Where there are three or four of these switches, junctions between the outer switches are provided to enable subscribers upon those boards to be connected. These junctions may be worked by signalling or by speaking direct to the operator concerned since they are so close together

It has been assumed that these subscribers all had metallic circuits, but where this is not the case the same board may easily be utilised Let us suppose that the subscribers all possess single lines. It is then only necessary to earth the B line soldering tags and the side of the indicator connected to the B line inner spring

Where metallic and single subscribers exist together, earthing the B line soldering tag would mean that when a single line was connected to a metallic the two A lines would be connected together, and the B line of the metallic circuit earthed. If the lines were short this would matter little, but were the metallic line a long one—as, for instance, a trunk line—then the noise created due to static induction would probably preclude conversation (page 136).

In order to avoid this, transformers have to be utilised The primary is connected to the single line with its other side earthed, and the secondary is connected to the metallic circuit This metallic circuit is thus not interfered with, there being no earth connected to it, and thus

M 2

the only disturbance upon it is that from the single line. Where only a few metallic circuits exist upon each board they are marked with a white ring, and a special pair of cords joined up with a transformer is used when it is necessary to connect them to a single line subscriber. When two single subscribers are connected together, the B line of the pegs is not required, but when two metallic subscribers are connected it is necessary.

To connect a subscriber to a Post Office junction, a transformer is inserted or not inserted at the Company's exchange as may be necessary, but the junctions are all metallic, and when a subscriber is connected earth must not be used upon it

At exchanges where all the lines are single ones, transformers are introduced upon the junctions.

Where the subscribers are half metallic and half single, a set of translator keys, in appearance very similar to a speaking key, is inserted by the side of the speaking keys. In the normal position, this key connects the A and B lines of the two pegs across directly When depressed, a transformer is inserted between the cords for connecting a single to a metallic subscriber or junction.

CHAPTER XXVII.

THE SERIES MULTIPLE.

Where a very large number of subscribers have to be dealt with in one exchange, a different method of working has to be adopted. If 3,000 subscribers were connected to sixty boards similar to those described in the last chapter, only about 1⅔ per cent. of the connections demanded would be for subscribers upon the same board, and thus a certain number of junctions would be required to each of the other fifty-nine boards. This

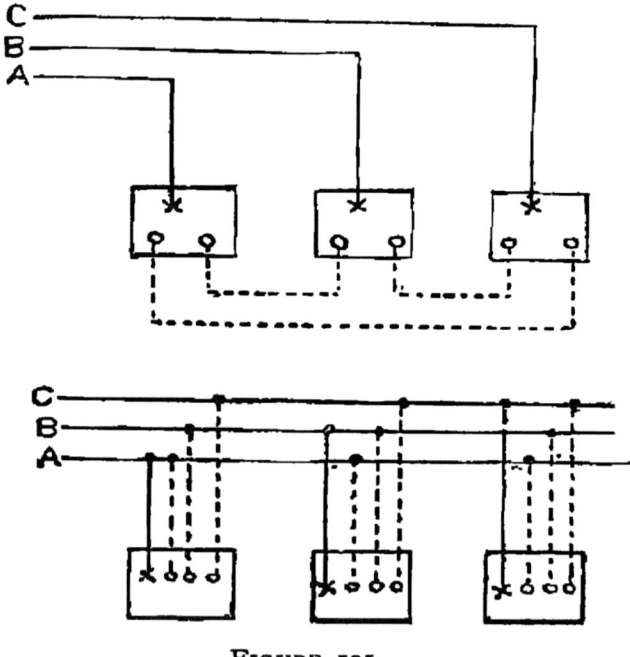

FIGURE 131.

could obviously be simplified by giving junctions to the central of each three operators, but even then scarcely 5 per cent. of the calls could be dealt with by one operator, and nineteen sets of junctions would be required to the twenty sets of three boards This would render the working of the boards very slow, and the number of junction lines required would be very large. The junctions between the switches might terminate upon switch-springs only, and then nineteen call keys would be required upon each section in order to instruct the various operators to put certain numbers on to certain junctions. This class of system may be termed the divided board system in contradistinction to the multiple system

The difference between the two systems is illustrated in Figure 131, where three subscribers each terminating upon three different boards are shewn. In the divided board or junction system, A, B, and C's lines terminate upon three different boards and are connected together by means of junctions. In the multiple system every subscriber's line is brought

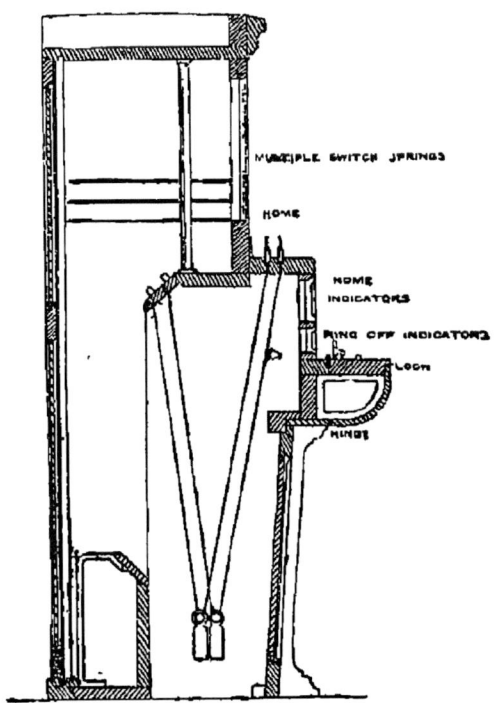

FIGURE 132.

to each board, and thus A may be connected to B or C at the first board without the services of another operator being necessary. The multiple system then consists in placing the whole of the subscribers within the reach of every operator. Each section of the multiple board is six feet six inches in length and contains the switch springs and indicators of the 200 subscribers—$i.e.$, the operators working this section answer the calls of 200 subscribers. Besides this the switch-springs of every subscriber upon the exchange are repeated upon the board. The switch-springs belonging to the subscribers attended to upon any section are termed the home switch-springs, and these are placed below the ordinary multiple. It will be obvious that it is not essential to the making of connections that the subscribers' numbers attended to upon a section should appear in the multiple upon that section, but in practice this omission is never made, as it would tend to confusion in operating.

The general appearance of a multiple switch is illustrated in Figure 132, and it will be seen how similar in section it is to the board described in the last chapter. Its length is practically six times as great. The home indicators, pegs, and speaking and ringing keys occupy the same positions as in the small board. The home switch-springs appear at the bottom of the multiple, the duplicated switch-springs appearing above them.

It has now been shown how a subscriber ringing up may be connected to any other subscriber he may ask for without the services of a second operator. It therefore remains to explain how an operator may know whether the subscriber asked for is or is not already connected and speaking. For instance, say No. 17 asks for No. 1236. Now No. 1236 may be connected at his own home switch-spring, or at any of the multiples. How, therefore, is the operator in charge of No. 17's line to know whether he is engaged or not?

This is accomplished in a very simple manner. The barrels of the switch-springs upon each subscriber's line are connected together—i.e., the barrel of No. 17's switch-springs on each multiple and upon his home switch-spring are all put into contact. The pegs used for making the connections have three instead of two points. The tip is the A line, the neck the B line, and the shoulder, which makes contact with the barrel of the switch-spring into which it is inserted, is connected to a small earthed battery. Thus the insertion of a peg anywhere, whether in the multiple or the home switch-spring of any particular subscriber puts this earthed battery upon the barrel of this subscriber's switch-spring throughout the exchange. The operator's telephone is earth-connected, and thus by touching the barrel of this subscriber a click is received in her telephone, thus indicating that the subscriber is engaged. The absence of the click shows that the subscriber is not engaged, and that the required connection may be made.

Five-point switch-springs are used in the series multiple. The subscribers' lines pass through the whole of the multiple switch-springs in series, as indicated in Figure 133. The A and B lines pass from the line springs to the inner springs, and thence to the next line and inner springs, and so on, the final inner springs (those of the home switch-spring) being joined to the home indicator. The B line has been dotted throughout to facilitate tracing. Thus it will be seen that by inserting a peg in any one of the switch-springs the A and B lines are picked up by the tip and neck of the peg. A bad connection between any one of the line and inner springs renders speaking difficult, but such faults are extremely easy to localise.

Connections of Engaged Test.

The test wires, as they are termed, are the wires connecting together the barrels of all the switch-springs belonging to a particular subscriber.

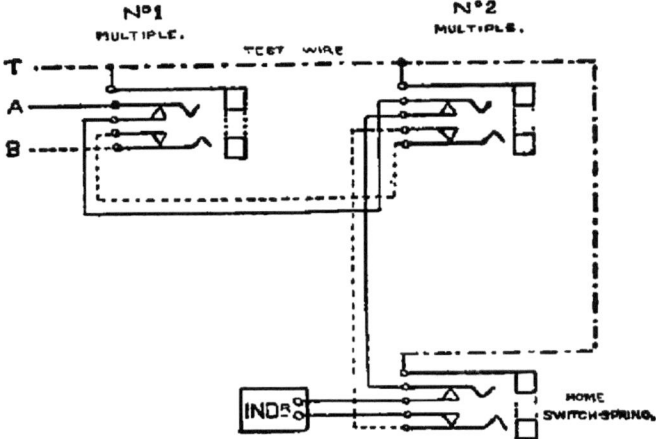

FIGURE 133.

A connection between No 17 and No. 1236 is shewn in skeleton in Figure 134. The connection is made at No 17's request, since a peg is

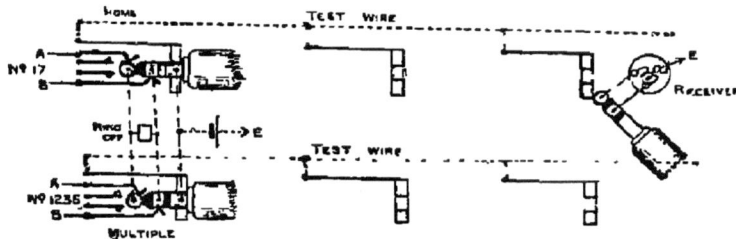

FIGURE 134.

inserted in his home switch-spring and one in No 1236 in the multiple Since No 17 has his home switch-spring below the first multiple the connection is made upon the first multiple. It will be seen that the two lines are connected together by the tip and neck of the two pegs The bodies of the pairs of cords are connected together to an earthed battery, and thus the test wires of No 17 and No 1236 are both joined to it By touching the barrel of either of these subscribers' switch-springs upon any of the multiples with the tip of the peg a click is received in the telephone, the centre of which is earthed for that purpose

The complete operating connections are precisely the same as in the case of the small 50-line board (Figure 130) We now see the object of dividing the induction coil and of the earth upon the centre of the receiver. In order to obtain a click in the receiver when the tip of

Method of Operating.   169

the peg touches the barrel of an engaged subscriber, it is necessary to have an earth upon the receiver. Now this earth can only be placed in the centre of the circuit, as, were it placed elsewhere, disturbances would be caused whenever an operator entered a circuit The earth is placed in the middle of the two coils of the receiver, and as there is half the secondary of the induction coil upon either side no disturbance is occasioned. When the speaking key is down the tip of the peg is connected through one coil of the receiver to earth, and it is in this way that the engaged click is received.

It has previously been pointed out that each multiple section contains 200 home switch-springs and indicators. These are dealt with by four operators. A multiple of the whole of the subscribers connected to an exchange is given to every four operators. Thus in an exchange of 2,000 subscribers, ten multiples and forty operators would be needed. This is, of course, exclusive of junctions, etc.

Each operator attends to the demands of fifty subscribers, and has twelve pairs of cords with speaking keys, etc, allotted to her. Frequently, however, the 200 lines are attended to by three operators, and the cords then have to be slightly re-arranged.

The procedure in case of a call is: Say No 17 rings up, his indicator falls upon the home section; his operator pegs in on the home switch-spring and gets the number of the wanted subscriber. Suppose this is No 1236 She takes the corresponding peg of the pair and touches the barrel of No. 1236's switch-spring on the multiple If she gets a click (the speaking key is meanwhile down) No 17 is informed that No. 1236 is engaged. If disengaged, the peg is pushed into the switch-spring, and the corresponding ringing key depressed Upon hearing the subscribers speak the operator raises the speaking key and does not come in circuit till the ring-off indicator is dropped by the subscribers turning their generators at the conclusion of their conversation.

A good point in connection with this system is that a triple connection is impossible. If two subscribers are connected and a peg is inserted into one of their switch-springs upon the multiple, one of the subscribers may be cut off, but it is not possible for the third man to listen to the conversation of the other two

An objection to the series multiple is that in an exchange of 5,000 subscribers, the A and B lines each pass through twenty-six moving contacts.

It may be mentioned that with the object of avoiding the use of three section pegs the seven-point switch-spring illustrated in Figure 100 (upon record table switch sections) are sometimes used. The barrel of the switch-spring is electrically separate from the remainder of the switch-spring. The long moving spring is connected to the test-wire of the subscriber to which the switch-spring refers. The other point with which the moving spring makes contact upon the insertion of a peg is connected to the engaged test battery Thus upon the insertion of a peg in any subscriber's switch-spring, the barrels of his switch-springs are connected to the engaged test battery. The barrel where the peg is inserted is, of course, disconnected from the moving spring by the insertion of that peg.

In mixed systems—*i e.*, partly metallic and partly single—translator keys are introduced, and the metallic circuits specially marked by a white ring. In single wire systems transformers are introduced upon the junctions.

Sometimes two switch-springs are allotted to each Post Office junction, the one for single and the other for metallic subscribers, a transformer in the former case being interpolated.

CHAPTER XXVIII.

The Self-Restoring Board.

The self-restoring indicator makes it possible to arrange our switch-springs upon the branching or parallel system. The A and B lines pass right along the line of boards and are teed off at each switch-spring. As the calling indicator upon the home switch-spring is also permanently teed across the loop, it is essential that when a peg is inserted in the multiple the corresponding home indicator should be locked, as otherwise calling currents would drop it, and the operator would never know whether the subscriber required attention or whether he was being rung up by another operator upon another multiple. Also it is clearly necessary to provide an engaged test.

The switch-springs employed are of a somewhat different form to any we have previously considered. There are three springs, and the barrel is divided into two parts. Three switch-springs and their connections are indicated in Figure 135. The front part of the barrel is used for the test

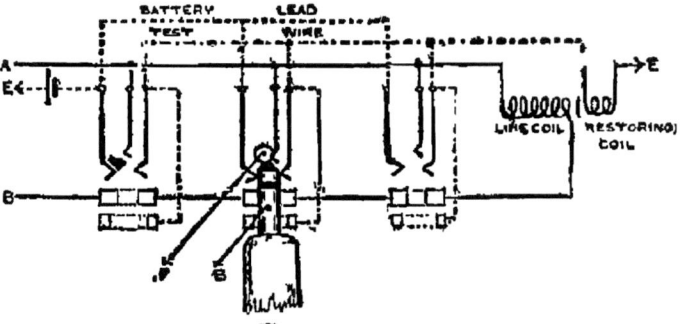

FIGURE 135.

wire, and the back part for the B line connection. Two springs of the switch-springs are placed opposite each other, and upon the insertion of a peg are connected together by the neck of the peg. The third spring of the switch-spring is the A line spring. The connections of the pegs are slightly different in this form of board. The two tips and the two bodies of the pegs are respectively connected together, the neck being left disconnected in each case. The insertion of a peg connects the A line to the tip and the B line to the body. Thus is the connection between the two lines of the metallic circuit effected.

172 Connections of Switch-Springs and Indicators.—Engaged Test.

It now remains to trace the engaged test and method of locking the self-restoring indicator. In Figure 135 a peg is inserted in the second multiple switch-spring. The battery which is used to lock the self-restoring indicator is also used for giving the engaged test. The circuit of the battery is along the battery lead through the two springs connected together by the neck on to the test wire, and thence through the restoring coil to earth back to the battery. This current locks the indicator, and thus ringing upon the circuit will not drop the home indicator. At the same time, the front barrel is connected to the earth battery

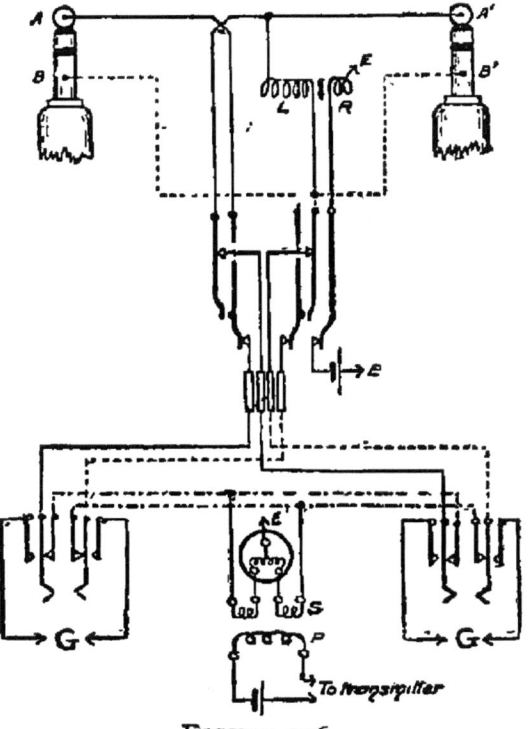

FIGURE 136.

The operating connections are very similar to those previously described, and so far as the engaged testing is concerned are precisely the same. The middle of the receiver is earthed exactly as in the connections previously described; thus by touching the front barrel with the tip of the peg a click in the receiver is heard if a peg is anywhere inserted in that particular subscriber's switch-spring. In the normal condition of affairs, the subscriber by ringing drops the self-restoring indicator. To answer the call, the operator inserts a peg and restores the indicator, and at the same time connects the battery to the test wire, thus engaging the subscriber throughout the room. The insertion of the corresponding peg into the wanted subscriber's switch-spring, after testing, locks his home indicator, and also engages him throughout the room.

The front barrel of the switch-spring is made larger than the inner or B line barrel, and thus the test wire is never connected to the body of the peg. Were this done, an earth would be introduced upon the B line of the loop, and this would, of course, cause disturbances.

In order to make the connection with the B line barrel perfectly secure,

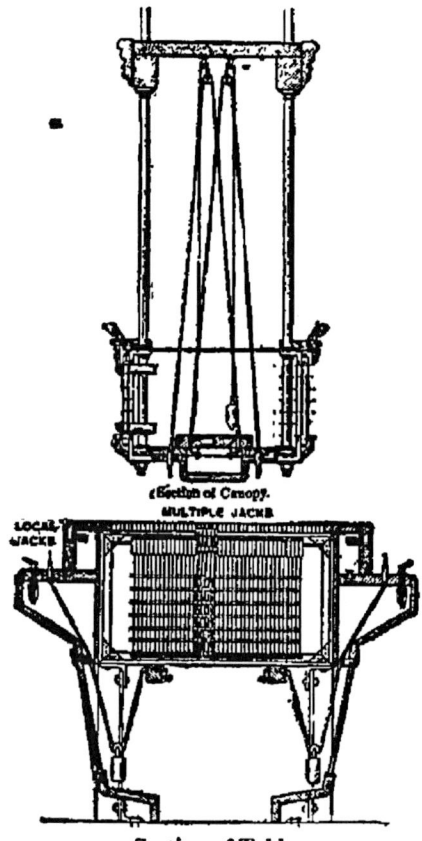

Section of Table
Flat Board with Self-Restoring Indicators
FIGURE 137.

an "umbrella spring" is employed. This consists of a brass spring let into the body of the peg.

The operator's connections beyond the four connection bars (Figure 136, are precisely the same as previously described, and the connections between the pegs and bars are not widely different. The ring-off indicator, which is of the self-restoring pattern, is teed across the cords permanently. The restoring coil is operated by a separate contact upon the speaking key. From the Figure 136 it will be seen that when the speaking key is depressed the indicator is restored.

In this system it is quite unnecessary to touch the indicators, since they are all worked automatically, and therefore they may be placed above the multiple, thus placing the switch-springs within easy reach of the operators. The relief afforded to operators by not having to restore the shutters by hand is not inconsiderable. The other details of the boards are precisely similar to the boards previously described.

In order to reduce the number of multiples necessary, the flat board has been introduced. Imagine the multiple switch-springs placed upon the flat. We may now put operators upon either side of the multiple, and thus roughly speaking only half the number of multiples will be necessary.

The keyboards and one cord of the pair (Figure 137) are placed upon a flat shelf below the level of the flat board. At right angles to the flat board are placed the home switch-springs. In the canopy suspended from the ceiling above the flat board are placed the self-restoring indicators corresponding to the subscribers' lines. Here also appear the corresponding cords of the pairs and the ring-off indicators. The electrical principles of the system are precisely the same as the system which has just been described. Two hundred subscribers, each dealt with by four operators, are placed upon either side of the multiple, i.e., one multiple is required for every four hundred subscribers. As before, twelve pairs of cords are allotted to each operator. These multiples are placed side by side, and thus the end operator reaches to the next multiple for subscribers which would be beyond reach were one multiple only provided. Thus, at the point where the multiple ends, a part of the multiple, termed a dummy section, has to be repeated for the use of the outside operators.

The flat board has not met with much favour save in this country, the objections urged against it being that it is impossible to effect repairs upon the multiple during the daytime, and the accumulations of dust which, being upon the flat, naturally result. Again, such things as pins, bits of black lead (i.e., pencil points), etc., cause trouble. With the upright board it is a very easy matter to remove any strip of switch-springs without disturbing the operators. A pump connected to a funnel is used to draw the dust from the switch-springs by suction, and to a great extent this gets over the difficulty. However, the question as to the desirability of flat boards is one which time alone can settle, but it may be mentioned that the National Telephone Company's Engineer-in-Chief, Mr. Dane

CHAPTER XXIX

THE CALL WIRE SYSTEM.

The call wire system consists in giving to every subscriber, besides his ordinary circuit to the exchange, access to a second circuit. This second circuit is common to about fifty subscribers, any one of which, by depression of a key, may place himself upon it. At the exchange the circuit terminates upon the speaking apparatus of the operator attending to the fifty subscribers' lines to which it is common. It is upon this circuit, termed the call wire, that the subscriber makes his demands for connections.

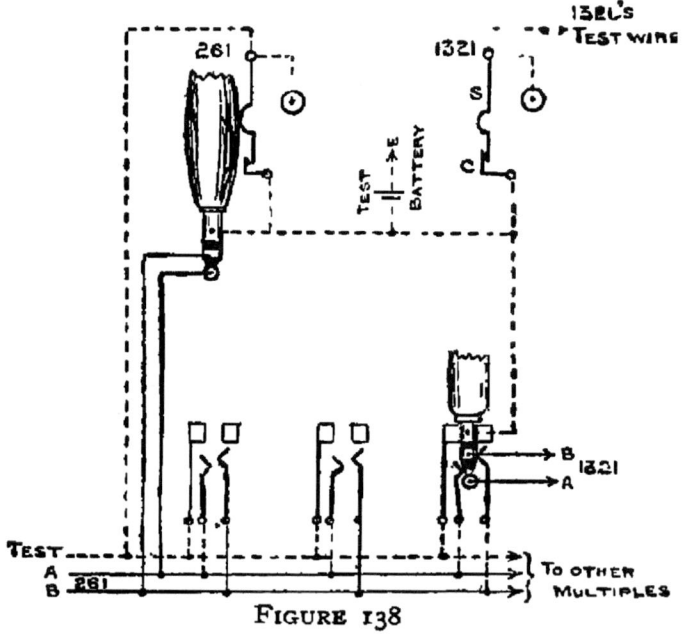

FIGURE 138

Since all instructions as to connections and disconnections are given over the call wire, it is clearly unnecessary to provide indicators or speaking keys at the exchange. The subscriber rings up his correspondent himself and thus speaking keys are not required. In the single cord system each subscriber's line terminates upon a peg, and is also connected to the multiple switch-springs, which merely consist of two springs and a barrel. The arrangement is depicted in Figure 138. No. 261's lines are connected to a peg and also to the multiple switch-springs shewn Thus, to connect No. 1321 to No 261, No. 1321's peg is inserted into No. 261's multiple switch-spring, and the connection is complete.

In front of each operator are placed the cords of the subscribers who have access to the call wire in that operator's charge These cords are placed in the canopy of switch, as the flat board system is again used here.

The question as to the engaged test has now to be considered. The pegs are made in three sections as before The third point is connected permanently to an earthed battery, thus the barrel of any switch-spring into which it is inserted is similarly connected. The barrels of the switch-springs belonging to a subscriber are all connected together, and thus the insertion of a peg joins the barrels of all his switch-springs to the earthed battery, thereby engaging him upon all the multiples. Thus the *called subscriber* is engaged. When the peg of the *calling subscriber* is pulled downwards to make a connection, the socket-spring S makes contact with the point C. Now C is joined to the earthed test battery and the spring S is joined to the subscriber's test wire . thus the pulling down of the peg engages the *calling subscriber* throughout the room.

It has previously been pointed out that the subscriber asks for connections upon his call wire. At the conclusion of the conversation the calling subscriber should again go upon his call wire and ask that the connection may be severed Let us suppose that he omits to do this or that the operator fails to sever the connection. As this request was made by No 1321 (Figure 138), No 261 is powerless to get the connection severed, since it is very improbable that he is on the same call wire as No 1321 Another point is that No 261 may require a connection shortly after he has spoken to No 1321. If now the connection were made by the operator, three subscribers' lines would be joined together and that without No 261's knowledge Therefore, it is necessary not only to test the line of the called subscriber, but also that of the calling subscriber Accordingly every subscriber's test wire is also taken to a small brass stud by the side of his peg If now No. 261 asks for a connection the operator touches the stud and, finding him engaged, tells him to ring up his correspondent and ask him to call off.

The operating connections are shewn in Figure 139. The call wire passes to the operator's telephone, and also through a ringing key to the service peg. It is also teed to a night control board and to a switch-spring upon the chief operator's desk The operator's telephone is permanently bridged across the call wire, so that she is always listening and ready to receive demands for connections The centre of the receiver is earthed and one side is connected to a flexible cord and thimble, which is usually fitted upon the second finger of the right hand This ebonite thimble carries a small brass stud, with which the testing is done.

The service peg is used for speaking to subscribers, or for other special purposes when necessary. In the normal state of affairs it is not required.

Night Arrangements.

The operator is unable to disconnect from the call wire save by the entire removal of her apparatus, and thus private conversations with subscribers are practically impossible, since they may be overheard by anyone coming upon the call wire or at the chief operator's desk.

The call wires are also teed to a night control switch so that at night calls may be quickly attended to. Normally the call wire is disconnected, and it is only when a subscriber places his instrument across it that it is connected. At this board a battery and indicator (as described in the case of Post Office up call wires) is connected to each call wire when the divided lever is moved over to the left (Figure 139). Immediately a subscriber depresses his call key this indicator falls. The night operator then moves the lever downwards (over to the right in the figure), thus connecting his telephone to the call wire. Having ascertained the numbers of the calling and called subscribers, the connection is made by a special pair of

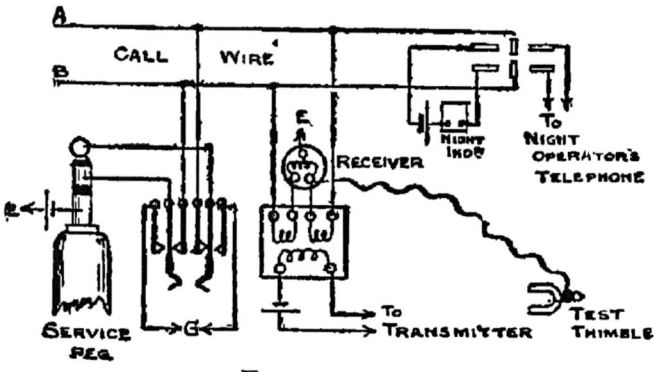

FIGURE 139.

cords upon the nearest multiple. Of course, when the day operators leave they remove their telephones, which would otherwise bridge across the call wire and actuate the night indicators.

Having considered the electrical details of the system, we may now pass to the construction of the system. To economically work a town with the call wire system, areas must be most carefully considered. Lead-covered paper cables containing either 153 or 204 metallic circuits are laid down to the various areas. These cables pass to standards where they are distributed to the various subscribers. The smaller the area the shorter is the length of wire required for the call wires. Since the call wires have to be arranged from geographical considerations—*i e.*, the distribution of the subscriber's lines—the subscribers upon any call wire are not arranged numerically, for instance, No. 3004 may be next door to No. 13. These two subscribers would, of course, be upon the same call wire.

At the exchange the cables are cross-connected, so that the subscribers' lines appear upon the test board in numerical order, thence they pass to the tags which are connected to the multiples round the room. These must clearly be in numerical order. Now the position of the pegs is that of the call wires, since the subscribers' pegs must all be within the reach of the operator dealing with the corresponding call wires. The wires have then again to be cross-connected to the cord positions. This board is termed the intermediate cross-connection field.

The advantages of this system may readily be summarised: We have the advantages and disadvantages of the flat board. The fact that in a breakdown of a call wire fifty subscribers are stopped, and are quite powerless until the call wire is repaired. There is also the possibility of the call wire being stopped by two subscribers disputing. Again, office boys can cause endless trouble by singing, whistling, or shouting upon the call wire, and since it may emanate from any of the fifty subscribers it is difficult to locate. Another point is that by listening upon one's call wire one might ascertain with whom every subscriber upon that call wire does his business. If two subscribers in precisely the same business are upon the same call wire much mischief may accrue from this source. The fact that the subscribers ring their own correspondents is a notable advantage.

In regard to the switching, the main objection is the fact that the called subscriber cannot get disconnected without calling up the calling subscriber. This, however, is a trouble which may readily be overcome by the use of a device which would drop a ring-off indicator upon *either* subscriber depressing a key.

CHAPTER XXX.

THE POST OFFICE MULTIPLE SYSTEM.

At Newcastle it was early necessary to provide a multiple switch, and to still retain the permanent current system. The advantages of this latter system are that an automatic ring-off signal is obtained from the subscriber, and, further, that the operator can always tell by glancing at any indicator exactly what is happening upon the circuit to which that indicator is attached.

The Newcastle system presents some notable advantages over any other system which has yet been propounded, inasmuch as it combines the advantages of the parallel multiple without its disadvantages. There is an arrangement by which, when two subscribers are conversing, the accidental connection of a third entirely short-circuits all three, thus stopping, and at the same time advising, the operator This is the most notable advantage. The system is also a secret one

At the subscriber's office a telephone having two receivers and switch-arms is used. This is of the universal type previously described, but has two extra contacts upon the right hand switch-arm. In the normal state of affairs a permanent current flows through the telephone relay to the exchange, there deflecting the needle of the non-polarised indicator relay permanently connected to the circuit over to the right, thus signifying that the circuit is disengaged. In order to call the exchange the left hand receiver is raised from the switch-arm This stops the permanent current, and causes the needle at the exchange to fall to the vertical, which, in this system, indicates a call At the same time the receiver and secondary of the induction coil are joined to the line, and thus when the operator speaks the subscriber hears Should the operator not answer immediately, the subscriber can vibrate the needle at the exchange by alternately raising and lowering the left switch-arm. Upon receipt of a reply from the operator the right hand receiver is removed and the demand is then given to the operator. The raising of this lever not only joins up the primary of the subscriber's telephone, but also reverses the direction of the permanent current which deflects the needle at the exchange to the left, thus indicating engaged. We have then three distinct indications for normal or disengaged, engaged, and calling. When a subscriber is through to another subscriber both their indicators are deflected to the left, showing engaged When they have concluded their conversation they replace their receivers upon the switch-arms and thus reverse their permanent currents, which again flow in the normal direction, deflecting the indicators to the right This is the operator's instruction to disconnect, which is done without remark

The subscriber's lines pass along the run of the multiple boards and are teed off to the respective switch-springs in each multiple as also to the home indicator (Figure 140). *En passant*, it may be remarked that it has been found unnecessary to duplicate the home switch-springs upon the multiple The switch-springs consist of four springs, of which the two inner ones are teed to the line and come into contact with the two sides of the peg, which is exactly similar to the peg described upon page 59 but for the fact that the end near the handle is rounded so as to fit into the circular opening of the switch-spring. The two outer or short-circuit springs project beyond the line springs and in the normal condition are connected together by means of the metal contact pin which passes through holes cut into the line springs but without touching them

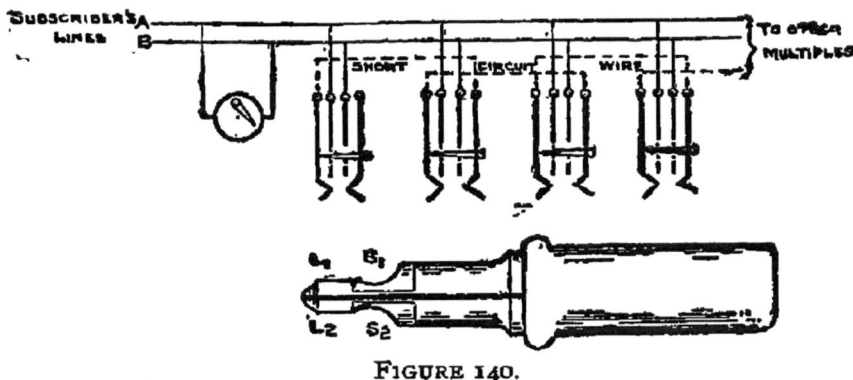

FIGURE 140.

In the case of trunk line operating in the Post Office multiple system the pairs of pegs and cords and apparatus by means of which the connections are made are of a very complicated nature. It is here necessary to distinguish between the two pegs of each pair. The answering peg is, as previously stated, of very similar construction to that described upon page 59. The other or calling peg is illustrated in Figure 140, and is of the same shape and size as the answering peg, but the centre of this peg contains two pieces of brass insulated by ebonite The ends of this peg L_1 and L_2 come into contact with the inner or line springs, thus picking up the A and B lines of the subscriber. The two segments S_1 and S_2 pick up either side of the short-circuit wire by means of the outer springs The object of this arrangement will be appreciated later. The outer or short-circuit springs are normally connected together by means of the brass contact pin The short-circuit wire runs from the A short-circuit spring to the B short-circuit spring of the following switch-spring throughout the multiple, as indicated in Figure 140.

Each pair of cords has attached to it a speaking key, which, in the normal condition "through" connects L_1 and S_1, also L_2 and S_2 of the detector peg and thus renders it precisely similar to the answering peg, which does not possess the separate segments. The top and bottom sides of the pegs are respectively connected across, and thus the arrangement is now identical with the simple pair of pegs and cords described on page 59.

Upon the receipt of a call (needle vertical or vibrating) the operator *first* moves over the speaking key of the pair of cords which it is proposed to use for the connection and *then* inserts the *answering* peg. In this way the operator's telephone is connected to the calling subscriber's line. Having ascertained the number of the required subscriber, the *detector* or calling peg is inserted into the wanted subscriber's switch-spring. Now L_1 and L_2 of the detector peg are connected to a detector which consists of nothing more or less than a galvanometer of high resistance. If the subscriber is disengaged, his permanent current will flow through the detector in such a direction as to deflect it to the right. If engaged it will be flowing in the opposite direction, and thus a deflection to the left will be observed. If the subscriber is calling, the needle will either hang vertically or will vibrate; thus it will be seen that by the insertion of this detector peg the operator can tell at a glance precisely what is happening upon any circuit. Now this is the engaged test. Should the required subscriber be engaged, the distant operator is informed and the answering peg is withdrawn. The detector peg is, however, allowed to remain, so that the operator may be made aware of the conclusion of the conversation by the reversal of the permanent currents.

If, however, the wanted subscriber be not engaged—*i.e.*, if the detector is deflected to the right—the operator momentarily depresses a key attached to the breast-plate transmitter. This energises the electro-magnets of the "combined call and detector switch" and the armature is attracted, thus making a series of fresh connections. Firstly, the detector is cut off, and a calling battery of sixteen cells is connected up to the wanted subscriber's line, thus ringing his bell. This calling battery does not cut off the operator's speaking set, and consequently upon the subscriber's response it only remains for the operator to go out of circuit and thus put the subscribers through. This is accomplished by the simple act of turning back the speaking key to the normal. By the deflection of the calling subscriber's indicators to the left the operator is automatically informed that the subscribers are through. The two subscribers' batteries are now both sending reversed permanent currents, and thus both their indicators are deflected to the left, and the insertion of a detector peg at any other multiple in either of the subscribers' lines will give a deflection to the left (engaged) upon the detector. Upon the conclusion of the conversation the subscribers replace their receivers, and this reverses the permanent current, deflecting the indicators attached to those subscribers to the right The operator who made the connection observes this, and removes the pegs.

It only now remains to be explained how triple switching is prevented, The insertion of an answering peg connects the long springs to the line springs, as indicated by the dotted lines in Figure 141. At the same time the contact between the two springs is broken by their being pushed apart by the insertion of the peg. If now two pegs are inserted into the switch-springs of the same subscriber upon two switch sections, the conditions of Figure 141 obtain—*i.e.*, the line is short-circuited The indicator immediately falls to the vertical, and thus the operator is made aware of the mistake. Now this is the reason for the different construction of the detector peg It is necessary to bridge the detector across the lines without disturbing a speaking subscriber. If now a detector were attached to an answering peg the lines would be short-circuited by this device. In order to avoid this the detector peg is made in four sections. When detecting S_1 and S_2 are disconnected, but immediately the detector is cut

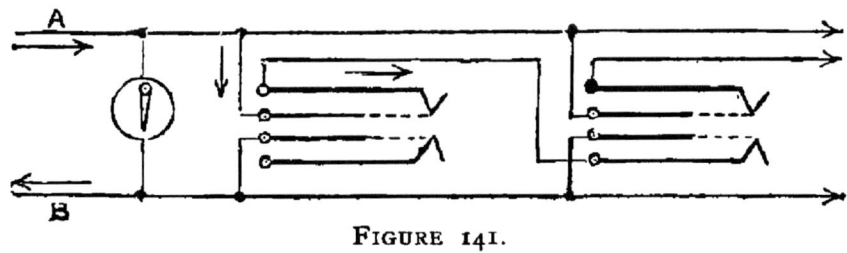

FIGURE 141.

out of circuit by depression of the call key, S_1 and S_2 of the detector peg are joined together, so that the insertion of a peg in the through position will at once short-circuit the subscribers, and the operator will at once observe the error. It is scarcely necessary to add that S_1 and S_2 are connected in the through position It will now be seen that, by causing the short-circuit springs to project beyond the line springs, operators are prevented from tapping circuits, as thereby the speaking subscribers and the operator would be short-circuited.

The combined call and detector switch is so arranged that after the first depression of the transmitter call key it is independent of it, the separate calling battery current flowing through its coils, and thus keeping them energised; in fact, the whole arrangement is bridged across the lines. This prevents the operators calling by means of a series of short rings.

In order that the introduction of the operator's telephone may not cause false signals upon the circuit of a calling subscriber, a battery is inserted in series with it, thus causing it to exactly resemble an engaged subscriber.

This battery also serves the double purpose of working the call switch upon the depression of the transmitter call key.

The system of trunk line working is very similar. The switch-springs at either end of a trunk line are arranged so that in the normal condition opposing permanent currents are sent to line through a relay. The insertion of a peg reverses the direction of the current. An indicator relay is permanently bridged across the lines, but its circuit passes through the local contacts of the first relay (Figure 142) In the case shewn the trunk is disengaged The indicators are deflected to the right by reason of the derived circuit across the lines. If now a peg be inserted at A the battery there is reversed. The two batteries now combine together, and the local circuit of the polarised relay at B is broken, and thus the indicator needle hangs vertically, indicating a call. At B the current in the relay is in the wrong direction to break the local circuit, and this needle goes over to the left. Upon the insertion of a peg at the distant end in order to reply that battery is reversed also, and the tongue of the relay goes back to its stop, thus again joining up the indicator. It should have been mentioned that the relay is biassed against the small current which normally flows through

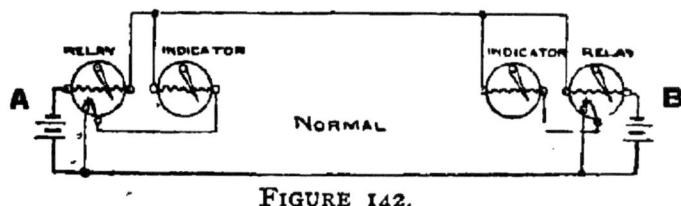

FIGURE 142.

it, and it is only upon its augmentation by the distant battery that the bias is overcome Both the indicators are now deflected to the left, indicating engaged.

It is scarcely necessary to point out that the battery upon the operator's telephone is so arranged as to connect the same poles to the lines as the trunk automatic calling batteries, in order to avoid derived circuits through it The subscriber's permanent current batteries are also similarly connected with respect to the trunk batteries.

Upon the conclusion of the conversation the subscribers replace their receivers, thus reversing their batteries, which causes them to join in series with the trunk battery at their own end. This current overcomes the bias of the relay, and the indicator falls to the vertical, thus advising the completion of the conversation. Precisely the same thing occurs at the distant end. In any case the removal of the peg at the controlling office brings about the same result

In working with the Company's local system, batteries are inserted across the junction lines to make the system resemble the above as closely as may be. A generator ringing key is added to each junction, and the connections are obtained by means of a down call wire. If a subscriber of the Company rings off, the local circuit of the junction indicator is broken, and the needle goes over to the right This is accomplished by means of a weighted bias.

Connections from trunk to trunk are made by means of special switch to switch junctions. A special circuit to each switch section is fixed upon every section. To transfer a connection to section five say, the operator inserts a peg into number five section call wire This deflects the indicator attached to that circuit to the left, and the operator answers and names a junction wire for the connection to be extended upon. Upon this junction there is no apparatus in bridge.

In the case of the local system the operating is slightly different from the method described in the case of trunk lines, but since exactly the same method may be used it was considered well to give it prominence. Instead of the pairs of cords being joined up with the operator's telephone and combined call and detector switch, they consist merely of pairs of plain two-section pegs and cords. The operating peg is quite separate, and the *modus operandi* is as follows :—Subscriber calls up; operator answers by inserting *her* peg; ascertains requirement, and withdraws; then inserts it into the called subscriber's switch-spring, and tests with the detector. If disengaged, she presses the telephone button, thus actuating the call-switch, and so rings up the called subscriber Upon receipt of his reply her peg is withdrawn, and the connection made by means of a pair of plain cords previously described. It will thus be seen that the functions of the plain cords and the special operating cord have been combined in the trunk-switch.

CHAPTER XXXI.

Miscellaneous Special Arrangements.

MANCHESTER JUNCTION ARRANGEMENTS. — Where the call wire system is in use at the local exchange some modifications in the method of working are desirable. One of the consequences of the call wire system is that the called subscriber is powerless to clear the connection himself. Hence when a trunk call arrives for a subscriber who is engaged locally as the called subscriber, some delay arises before the calling subscriber clears the connection. Now trunk lines are not kept waiting for this, and therefore an excess of junctions over the trunk lines is required. Six junctions are allotted to each section in place of the usual five.

In the ordinary system when a subscriber who is engaged locally is asked for by the Post Office, the Company's operator connects him to the junction line, but also comes into circuit herself when the subscriber is asked if he will take the trunk call. If he agrees, a twist of his generator will sever the connection, and the Company's operator by testing will at once observe when this has been done. Here it does not matter whether the subscriber is *calling* or *called* subscriber.

In the case of the call wire system each junction terminates in a peg at the Company's end, and upon a request being made for a certain subscriber to be placed upon a particular junction, that junction peg is pulled down and inserted into the multiple switch-spring bearing the number of the wanted subscriber, *without testing* to see whether he is engaged or not. Now not only is the subscriber's loop extended to the Post Office, but also his test-wire. There it passes through a telephone exchange galvanometer, one of which is allotted to each junction. If a subscriber is engaged locally the test battery sends a current along the test-wire through the galvanometer, producing a deflection to the right, thus advising the Post Office operator. The tip and neck of the junction peg when inserted into a subscriber's switch-spring extends the loop, and the body of the peg connects the body of the switch-spring to the third wire. The junction clearing arrangements are precisely the same as in the case of the ordinary system. The socket contact upon the junction peg joins up the junction clearing relay, so that when the peg is removed at the Post Office the lamp may be lighted.

This system throws upon the Post Office operator the responsibility of getting connections cleared.

It will be observed that the third wire passes from the top contacts of the eight-point switch-spring, through the galvanometer and through the three-point key (Figure 143) to earth. Where there are a large number of junctions to be dealt with, the whole of the switching cannot be done upon a single

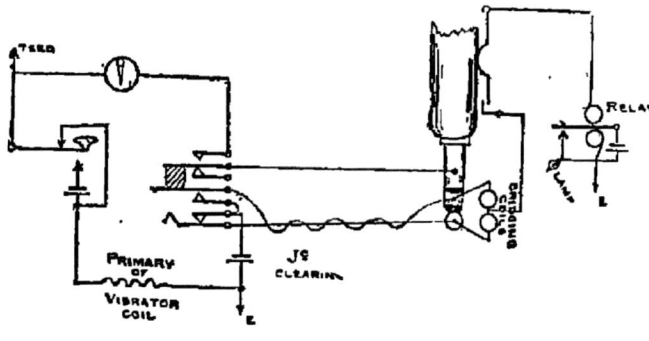

FIGURE 143.

multiple board Hence it is possible to get a subscriber connected to more than one junction. For instance, a subscriber who is speaking, say, to London from Manchester would not appreciate having half or one minute of his three minutes wasted by an explanation with a second

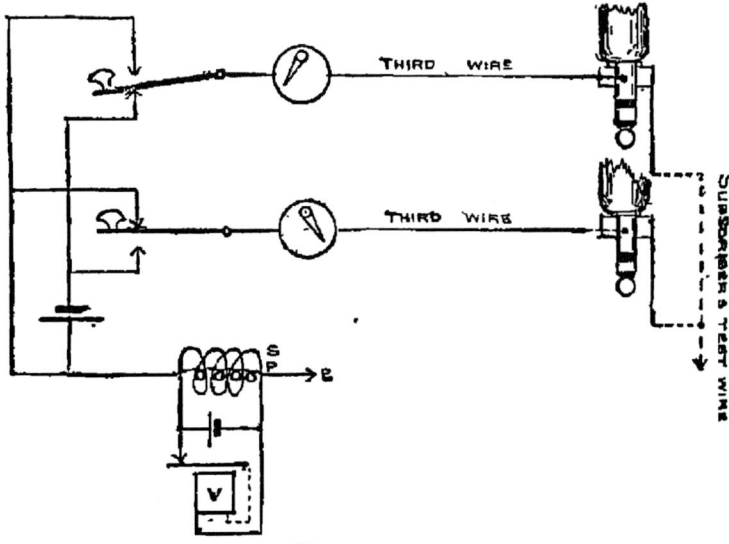

FIGURE 144.

operator, who wishes to tender a threepenny call from say Rochdale. It was therefore necessary to design an arrangement which would enable an operator at the Post Office to ascertain whether a wanted subscriber is engaged upon another junction. This is the object of the three-point key shewn in Figure 143 Depression of this key causes the exchange galvanometer to be deflected to the *left* if the subscriber is also connected to another junction.

The principle of the arrangement is shewn in Figure 144, where one subscriber is shewn connected to two junctions, *i e.*, so far as signalling is concerned. The test-wire of a subscriber who is not engaged locally is disconnected, and therefore the depression of the trunk engaged test key does not affect the galvanometer. Now in the case illustrated it will be seen that the current passes along the first third wire, along the subscriber's test wire, which is connected to earth through the second third wire to which that subscriber is connected. Thus, when a subscriber is connected to two or more junctions the test wire is earthed, and, therefore, the depression of the trunk engaged test key informs the Post Office operator, who waits till the conversation is finished.

Now the Company's engaged test battery is of the same voltage as the trunk engaged test battery, therefore a subscriber engaged locally only will merely cause the needle to fall from a deflection to the right to the vertical position. If engaged on a junction also the needle deflects to the left

If a subscriber is asked for (locally) several times, and tests engaged, it is usual for the operator to enter his circuit by means of the service peg, and inform him that someone wishes to speak to him. It would be most objectionable to have conversations upon trunk lines interrupted in this way.

The test wire of any subscriber connected upon a junction is put to earth through the telephone exchange galvanometer upon the junction to which he is connected. The Company upon testing get a click, due to this earth. Now, in order to render the test distinctive, the primary of an induction coil is included in the main earth at the Post Office. The secondary is joined up with a vibrating sounder and battery, so that an alternating current of sufficient frequency to produce a musical " hum " is always included in the Post Office earth ; thus any of the Company's operators testing a subscriber who is connected to a junction line hear a musical note, which is their instruction not to enter the circuit as the subscriber is speaking upon a trunk line If the subscriber is engaged locally then a click merely is heard. The arrangement is indicated in Figure 144.

GLASGOW JUNCTION ARRANGEMENTS.—At Glasgow the Company's system is a mixed one, and in addition to this it is operated upon the call wire system. Here some very awkward arrangements have to be made. Every junction is furnished with three pegs. The first takes the junction loop direct for metallic subscribers (distinguished by a white circle round the switch-spring upon the multiple), the second includes a transformer for single wire subscribers, and the third peg is connected to the third wire of the junction and terminates at the Post Office in an exchange galvanometer.

The procedure is as follows:—The Post Office ask for a number to be placed upon a particular junction. First, the special peg, which is short, connects the subscriber's test wire through the Post Office exchange galvanometer, in circuit with which is placed a small battery. If engaged locally the subscriber's test wire is to earth, and a deflection is observed upon the galvanometer. If no deflection is observed, the Post Office operator asks for the subscriber's line to be joined through to the junction. If a deflection is observed, the short peg is left in the switch-spring until the Company's operator is told upon the call wire that the subscriber is clear.

This cumbrous arrangement has been found to be imperative as the simpler system in use at Manchester cannot be employed on account of the form of a switch-spring used by the Company. This system may be regarded as a tentative one, pending alterations which would render the simpler system applicable.

DIFFERENTIAL SELF-RESTORING INDICATORS.—In the case of A and B sections, in order to guard against the possibility of failure of the service circuit, one or more of the junction lines are equipped with self-restoring indicators; indeed, this is why the three self-restoring indicators are provided. It has, however, been pointed out that the connection of the indicator between the two inner springs of the switch-springs prevents the use of automatic clearing, and it is to avoid this difficulty that the differential indicator is provided. The centre of the line coil is connected to the junction clearing battery, and the inner springs of the junction switch-spring are connected to the ends of the line coil in the ordinary way. Since the indicator is differential, the clearing current splitting equally through the two half coils produces no effect upon it.

The indicator is wound to a much lower resistance than is usual, each half coil having a resistance of 50ω only.

THREE-CONTACT GENERATORS.—In order to avoid the complications shewn in Figure 82, a three-contact generator has been designed. Instead of the power or hand generator being connected up to all the sections, and exchangeable by means of a single two-way switch, the hand generator itself makes the requisite changes. In the normal position of the three-contact generator the power generator is joined to the particular section to which it is attached. Upon revolving the hand generator the power generator is cut off and the un-short-circuited hand generator substituted. This avoids all switches and makes each section complete in itself.

NIGHT ARRANGEMENTS.—The majority of the smaller Post Offices close at 8 p.m., and it becomes necessary to provide a night service, and at the same time retain the control of the circuits. At 8 p.m. all the smaller Post Offices which are not open all night are put through upon one or two main trunk lines to the Company's exchange. The trunk line is then extended to the larger Post Office, which is open all night. For instance, Barrow-in-Furness puts the Blackburn-Barrow trunk through to the Company by means of a junction line, which at the Company's end is fitted with an indicator. At Blackburn, this trunk is extended to Manchester by means of a Blackburn-Manchester trunk. A peg is inserted at Manchester so as to remove the permanent currents, thus working the circuit as an open one, and ringing by generator. Similarly a couple of Manchester-Blackburn trunks would be extended to the Company's exchange at Blackburn. Now one end of these lines is under the control of a Post Office open all night. If a Blackburn subscriber wished to speak to a Barrow subscriber, the Blackburn National would ring up Manchester Post Office, who would ring Barrow National. This seems somewhat roundabout, but it achieves the required object—viz., dispenses with night attendance at the small Post Offices, and yet leaves the complete control of the night traffic in the hands of the Post Office.

It will be seen that at night there are a very large number of trunk lines which are not in use. For instance, three or four of the twenty-seven circuits between Manchester and Liverpool would amply suffice to carry the traffic even at the busiest periods. Now in order to reduce the space occupied by the working trunks, a switch is arranged which throws all the working trunk lines on to, say, the first ten sections. A large removable label is provided for indicating the alterations which have been made.

At present the switch used for concentrating the trunks at night merely consists of a trunk test tablet, the test holes and U links being used as a switch. In course of time it may be found worth while to concentrate the trunks upon a special board accommodating from thirty to fifty lines, and in this event it is probable that a simpler switching arrangement could readily be designed.

INTERMEDIATE STATIONS UPON TRUNK LINES.—It is occasionally advantageous to place an intermediate station upon a trunk circuit. This can only be satisfactorily done where the traffic of the intermediate office is small.

The principle of the method consists in dividing the trunk circuit into two halves at the intermediate office and connecting them together by means of a pair of cords. A condenser is included in the ring-off circuit at the intermediate office, so that alternating currents only affect the apparatus. Thus the primary battery signalling between the terminal offices does not affect the intermediate one. To call this office, the terminal offices rings with the red button. The disengaged side is cut off by removing the peg, thus connecting up a polarised indicator relay and permanent currents. The circuit is then entered by means of the speaking key. This virtually divides the circuit into two. The disengaged side is joined up to the permanent current relay, and thus the terminal office is not disturbed. Any call would be received upon the relay and would then be answered by the intermediate office pegging into the second switch-spring. Now when the intermediate office connects a subscriber the condenser is short-circuited by inserting a solid brass plug in the special switch-spring. Thus when the

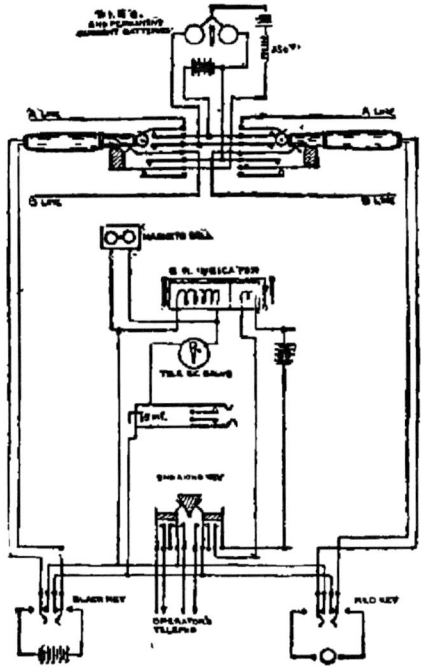

FIGURE 145.

terminal office removes the peg the exchange galvanometer is deflected. In order to receive calls a magneto bell is joined in parallel with the self-restoring indicator and exchange galvanometer.

If the intermediate office wishes to enter the circuit to speak to one of the terminal offices it is necessary to first ascertain whether the circuit is disengaged. By inserting the brass peg the exchange galvanometer is directly joined up. If the circuit is disengaged the permanent currents deflect the galvanometer. If not, no deflection is observed, and in the latter case the peg is left in, and the circuit is entered upon the conclusion of the conversation, when the permanent currents are restored.

The whole arrangement is indicated in Figure 145, where the circuit is shewn in the normal condition. Obviously, if the exchange galvanometer were left directly in the circuit, both the terminal circuit indicators would be actuated; hence the condenser, which, whilst it stops direct, permits alternating currents to pass.

SINGLE WIRE TRUNK LINES.—At the transfer of the trunk lines to the Post Office a few single wire trunk lines existed, and it was therefore necessary to slightly modify the present system of working in order to meet this case. As it is the intention to double all these circuits as early as possible, a very brief mention of the arrangement adopted will suffice.

In the normal state of affairs the circuit is joined up precisely the same as an ordinary trunk circuit, save that the B line is to earth and that the main permanent current battery is increased to nine cells, so that the distant local circuit of the relay is closed upon the insertion of a peg at the home end. In this respect it is independent of the trunk ringing battery. Upon the insertion of a peg a transformer is joined up, through which the speaking takes place.

SUPERVISOR'S SWITCH SECTION.—Experience has shewn the desirability of providing a means of communication with the supervisor of the exchange, and also a means by which the working of any section might be checked, and therefore a switch for the purpose has been provided at all the larger exchanges. It consists of a transfer circuit from each switch section to the control switch, a series of switch-springs each teed on to the operator's telephone, and also a set of switches for bunching and throwing the up call wires or record table circuits, as the case may be, on to special indicators placed upon the local switch. The transfer circuits are placed upon one of the vacant switch-springs and visuals upon the sections, and are marked "supervisor." At the control switch the switch-springs and visuals (which are in strips of twenty) are marked with the number of the switch section to which they correspond.

The receiver springs of each switch telephone connector are taken to a two-point switch-spring in every way similar to those used for the local switch junctions. Thus every operator's speaking circuit is permanently connected to the control switch, so that by inserting a peg connected to the speaking set it is possible to listen to and check the working of any section in the room. The instructions or other remarks addressed to the operator, as well as the operator's own conversation, may be listened to at this control board, thus rendering it possible for an inexperienced operator to receive assistance from the superintendent, which is a most valuable aid.

At the top of the supervisor's switch-section is placed a row of ten plug keys. These are of exactly the same pattern as the plug keys shewn on page 68. The up call wires are each teed on to the long springs of the plug keys, the top and bottom inner springs of which are respectively teed together to a single circuit going to the local switch. In the normal condition, when all the plug keys are in, the teed connections from the call wires to the supervisor's switch-section are disconnected. When all the plug keys are pulled out the whole of the up call wires are bunched on to the special circuit going to the local switch. This circuit passes on to a plug key having six springs, and being, as regards contacts, exactly similar to a ringing key. In the normal position the bunched call wires are connected to a battery and indicator arranged as described in the case of the Company's system (page 177)—*i.e.*, immediately a call wire is connected, by an operator going upon it, the indicator drops. When the key is pulled forward the call wires are thrown on to the local switch operator's telephone.

At the supervisor's switch section the plug keys are provided with a brass bar and screw which will clamp the plug keys either in or out, thus preventing the disconnection of a call wire by an accidental touch.

SPECIAL KEYBOARD.—Experience has shewn that the provision of separate ringing keys for each pair of cords is not absolutely necessary, and it is in contemplation to reduce the number. As it is necessary to ring with the generator upon transformer circuits (the outsides of superimposed circuits), three ringing keys are necessary—viz., two keys (a black and a red) for the black pegs and a red one for the red pegs. This set of three keys would replace the present twelve. The connections would have to be re-arranged and additional contacts added to the speaking keys—in fact, the connections would be very similar to those employed by the Company (page 162). The speaking key would have to pass on both the lines from both pegs on to the common ringing keys, whence they would pass to the operator's telephone.

At the same time it has been proposed to put in two common keys through which the cords would pass after leaving the depressed speaking key. The object of this is to enable an operator to cut off either cord, whilst speaking upon the other, without removing the pegs. As the system is an automatic one the removal of pegs gives clearing signals, and this causes delay when it becomes necessary to ask the originating subscriber if, say, he will have his conversation extended to six minutes. The arrangement is being tried experimentally, as experience only can shew whether the improvement is of practical value.

CORD TESTING.—In any telephone exchange the weakest point is unquestionably the cords. These are usually of one of two types, the one having the two conductors lightly covered and wrapped spirally with wire covered by a spiral braiding; the other cord does not contain any wire, being packed with cotton.

It is in contemplation to replace the present form of brass pegs by aluminium, and at the same time to use a cord of about half the diameter of the present form. This cord consists of two tinsel conductors suitably insulated with cotton and encased in a woven covering. The openings at the ends of the pegs are considerably narrowed, and the cord can readily be knotted inside. At the same time the weight which holds the cords taut is very considerably reduced. However, some time will have to elapse before it can be said definitely whether this is in reality the improvement it appears.

The testing of cords and pegs is a most important matter. A special piece of apparatus, designed to detect cord faults before they become sufficiently pronounced to cause disturbance to the working, has recently been designed. It consists of four switch-springs, a press key, and two 20ω resistance coils, which latter are used as the ratio arms of a Wheatstone bridge in the test for equality of conductor resistance. One of these coils is also in circuit during the other tests. The cord tester, which tests both cords of a pair at once, is used in conjunction with an ordinary Q. and I. detector, connected to it by a suitable length of two-conductor flexible cord. During tests the instrument may be held in one hand, and the detector placed in any convenient position not too near the hand generator. The requisite battery power is connected to the instrument by means of a pair of plain cords, one end of which is inserted in a switch-spring marked Testing Battery, upon the sections under test. It is only necessary to provide one such switch-spring upon every third section. The trunk ringing battery ($12v$) furnishes a sufficient voltage for the test, and is therefore made to serve the double purpose.

Since it is found that the presence of the ring-off indicators renders the tests far less sensitive than they would otherwise be, their disconnection has been provided for by means of wire U links placed immediately below them.

The equality test is made by inserting the two pegs of the pair of cords under test in the first and second switch-spring of the tester. The wire links are all withdrawn prior to the making of any of the tests. This joins up the two 20ω coils as the proportionals, and the A and B lines of the cords as the third and fourth arms of a Wheatstone bridge. Depression of the key now connects the galvanometer across the junctions of the cords and the 20ω coils. Absence of, or a very small, deflection indicates a satisfactory condition. It may, however, be remarked that the cords should be moved about during the progress of the tests since intermittent faults are more frequent with cords than with any other telephone appliance. If both cords were disconnected, or if both were of very high resistance, no deflection would be given by the equality test, and therefore the continuity test is provided. The pair of pegs are now inserted in the second and third switch-springs, and the key again depressed. A large deflection will result if the continuity is perfect. The magnitude of the deflection is a measure of the condition of the cord in respect of its conductor resistance. The third and last test is made by withdrawing one peg from the second switch-spring, *i.e.*, with one peg in the third switch-spring. Depression of the key now tests for contact, the absence of which is revealed by the absence of a deflection upon the testing galvanometer.

For small exchanges, where the provision of a contesting set is not considered necessary, the cords should be tested by inserting one peg in the transmitter switch-spring of the switch telephone connector, whilst the receiver is placed in its usual position and is employed for listening upon. The depression of the speaking key attached to the cord under test results in a click being heard in the receiver if the cord is perfect, whilst noise when the cord is moved about or absence of the click indicates a fault. This test is not so complete as the one previously described.

AUXILIARY RECEIVER.—In the case of very long distance calls operators frequently experience difficulty in hearing, owing largely to the noise of the switch-room and to the inefficiency of the ordinary head-gear receiver. To avoid this a receiver of an improved watch pattern joined in parallel with the operator's telephone is provided on sections where these long-distance calls are dealt with. The receiver when not in use rests upon a switch-arm which cuts it out of circuit.

CHAPTER XXXII.

SWITCH SECTION FAULTS.

In tracing faults upon telephone circuits generally, the first thing to be ascertained is in what part of the circuit the fault lies. In order to form an opinion as to where a fault is it is best to obtain as many conditions as possible. Generally, one may divide a telephone circuit into primary, secondary, and signalling circuits. Having found out in what circuit a particular fault lies it is best to consider how much of this circuit is common to another circuit which has been proved perfect. For instance, suppose it is stated that a particular circuit is out of order. Ring up the distant station. Upon hearing an answering ring, next try to speak. The ringing has proved the lines and the whole of the connections through which the ringing is performed. If now we are unable to converse, this may be due to faults in either of the secondary circuits or in one of the primary circuits. If now we can hear the distant speaker but are unable to reply, the fault is in our own primary circuit, or is due to the distant receiver being short-circuited The former may readily be proved by blowing upon the transmitter. If the sound cannot be heard, then clearly the fault is in our own primary circuit. In this case conversation may be carried on by shouting through the receiver.

Again, suppose we can only ring in one direction but can speak perfectly in both directions. This fault is in the ringing generator, which is not breaking the short-circuit across the generator. If we cannot ring or speak in either direction the fault is in the line or main circuit. By following out this method of locating faults systematically an intuitive sense is developed, and a fault is localised in a tenth of the time which it would take to mention even the order in which the tests should be taken In the case of complicated faults, unless followed out systematically, an hour or two is easily wasted where ten minutes should suffice.

A fault which sometimes leads one to form erroneous conclusions is that due to a disconnection in the middle of a long circuit Now, it is possible to speak through a disconnection. This effect is due to the capacity of the circuit. The current passes along the perfect wire through the distant telephone, thence along the disconnected wire through the air between it and the earth, and thence back to the other side of the disconnected wire and back to the original telephone. If the disconnection is very near either station the capacity of the short length of wire is so small as to render it impossible to speak through it, since the capacity through which we speak is the capacity of the two broken lengths of wire in cascade, *i.e.*, less than the capacity of the shorter length of wire. The speaking will in any case be scarcely as loud as if the circuit were perfect.

In dealing with faults upon trunk circuits it is possible to again sub-divide the circuit into main and signalling. If we are unable to speak or signal over a circuit the fault is clearly in the main circuit. This may readily be proved from the test board. The location of line faults presents little or no difficulty and will not be specially dealt with here.*

The faults most commonly occurring in the trunk signalling circuit are faults in the trunk switch-springs. In the event of a total disconnection in main circuit between the test board and the switch section it is not possible either to speak or signal. If we are able to speak to but not signal the distant office, the fault is in the circuit between the two inner springs of their trunk switch-spring. Were the circuit of our exchange galvanometer merely disconnected, we should register a call upon dropping our speaking key or upon depressing the trunk ringing key

If the needle of the trunk relay still remains to the right when a peg is inserted, the bottom and central springs are probably not breaking contact.

A disconnection in the main permanent current battery causes the distant office to be unable to signal us, but does not affect our signalling them. The same effect would be caused by a disconnection anywhere in the circuit between the two inner springs, but if this fault were in the right hand coil of the relay the needle would hang vertically in the normal position, owing to the disconnection of the local permanent current circuit.

When a faulty peg has been replaced it sometimes happens that the tip and body get reversed. This causes no trouble until the trunk ringing key is depressed, when the indicator relay will be deflected to the right.

The A and B lines of a trunk can always be proved by inserting a peg, when, if the deflection is to the left, the lines should be crossed at the test board. Both trunk indicators will be permanently deflected to the left till this is done. A short-circuit upon the line or contact between the two inner springs of the trunk switch-spring will also cause a permanent deflection to the left.

A faulty cord is at once detected by an operator, as the subscribers connected cannot converse. If upon changing the pegs conversation is easy the fault is in the pegs. As a rule, the moment an operator experiences difficulty the cords are changed.

If the ringing keys stick at all, or the long springs do not make a good contact with their normal stops, intermittent disconnection will occur.

---

* The reader will find all the information required upon the subject from Chapter XXII. and from another work by the present writer, viz., "Electricity in its Application to Telegraphy."

In cases where cords are reported to be faulty and are subsequently found to be in good order, it is as well to examine the ringing keys.

The ringing and speaking keys are fortunately very free from faults. They are, however, fairly easy to trace in the majority of cases when they do occur. If the fault affects all the speaking keys it is in the part of the circuit common to all. The next thing to ascertain is whether the fault is in the operator's telephone. A fault in the primary is evidenced by ability to hear but not speak. Reversing the pegs puts on another battery If the fault is still present, it should be traced through the switch telephone connector to the speaking keys. The effect of a rod of the speaking key becoming worn or otherwise too short is to permanently join up the transmitter-battery, thus running it down very rapidly.

The most awkward fault to deal with is a slight contact between the speaking keys. This is frequently due to careless soldering or displaced wires. To find out where the fault is, drop all the speaking keys but the first, and then depress the corresponding red button. If the generator can be heard raise the keys one by one till the sound is removed. The key removing the sound is the faulty one Repeat the experiment with each key in turn until the key causing the trouble is found. Having done this, nothing but careful inspection and frequent repetition of the test will serve In cases of this kind always use a diagram, and get as many conditions in which the fault does or does not appear as possible

A fault which appears somewhat mysterious at a first glance is that two circuits, both silent separately, are noisy when connected together. This is due to an earth fault upon the shorter circuit. A subscriber's line *may* be perfectly silent and yet have a full earth upon it, but immediately it is put through upon a long trunk line noise results, due to the fact that the fault upsets the balance upon the trunk line. This fault frequently appears in the case of single wire subscribers, owing to a fault in the Company's repeater key or due to a contact between the primary and secondary of the inserted transformer. An earth fault upon a junction causes similar trouble.

Junctions should be *absolutely* silent. If the slightest sound can be heard steps should be taken to ascertain the cause

Earths upon junction lines further run down and short-circuit the junction clearing battery The lightning protectors may be tested when this occurs. To prove where the trouble comes in, a galvanometer should be inserted in the path of the clearing battery at a slack time, and the sections watched and disconnected one by one till the fault is found. In the normal state of affairs no current should be sent out.

Disconnections upon the call keys are very rare, and are quite easy to trace.

Faults in the operator's telephone circuit are usually in the pegs. This may at once be found out by changing the set. In the transmitter occasionally the switch does not make contact, but the most common thing is for a layer of dirt to form between the fixed holder and the revolving axle upon which the transmitter is fixed.

Faults in the switch telephone connectors generally should be traced by ascertaining in what part of the circuit the fault lies, and then by careful inspection or, as a final resource, tracing with a detector and battery. It may, however, be pointed out that the primary circuit may be proved by inserting one peg of a pair. A deflection will be observed upon the exchange galvanometer *upon the depression of a speaking key* if the circuit is perfect.

Faults in the local circuits are very common, usually being due to the faulty adjustment of an indicator. Having ascertained that the fault is not in the trunk relays by touching each armature with a capstan spike or "tommy," inspect the self-restoring indicators. The fault will then usually be very evident. In case of a serious fault disconnect all the self-restoring indicators and test with a galvanometer and battery.

Upon the record table switch sections an earth fault upon any circuit causes the indicator to be thrown. If the A and B lines become crossed, the visual vibrates if a subscriber happens to ring upon it. Short-circuits easily occur if the ebonite handle of the plug-key gets loose and the key enters too far. Again a short-circuit of the augmenting battery may occur as a result of one of the plug-key springs not breaking contact. Where secondary cells are used these faults blow the fuses, and are at once detected. Knowing that a short-circuit takes place upon, say, the first part or calling battery, pull out all the plug-keys, and return them one by one till the short circuit again appears.

Faults upon the transfer boards are not always easy to trace, owing to the huge number of teed connections. Of course, faults in the speaking circuits are very simple to deal with, and need no comment. The commonest fault upon a transfer board is the short-circuit of the three springs. A disconnection of the signalling wire results in neither section nor transfer board being able to signal upon the circuit. The same remark applies to a disconnection in either visual.

If a short circuit occurs upon a section, that section's fuse is blown, and the fault may then be traced by inspection of the switch-springs upon inserting a peg in each in succession. The same general procedure is recommended in the case of the transfer board.

Wherever single wire subscribers exist a transformer is inserted when that subscriber speaks upon a trunk line. If now the distant subscriber has a single line a second transformer is introduced upon the circuit. If now the call chances to be put through upon a transformer circuit, two more are introduced. Speaking through four transformers is always very difficult, to say the least of it. Now should these subscribers be so unfortunate as to get put through to the Company's exchange from a sub-exchange upon a superimposed junction, two more transformers may be interpolated. In cases of complaint of inability to hear, a little inquiry in reference to the possible number of transformers will well repay the time spent. Again these remarks apply with even greater force where two superimposed trunk lines are connected together This, however, can only happen by error upon the part of the operators, as distinct instructions are given that the superimposed circuits themselves should be used in such cases Again cords which are partially short-circuited should be looked for if all other explanations fail.

CHAPTER XXXIII.

RECENT ADVANCES IN SWITCHBOARD DESIGN.

THE CENTRAL BATTERY AUTOMATIC MULTIPLE SYSTEM.—This system, known in America as the "relay board," provides signals which are entirely automatic in the action, *i.e.*, the removal of the receiver from the switch-hook at the subscriber's end lights a calling lamp, and its replacement, upon the completion of a conversation, lights a clearing lamp. At the same time the provision of batteries at the subscriber's offices is avoided by the supply of the current necessary for both signalling and speaking from the exchange to which they are joined. It is this system which the Department propose to use for their competitive telephone scheme in London, and though the details of the junction arrangements, &c., cannot yet be stated, a general description may prove of some interest.

The switch-springs are of the ordinary three-point character, save that their size has been reduced till a strip of twenty now occupies only $7\frac{7}{8}$ ins. $\times \frac{3}{8}$ in., thus leaving $\frac{1}{8}$ in in either direction for fitting The line springs and the body are teed throughout the multiple as described in the case of the call-wire system (page 175).

A skeleton diagram of the connections of the subscriber's end and its circuit at the exchange is shown in figure 146.

In the normal position the magneto bell and condenser C only are joined up in series between the two lines. This leaves the circuit disconnected for continuous currents, whilst the alternating currents from a generator will pass through both condenser and bell, so effecting a ring. A portion of this ringing current will pass through the primary P and secondary S of the induction coil and through the receiver. This derived circuit is, however, of little consequence, and may be dismissed from consideration with the remark that it entails a little wasted energy

The removal of the receiver from the switch-hook joins up the primary of the induction coil and the transmitter in series across the line. This makes a circuit for the 24 volt battery through the line relay L R, through the third to the fourth spring of the cut-off relay C R on to the B line through the transmitter and primary of the induction coil on to the A line, thence through the second and first springs of the cut-off relay back to the negative pole of the battery. This current causes the line relay L R to attract its armature, so completing the circuit of the 24 volt battery through the calling lamp L which now glows The current circulating through the primary of the induction coil replaces that usually derived from primary batteries. Variations in the resistance of the transmitter cause variations in the current circulating through

P, and thus currents are induced in the secondary S. The currents flow through the receiver and condenser C, on to the B line and through the distant subscriber's secondary and receiver back to the A line, and thence through the primary P to the secondary. It will be noticed that the secondary and receiver are permanently shunted by the transmitter and also by primary and magneto bell. The latter is of no moment, owing to the high self-induction of the bell. In receiving speech a portion of the current flows through the secondary and receiver, whilst the remainder circulates through the primary and transmitter, thus inducing currents in the secondary. The received speaking is thus made up of two parts, the direct current through the receiver, and that produced by induction from the portion of the current circulating in the primary. These currents add together, and so but little diminution in the received speaking is observed. The transmitted speaking similarly consists of two parts adding their effects together, viz., the variation of the current along the line wires plus the currents induced in the secondary as a result of that variation. It may also be pointed out that the induction coil is of very different dimensions to those used with individual battery systems, the primary having a resistance of 15ω and the secondary 30ω.

It may now be well to detail the method of operating in order to render the subsequent electrical details the more clear. It has already been stated that each subscriber's line is furnished with a calling lamp which is lighted by removal of the receiver. This lamp is cut out of circuit by the insertion of a peg in the home switch-spring. The operating is accomplished by means of pairs of pegs and cords together with their usual accompaniment of speaking and ringing keys. Instead of the usual ring off indicator two lamps are used, one indicating the conditions on the answering peg side, and the other those on the calling peg side. These lamps glow when the corresponding receivers are upon their hooks, and are dark when the receivers are raised. We are now in a position to follow the whole of the operating movements.

The calling subscriber lights his calling lamp by removing his receiver from its switch hook. The operator upon observing the lamp alight inserts her answering peg into the home switch-spring, so extinguishing the calling lamp. By depressing the speaking key attached to the pair of cords, the number of the wanted subscriber is obtained, and the latter's line tested in the ordinary way by means of the tip of the corresponding peg. If disengaged the peg is pushed home and the ringing key depressed. Since the calling subscriber has his receiver off the hook his clearing lamp is dark. The called subscriber's lamp, on the contrary, is now glowing, since his receiver is still hung up. Upon removing it to reply his clearing lamp also darkens. When the subscribers have finished their conversation both restore their receivers to the hooks, and so both lamps light, and this constitutes the operator's instruction to disconnect. If one lamp only glows the operator takes no notice, since this merely means that one subscriber only has left the telephone—possibly in quest of information.

262   *Central Battery System.*

Pegging into a line renders it impossible for its calling lamp to be lighted. This state of affairs is analogous to the locking of the self-restoring coil detailed on page 172. The double-tongued cut-off relay C R, figure 146, which is connected to the barrel of the subscriber's switch-springs and test wire, is responsible for the disconnection of the calling lamp circuits. The energising of this relay causes the armature to descend, so breaking the contacts between all four springs, and thus cutting off the whole of the apparatus shewn at the exchange end of the subscriber's circuit

The calling and answering pegs P_1 and P_2 are connected together by means of a four-coil transformer T_1 and T_2 in the centre of which appears a 24-volt battery. In series with each side of the transformer are the clearing relays R_1 and R_2. The insertion of the peg P_1 into the switch-spring S_1 causes a current to flow from the positive pole of the battery through the clearing lamp L_1, 90ω resistance coil to the third point of the peg, and thence through the body of the switch-spring S_1, through the cut-off relay C R to earth, and so back to the negative pole of the battery. This causes the lamp L_1 to glow and also cuts off all the subscriber's calling apparatus by actuation of the cut-off relay C R. The clearing lamp L_1 glows until the receiver is raised from the switch-hook,

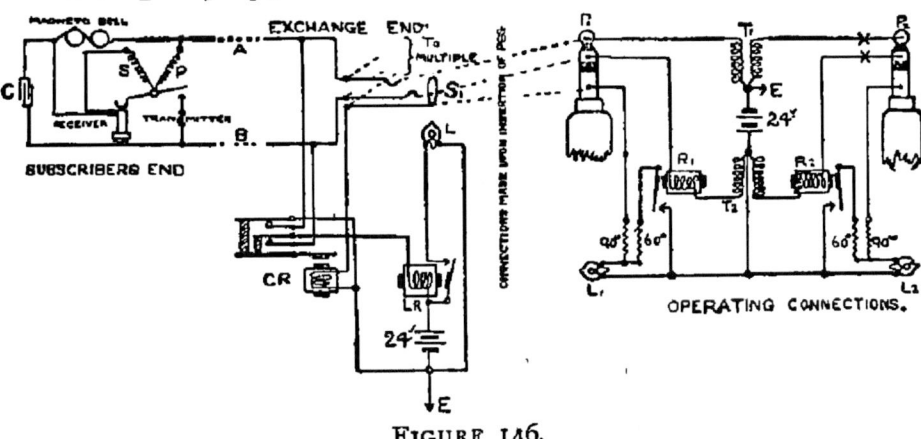

FIGURE 146.

when another circuit is formed from the positive pole of the battery through the coil of the transfomer T_2, and cut-off relay R_1 along the B line through the subscriber's transmitter and primary of his induction coil, along the A line and back to the battery through T_1. This provides the speaking current; and also by actuating R_1, places a shunt of 60ω across the lamp L_1, so darkening it. Precisely the same remarks apply to R_2 and the other side of the transformer. The speaking currents induced in the secondaries of the induction coils pass through the transformer and induce similar currents upon the other side.

For the sake of simplicity the operator's speaking apparatus has been omitted from the operating connections, and the calling and clearing batteries have been shewn separately for the same reason   In practice only one battery, consisting of secondary cells of very large size, is employed for the whole exchange. The speaking key is merely a tap across the lines at the point marked by crosses, and the ringing keys are interpolated in the usual manner

It will now be apparent that the calling apparatus is removed from a subscriber's circuit immediately a peg is inserted either in the home or one of his multiple switch-springs ; also that the lamps L_1 and L_2 shew exactly what is happening upon either side of the cords. It is not until both clearing lamps glow that the operator disconnects.

Junctions to exchanges where the same system is being operated are worked in a very similar manner. Each junction terminates in a peg, with a four-coil transformer interpolated. Two lamps are provided, one of which glows when the *distant* calling subscriber hangs up his receiver, and the other when the called subscriber does so. At the first exchange the two lamps in the pair of cords light in the ordinary way, one for the calling subscriber and one for the called subscriber.

Junctions to exchanges where a different system is employed are worked by the adoption of an altogether different plan. Condensers are inserted in either side of the junction-loop, and the signalling upon the junction side is effected by means of a self-restoring indicator placed upon the sub-exchange side. To work with the trunk line system of this country some such arrangements may be necessary, but these details will probably not be finally settled until the system has been in operation some time.

THE KELLOG SYSTEM.—This system has for its object the increase of the capacity of a telephone exchange. When the number of subscribers to an exchange reaches 10,000, the limit of the multiple is very nearly obtained. Again, were it possible to construct a multiple of say forty or fifty thousand, the cost of providing for new subscribers would be a largely increasing quantity as the exchange grew.

Four multiple boards are provided: the first, or A board, containing a multiple of subscribers, 1 to 10,000 ; the second, or B board, 10,001 to 20,000 ; the C board, 20,001 to 30,000 ; and the D board, 30,001 to 40,000. Each subscriber has four indicators and four home-jacks, one upon each of the multiple boards, A, B, C, and D. He is provided with a generator of special construction, and four keys, A, B, C, and D. Depression of the A key sends a positive current along the A line upon turning the generator. Depression of the B key sends a negative current along the same line. Similarly C and D respectively send positive or negative currents along the B line. At the exchange each line passes through two polarised indicators, and it will thus be seen that by depressing the suitable key any one of the four indicators may be actuated without affecting the others. The insertion of a peg in either the home or multiple switch-springs cuts out the whole of the indicators.

The subscriber who desires a connection rings up on the board to which his correspondent is connected, *i.e.*, if the number were 15,361, he would ring up on the "B" board. Each subscriber's calls are therefore divided into four parts, which, in the aggregate, may be considered equal parts, and therefore each operator is able to deal with four times as many subscribers' lines upon each board. So, instead of 200 lines per multiple section, 800 are connected, and the same result is obtained with the equivalent of four multiple boards of ten thousand each, plus the extra home switch-springs and indicators as would be obtained by the construction of a 40,000-line multiple, were such a thing possible. It will therefore be seen that, by the employment of this method, every connection is dealt with by one operator only, and thus the waste of time inseparable from junction-worked systems is avoided.

THE CHICAGO EXPRESS SYSTEM.—This system, which is a non-multiple or divided board one, has for its object the increase of the number of subscribers which may be connected to a single exchange, and also the even distribution of work amongst the various operators. Every call is, however, dealt with by three operators, and thus a slight increase in the time required to make a connection by this system as against a multiple system is observed.

The first or "Y" operator, as she is termed, does not answer any calls, and speaking apparatus is not therefore required. Her sole duty consists in plugging subscribers who call up through to the operators who answer the calls, *i.e.*, we may imagine the "Y" operator as evenly distributing the calls between two A operators. Upon the removal of the subscriber's telephone from the hook a lamp lights in front of the Y operator, who immediately connects him to a junction to one of the A operators. This A operator answers his call and extends him, by means of a junction, to the B operator, who has charge of the circuit to which he desires to be connected. The B operator is instructed by call wire as to the connection to be made. These junctions are all worked automatically, the insertion and removal of the pegs giving the requisite signals. The A operator has complete control of the connections and has two lamps in her cords, one for the calling and one for the called subscriber, and it is not till both glow that the connection is severed. The removal of the pegs from the junction to the Y and B operators by actuating the corresponding signals, advise the conclusion of the conversation.

SABIN'S DIVIDED BOARD SYSTEM.—The distinctive feature of this system is that the junctions between the switches are multipled in such a way as to greatly reduce their number.

The operators are divided into two classes, the "A" and the "B" operators, and are seated side by side. The A operators answer all calls from the subscriber's lines to which they attend, whilst the B operators only connect incoming junction calls to the subscribers' lines in their charge.

The A operators have junctions to each B section in the room, but the junctions are multipled to the A operators, *i.e.*, No. 1 junction to No. 10 B operator appears on every A operator's section. Since the B operator selects the junction it is not possible for an A operator to peg on to an already engaged junction.

The procedure is as follows :—The subscriber lights his calling lamp by the removal of his receiver. The A operator extinguishes this by pegging in. Having ascertained the number of the wanted subscriber, the operator goes on to the call wire to the B section upon which the subscriber's line is connected, and asks for the wanted subscriber. The B operator names the junction, upon which she connects him, and by depressing her ringing key calls him up. Until he answers, a white lamp glows. The connection is now complete.

Upon conclusion of the conversation the subscribers replace their receivers. This act lights the A operator's lamp in circuit with the connecting cord and also a red lamp in circuit with the B operator's cord. The pegs are all withdrawn, and all signals and connections return to the normal.

It may perhaps be well to explain that upon the board directly in front of an A operator appear all the multipled junctions, together with connecting pegs and cords and call-wires. Directly in front of the B are the subscribers' switch-springs and indicators, together with the ends of all the multipled junctions, &c., which terminate in pegs. Thus both the A and B operators have access to the particular set of subscribers' lines to which they attend—A to answer the subscribers' calls and pass them forward to the required B operator, and the B operator to answer and connect all incoming calls over the office junctions to the subscribers in her charge.

RECENT MINOR IMPROVEMENTS.—*Engaged subscribers.*—In order to avoid the necessity of an operator telling calling subscribers that their correspondent is "engaged," a switch spring connected to a telephone and phonograph is employed. The phonograph incessantly repeats "Line engaged; call again": and instead of the operator telling a subscriber that his correspondent is engaged, his line is plugged on to the phonograph for a few seconds. The relief thus afforded is not inconsiderable.

Automatic ringing.—Instead of calling by a series of rings given by the repeated depression of a ringing-key, upon depressing the ringing-key the subscriber's bell rings intermittently for certain definite periods, until the circuit is broken by the removal of the subscriber's telephone from the hook.

EQUAL DISTRIBUTION OF WORK.—An attempt to secure this object has been made by providing junctions from each operator to a neighbouring one. Any operator having more than two calls on hand, pegs the remainder on to one of these relief junctions. The operator on the section at the end of the junction answers the call, or pegs it on to another operator until it finds its level. It is well known that the capacity of an operator's hands largely exceeds that of her voice, and therefore the passing-on of calls in excess of her ability to deal with along automatically-worked junctions presents no difficulty. By thus distributing the work each operator is able to attend to a large number of subscribers, and thus the number of multiples necessary is reduced.

APPENDIX A.

THE KR LAW.

If a battery be connected to a circuit possessing resistance and capacity, a certain time elapses before the current attains its maximum value. A telegraphic or telephonic circuit possesses both resistance and capacity, and it is not possible for a current to attain its maximum value in an infinitely short time. In telegraphy this means that the speed of signalling cannot be indefinitely increased. Lord Kelvin (then Sir William Thomson) investigated the question of the propagation of electric currents along wires possessing distributed capacity and resistance, and as a result the speed of signalling upon any cable can be calculated from the dimensions, or, what is more to the point, the dimensions can be determined which will permit a given speed of working. This law applies equally to telephonic circuits, but it has to be stated in a far more general way, owing to the fact that the problem of speech transmission is too complicated, and requires so many conditions that a complete mathematical statement of the conditions and a solution has so far been impossible.

Kelvin found that the time taken for a current to arrive at a certain fraction of its maximum value was inversely proportional to the product of the total resistance and capacity of the circuit. The limiting values at which speech was possible were determined experimentally by Preece. The results obtained, after a large number of experiments, were as follows :—

Conductor.	Speech possible up to KR (m f. × ohms).	Speech commercially practicable up to KR.
Copper (open wire)	15,000	10,000
Copper (cables and underground)	12,000	8,000
Iron (open wire)	10,000	5,000

This rule is known as the KR law, and is one about which much disparity of opinion exists. These values were determined several years ago, before the granular transmitters had attained their present perfection, and there is little doubt that the values given on the previous page will not hold strictly to-day.

The lower value for iron wire is due to the fact that iron is a magnetic substance. The currents flowing along it magnetise it and thus increase its self-inductance, thereby adding a certain amount of retardation (which is absent in the case of copper). The difference in the KR between open and covered conductors is largely a matter of insulation resistance. In the case of open wires the insulation is lower, and the wire has more points for discharging. It is found in practice that the insulation of a telephone circuit may fall to one quarter of its conductor resistance before speech is affected In this condition the circuit is at its best working value. The lower the insulation of a circuit the more rapidly will a current attain its maximum value; but it has to be recollected that this will be of little service if the current is thereby rendered so small as to be unable to produce its effects. The working power upon a telephone circuit cannot be increased by any known means. The design of a telephone relay has hitherto proved impracticable.

A single wire circuit with an earth return has theoretically the same working value as a metallic circuit of the same length and material. This is due to the fact that the capacity of the metallic circuit is only half that of the single wire. The capacities of the two wires of the loop are in cascade and therefore jointly are half either of them. The resistance of the metallic circuit is, however, double that of the single wire and therefore the product KR is the same. In practice the capacity is ·6 instead of half the single wire value.

The effect of capacity or self-induction and resistance or all three is to distort speech through a telephone. The distortion is due to the fact that the length of time that a current takes to arrive at its maximum strength depends not only upon the values of the resistance, capacity, and self-inductance, or, as the combination of all three is frequently termed, the reactance, but also upon the frequency of the currents. A current which changes in direction 1,000 times per second will be retarded more than one which reverses 500 times. Now articulate speech gives rise to a series of most complicated waves of current. If any particular wave be taken and carefully analysed, it will be found that it is possible to split it up into a number of waves of the simple sine type. The fundamental heavy wave is the wave which gives the sound its pitch. Allied with it there are a large number of smaller waves in octaves and in harmony above and below the fundamental, and perhaps arranged in a still more complicated fashion. These smaller waves, or overtones as they are termed, are of much greater frequency, and are therefore retarded more than the fundamental—*i.e.*, the overtones are displaced with respect to the fundamentals,—and when this displacement exceeds a certain amount speech becomes impossible owing to the speech losing its *timbre*. Thus it will be seen that pitch and volume of sound accurately specified includes *timbre*. It is to Helmholtz that much of our modern theory of sound owes its origin and its development.

A controversy has arisen in reference to the possibility of mutual induction between the wires constituting a metallic circuit. On the one hand it is stated that this can occur, and that, by bringing the wires closer together, a point may be reached where the beneficial effects of the currents flowing in one wire, and thus inducing currents of opposite sense in the other wire, thereby assisting the rise of the current, may be sufficient to satisfy the circuit's capacity and thus produce a distortionless circuit. Upon the other hand this action, if it exist, is termed diminution of the self-inductance, and the principle stated is the one upon which the most inefficient circuit would be designed. Experiments will probably settle this matter conclusively ere long.

APPENDIX B.

CAPACITY AND RESISTANCE OF LINE WIRES. (A. EDEN.)
Copper Wire.

Gauge.	Resistance per mile.	Capacity to earth.	Capacity wire to wire.
100 lbs.	8·782 ω	·0144 m.f.	·00864 m.f.
150 ,,	5·855 ω	·0147 ,,	·00882 ,,
200 ,,	4·391 ω	·015 ,,	·009 ,,
300 ,,	2·928 ω	·0153 ,,	·00918 ,,
400 ,,	2·195 ω	·0156 ,,	·00936 ,,
600 ,,	1·464 ω	·0158 ,,	·00948 ,,
800 ,,	1·098 ω	·016 ,,	·0096 ,,

Note.—It will be seen that the capacity to earth is 1·6 times the capacity measured wire to wire, or in other words a metallic circuit has ·6 of the capacity of a single wire of the same loop. Six per cent. should be taken off these values for the winter. The table assumes average distribution of trees, and twelve wires upon the poles at an average height of thirty feet above the ground. Twenty-eight per cent. should be taken off if only one circuit upon the poles.

Wires placed underground, No. 7 prepared G.P. wire, averages ·3 m.f. per mile, whilst paper cable averages about ·08 only.

Hard Drawn Copper Wire.

Weight per mile (lbs.).			Approximate Standard Wire Gauge.	Diameter (inches)			Resistance in Standard Ohms per mile at 60° F. of Standard size.	Minimum breaking stress (lbs.).
Stand.	Max.	Min.		Stand.	Max.	Min.		
100	100½	97½	14	·079	·080	·078	8·782	330
150	153¾	146¼	13	·097	·098	·0955	5·855	490
200	205	195	11½	·112	·11325	·1105	4·391	650
300	307½	292½	9½	·137	·13875	·13525	2·928	950
400	410	390	8	·158	·16025	·1555	2·195	1,250
600	615	585	6	·194	·196	·191	1·464	1,800
800	820	780	4½	·224	·226	·2205	1·098	2,400

To convert B.A ohms to standard ohms.—Multiply by ·9866.
To convert standard ohms to B.A. ohms:—Multiply by 1·0136.

APPENDIX C.

CROSS-CONNECTION STRIPS.

Signalling Side.

Tag.	A Section.	B Section.	C Section
1, 2	Local P.C. 1 ..	Local P.C. 1 ..	Local P.C. 1
3, 4	,, 2 ,.	,, 2 ..	,, 2
5, 6	———	,, 3 ..	,, 3
7, 8	———	,, 4 ..	,, 4
9, 10	———	,, 5 ..	,, 5
11, 12	Main P.C. 1 ..	Main P.C. 1 ..	Main P.C 1
13, 14	,, 2 ..	,, 2 ..	,, 2
15, 16	———	,, 3 ..	,, 3
17, 18	———	,, 4 ..	,, 4
19, 20	———	,, 5 ..	,, 5
21, 22	———	———	Transfer Circuit 1 dis.
23, 24	———	———	Transfer Circuit 2 dis.
25, 26	———	———	Transfer Circuit 3 dis.
27, 28	———	———	Transfer Circuit 4 dis.
29, 30	———	———	Transfer Circuit 5 dis.
31, 32	———	———	Transfer Circuit 6 dis.
33, 34	———	———	Transfer Circuit 7 dis.
35, 36	———	———	Transfer Circuit 8 dis.

Cross-Connection Strips.

SIGNALLING SIDE.—*continued*.

Tag	A Section.	B Section.	C Section.
37	—	—	Transfer Circuit 9 dis.
38			
39	} Service S.R.I. bat'ry	Service S.R.I. bat'ry	Transfer Circuit 10 dis.
40			
41	} S R. Indctor. bat'ry	S R. Indicator bat'ry	S.R. Indicator battery
42			
43	} ,, local	,, local	,, local
44			
45	} P.I. No 2 ,,	P.I. No 2 ,,	P.I. No. 2 local
46			
47	} Dis.	Transfer battery	Transfer battery
48			
49	P.I.R.B. 1 local +	P.I.R.B. 1 local +	P.I.R.B. 1 local +
50	,, 2 ,, ,,	,, 2 ,, ,,	,, 2 ,, ,,
51	,, 3 ,, ,,	,, 3 ,, ,,	,, 3 ,, ,,
52	,, 4 ,, ,,	,, 4 ,, ,,	,, 4 ,, ,,
53	,, 5 ,, ,,	,, 5 ,, ,,	,, 5 ,, ,,
54	P.I.R.B. locals −	P.I.R.B. locals −	P.I.R.B. locals −
55	} Trunk Ringing	Trunk Ringing	Trunk Ringing
56			
57	} Generator	Generator	Generator
58			
59	} —	—	—
60			
61	Transmitter 1 + Split	Transmitter 1 + Split	Transmitter 1 + Split
62			
63	Transmitter 2 − dis.	Transmitter 2 − dis.	Transmitter 2 − dis.
64			
65	} —	—	—
66			
67	Junction Clearing dis	Junction Clearing dis.	Junction Clearing dis.
68			
69	} —	—	—
70			
71	} —	—	—
72			

In every case where two tags are bracketed the odd number is a positive and the even number a negative lead.

Cross-Connection Strips.

SPEAKING SIDE.

Tag.	A Section.		B Section		C Section.	
73, 74	P.O. Subscriber	1	P.O. Subscriber	1	P.O. Subscriber	1
75, 76	,,	2	,,	2	,,	2
77, 78	,,	3	,,	3	,,	3
79, 80	,,	4	,,	4	,,	4
81, 82	,,	5	,,	5	,,	5
83, 84	,,	6	,,	6	Transfer Cct.	1
85, 86	,,	7	,,	7	,,	2
87, 88	,,	8	,,	8	,,	3
89, 90	,,	9	,,	9	,,	4
91, 92	,,	10	,,	10	,,	5
93, 94	———		Transfer Cct.	1	,,	6
95, 96	———		,,	2	,,	7
97, 98	Service	1	Service	1	,,	8
99, 100	,,	2	,,	2	,,	9
101, 102	,,	3	,,	3	,,	10
103, 104	———		N. T. Co. Junction	1	N. T Co Junction	1
105, 106	———		,,	2	,,	2
107, 108	———		,,	3	,,	3
109, 110	———		,,	4	,,	4
111, 112	———		,,	5	,,	5
113, 114	———		———		P.O. Ex. Junction	1
115, 116	———		———		,,	2
117, 118	———		———		,,	3

Cross-Connection Strips.

Speaking Side.—*continued*.

Tag	A Section.	B Section.	C Section.
119, 120	———	———	P.O. Ex. Junction 4
121, 122	———	———	,, 5
123, 124	Trunk 1	Trunk 1	Trunk 1
125, 126	,, ... 2	,, ... 2	,, ... 2
127, 128	———	,, ... 3	,, ... 3
129, 130	———	,, ... 4	,, ... 4
131, 132	———	,, ... 5	,, ... 5
133, 134	———	———	N T. Co. Call Wire.
135, 136	———	———	P.O. Ex. ,, ,,
137, 138	———	———	Transfer ,, ,,
139, 140	———	———	———
141, 142	———	———	———
143, 144	———	———	———

In every case the odd number is the B line and the even number the A line.

Where 20 transfers have to be provided two extra cross-connection strips, one for signalling and one for speaking circuits, are added.

Where secondary batteries are employed tags 61 and 63 should be teed together.

INDEX.

A

	PAGE
A and B lines	36
A and B transfer circuits	107
ABC Wheatstone	57
Absolute units	5
Accumulators	113, 152
Ader transmitter	25
,, receiver	18
Agglomerate, Leclanché	40
Ammeter	157
Amplitude of vibration	2
A operators	204
Armature, Siemens	45
Arms, 48-inch	135
Arresters. See lightning protectors.	
A switch section	38
Automatic clearing of junctions	94, 188
,, ,, on service circuits	100
,, ,, Stock Ex. circuits	128
,, cut-out for generator	48
,, signalling	58
,, switch	157
Auxiliary receiver	194

B

Batteries, bichromate	159
,, Leclanché	40
,, E P S. K7	152
Battery ringing telephone station	36
,, speaking	42
,, tablet	147
,, trunk ringing	90
Bell Blake station	52
Bell, Prof.	1
Bell receiver	4
,, ,, theory of	6
,, ,, ,, dimensions	8, 9
Bells, short-circuiting	35
,, magneto	44
,, trembler	34
Berliner transmitter	25
Bidwell, Shelford	15
Blake transmitter	26
B operator	204
Bourseul	1
Breastplate transmitter	86
Bridge, intermediate station	56
Bridging coils	94, 118, 128
B switch section	93

C

	PAGE
Call-office circuits	123
Call wire key	101
,, wires on supervisor's switch	192
,, wire system	185
,, ,, to local switch	105
Capacity of line wire	209
Carbon, resistance of	15
Cell voltaic	5
Central battery system	200
Charging switches	158
Chemistry of Leclanché cell	40
Chicago express system	204
Coils, bridging	94, 118, 128
Collier-Marr receiver	21
Combination key	109
Concentration of trunks at night	189
Condensation waves	2
Condenser	95, 106, 190, 200
Connections—	
Battery worked station	36
Bell Blake set	49
Call wire system	175
,, ,, night control switch	177
Central battery system	202
Counter communication switch for 1 cabinet	123
Counter communication switch for 5 cabinets	126, 127
Generators, hand and power	95
Intermediate stations on trunk lines	190
Junction clearing	94
Junctions to N. T. Co	90
Local contacts	91
Local switch (P O) junctions	105
,, ,, standard board	161
Local switch standard board operating	162
Newcastle system	180
P.O. local switch	68
,, ,, ,, operating	69
,, subscribers on trunk switch	89
,, telephone	55
,, ,, for permanent currents	61
R.C.J. circuit on trunk switch	120
,, switch section	115
Record table switch section	119

Index.

Connections—*contd*.

	PAGE
Record table tablet	102
Self-restoring board	171
,, ,, operating	172
Series, multiple	168
Service circuit	89
Superimposed circuit	141
Switch telephone connector	84
Transfer board, A circuits	113
,, ,, B ,,	111
,, circuits, B sections	98
,, ,, C ,,	103
Trunk engaged test	186
,, line permanent current signalling	72
Trunk line operating	82
Universal trunk battery tablet	158
,, ,, signalling	154
Up service circuit multipled	99
Cordeaux's insulator	135
Core of induction coil	16
Cord testing	192
Counter communication switch for 1 cabinet	124
Counter communication switch for 5 cabinets	126
Cross connections	150
Cross connection strips 72, 92, 112, 148, 159	
,, ,, ,, appropriation	210
Crossing system for prevention of induction	133
Crossley transmitter	24
C switch section	103
Current, effects of	4
,, methods of producing	5

D

Deckert transmitter	30
Detector for Newcastle system	181
,, Q and I.	193
Diaphragm	3
,, silk	87
Direct junction circuits	118
Distribution of work	205
Divided board systems	204
Double pole receiver	20
Du Moncel	9
Dust extraction	174
Dynamic induction	131
Dynamotor	96

E

Earths, effect of, on short lines	135
Eden	209
Energy, chemical and electrical	5
,, transformations of	8

	PAGE
Engaged test 168, 172, 176, 181, 186, 205	
Ericsson switch-board telephone	56
,, table set	52
,, transmitter	86
Exchange, principle of	57

F

Faults in switch sections	195
,, key-board and junctions	197
,, local circuits	198
,, trunk signalling circuit	196
Flat boards	174
Fundamental tone	207
Fuse tablet	153, 156
,, ,, arrangement	157

G

Galvanometer telephone exchange 75, 128, 185	
Generator, magneto	46, 91
,, three-contact	188
Glasgow junction arrangements	187
Gouloubitzky receiver	17
Gower-Bell station	53
Gower receiver	20
,, transmitter	25
Granular transmitters	28

H

Headgear receiver	86
Helmholtz	208
Hughes, Prof.	14
,, ,, microphone	14
Hunnings' cone transmitter	30
,, transmitter	28

I

Indicator, calling drop	161
Polarised No. 2	60
Relay polarised B	64
,, non-polarised B	140
Ring-off tubular	161
Self-restoring	76, 99, 171
Visual 96, 104, 109, 115, 119	
Induction coil, principle of	13
,, ,, for P.O. telephone	55
,, ,, examples of use 85, 102, 163, 187, 201	
Induction of electric current	12
Inductive disturbances	130
Insulators	135
Intermediate stations	56
,, ,, on trunk lines	189

J

	PAGE
Jacks. See switch-springs.	
Joint microphonic	16
Junctions—	
To N. T. Co.	70, 93
Automatic clearing of	94
Central battery system	203
Chicago express system	204
Direct circuits	118
Newcastle system	184
Operating of	90
P.O. local switch	105
Sabin's divided board system	204
Junction transfer section	122

K

Kellog system	203
Kelvin	206
Keyboard special	192
Keys, call-wire	101
Combination	109
Plug	68, 116
Ringing	79, 162, 172
Speaking	81, 162, 172
K R law	206

L

Lamps	115, 201, 204
Leclanché cell	40
Lightning protectors	144, 159
Lines of force	4
Line wire, resistance and capacity of	209
Listening keys. See speaking keys.	
Local circuit	55, 155
,, contacts	92
,, system N T. Co.	160–178
,, ,, Newcastle	184
Local system permanent current	57
,, ,, P O trunk exchange	67
Lodge O.J.	4

M

Magnetic circuit of induction coil	16
,, field	4
,, tick	1, 9
Magnetism residual	16
Magneto bell	44
,, generator	46, 91
,, worked telephone station	49
Manchester junction arrangements	185
Maxwell	4
Mechanical telephone	3
Mercadier	8
Microphone	14
Microphonic joint	16

	PAGE
Micro-telephone. See switchboard telephone.	
Mix and Genest transmitter	25
Mixed circuit working	163, 170
Mosley transmitter	29
Motor generator	95
Multiple switchboards	165
Mutual induction	77, 208

N

National Telephone Company's systems	160–178
Night arrangements for trunk lines	189
,, ,, ,, call-wire system	177
Non-polarised indicator relay	140

O

Ohm's law	11
Overhearing	130, 143
,, between contiguous indicators	77
Overhearing on operators' telephones	154
,, on record table circuits	117
Overtones	207

P

Packing difficulty	29
Pegs, circular	67
,, ,, 3-point	167
,, detector	181
,, double circular	85
,, flat old form	59
Permanent current battery—	
Counter switch	124
Trunk local	71
,, main	71
System	61
Universal working	155
Permanent current working local system	57
Permanent current working, trunk lines	70
Persistent vibration	2
Phelp's pony crown receiver	17
Phonograph, use of, in telephony	205
Pitch	2
Plug-key	116, 191
Plus circuits	138
Polarised indicator relay	64
P O. telephone	54, 159
Primary circuit	36
,, coil	12
Protectors, Lightning	144, 159

R

Rarefaction waves	2
R.C J. circuits	114

Index.

	PAGE
R.C.J. circuits, method of working	120
,, ,, terminated on switch sections	119
Receivers—	
Ader	18
Bell	17
Collier-Marr	21
Double pole	20
Gouloubitzky	17
Gower	20
Headgear form	86
Phelp's pony crown	17
Swiss administration	17
Watch	22, 86
Record table—	100
Circuits	113
,, calling at night	117
,, method of working	117
Switch section	115
Tablet	102
Reed ringers	95
Reis	1
Relay Board System	200
Relays—	55, 60, 117, 120
Non-polarised indicator B	140
N. T. Co.'s on record circuits	117
Polarised indicator B	64
Repeater See transformer.	
Residual magnetism	16
Retard coil	117
Ringing, automatic	205
,, circuit, resistance inserted	156
,, ,, trunk switch sections	80
,, keys	79, 162, 172

S

Sabin's divided board system	204
Secondary cells	113, 152
,, coil	12
Secrecy of communication	58
Self-induction	78, 145, 207
Self-restoring indicator	76, 99, 171
,, ,, differential	188
,, ,, multiple	171
Series multiple	165
Service circuits	89, 99
,, ,, failure of	188
,, ,, automatic signalling on	100
Shelford-Bidwell	15
Siemen's armature	45
Silence cabinets	123
Sine waves	207
Single wire circuits, KR of	207
,, ,, ,, N. T. Co	163, 170
,, ,, trunk circuits	191
Six-block agglomerate cell	42

	PAGE
Socket contacts	94, 114, 122, 176
Solid back transmitter	32, 86
Sound, definition of, &c.	1
Sounders, vibrating	106
Speaking battery switches	157
Speaking circuit, skeleton of	37
,, keys	81, 162, 172
,, plug	68
Speech, principle of transmission of	3
Square, preservation of	133
Static induction	130
Stock Exchange circuits	127
Sub-exchanges	122
Subscribers connected to trunk switches	89
Subscriber's switch, new form	68
Superimposed circuits	137
,, ,, conditions necessary	139
,, ,, testing of	143
Supervisor's switch section	191
Sur excitateur	18
Switch-arms	36, 38, 39
Switch-boards—	
Flat form	174
Newcastle system	179
P.O. local new form	64
,, ,, old form	59
Standard for 50 lines	160
Self-restoring multiple	171
Series multiple	165
Switchboard telephone	56, 85
,, ,, tablet	63
Switch-springs—	57
2-point	105, 191
3 ,,	175, 200
5 ,,	73, 83, 89, 90, 94, 105, 115, 126, 149, 161, 171
7 ,,	115
8 ,,	74, 89, 97, 99, 103, 111, 119, 126
Old form	59
Switch section—	
A	88
B	93
C	103
Record table	115
R C J.	121
Switch telephone connector	84, 102
Symmetrical twist system	133

T

Table telephones	52, 56
Tags connecting. See cross connection strips.	
Test boards	144, 149
Test cases	144

	PAGE
Test holes	144
Test-room appliances	144
Test tablets, 25 circuit (line)—	146
40 circuit (line)	145
Test tablets, 60 circuit (line)	149
32 circuit (battery)	147
Test wire	168, 172, 176, 181, 185, 205
Theory of Bell telephone	6
Theory of microphone	14
Through wires	144
Timbre	3, 207
Transfer board	107
Transfer circuits, B sections—	96
C sections	103
Junction section	122
Method of working	111
Necessity for	96
Number required	104
Principle of working	97
Transformers	137, 163
,, serious effects of	199
Transformer circuits	142
Translator keys	164
Transmitters—	
Ader	25
Berliner	25
Blake	26
Breastplate	33, 86
Crossley	24
Deckert	30
Edison	10
Ericsson	33
Gower	25
Granular	28
Hunnings	28
Hunnings' cone	30
Mix and Genest	25
Mosley	29

	PAGE
Transmitters—*contd.*	
Solid back	32
Worked by universal battery	153
Trembler bell	34
Triple switching	182
Trunk engaged tests	186, 187
Trunk line permanent current system principle	70
Tuning fork	2
Twisting of circuits	133

U

	PAGE
U links	141
U links wire	193
Umbrella spring	173
Up-call wires	191
Universal battery system	152
,, ,, ,, primary batteries	158
Universal permanent current working	155

V

	PAGE
Vibrating sounders	106
Visual indicators	96, 104, 109, 115, 119
Volume of sound	2

W

	PAGE
Watch receiver	22, 86
Wave, definition of	2
Wires, capacity and resistance of	209

Y

	PAGE
Y operators	204

Z

	PAGE
Zincs shallow circular	43

A MANUAL OF TELEPHONY. By Sir W. H. Preece, F.R.S., Past President of the Inst. of Electrical Engineers, late Engineer-in-Chief and Electrician at the General Post Office; and A. J. Stubbs, A.I.E.E., Technical Officer, General Post Office. With Illustrations, Appendix, Tables, and full Index. 15s.

CONTENTS.

- I. Transmitters and Receivers.
- II. Apparatus and Circuits.
- III. Simple Telephone Exchange Systems.
- IV. Multiple Switches.
- V. Miscellaneous Switching and other Systems.
- VI. Construction, Wires and Cables.

"The most complete epitome of present-day telephonic practice."
Electrical Engineer.

THE PRACTICAL TELEPHONE HANDBOOK. By J. Poole (Wh.Sc.), A.I.E.E. With 288 Illustrations. 5s.

"This essentially practical book is published at an opportune moment."
Electrician.

ELECTRICITY IN ITS APPLICATION TO TELEGRAPHY. A Practical Handbook covering the Syllabus of the new Technical Examinations. Adopted by the Post Office Telegraph Department. By T. E. Herbert, Engineer of Postal Telegraphs. With 50 Illustrations. Crown 8vo. Cloth. 3s. 6d.

WIRELESS TELEGRAPHY AND HERTZIAN WAVES. By S. R. Bottone. With 35 Illustrations. Crown 8vo. Cloth. 3s.

ELECTRIC INSTRUMENT MAKING FOR AMATEURS. By S. R. Bottone. With 96 Illustrations. 3s. 6d.

ELECTRIC BELLS. A Practical Book for Practical Men. By S. R. Bottone. With 99 Illustrations. 3s.

Catalogue of Works on Electricity, &c., post free.

WHITTAKER & CO.,
White Hart Street, Paternoster Square, London, E.C.

THE ELECTRIC TELEPHONE. By Edwin J. Houston, Ph.D., and A. E. Kennelly, D.Sc. With 143 Illustrations. Crown 8vo. Cloth. 5s.

ELECTRIC TELEGRAPHY. By Edwin J. Houston, Ph.D., and A. E. Kennelly, D.Sc. With 163 Illustrations. Crown 8vo. Cloth. 5s.

MAGNETISM AND ELECTRICITY, AN ELEMENTARY COURSE OF PRACTICAL EXERCISES IN. By J. R. Ashworth, M.Sc., F.Phys.Soc., Lecturer in Physics, Rochdale Municipal Technical School. Crown 8vo. 2s. 6d.

ELECTRICITY & MAGNETISM, FIRST BOOK OF. By W. Perren Maycock, M.I.E.E. With 107 Illustrations. 2s. 6d.

"Students who purchase a copy and carefully study it will obtain an excellent groundwork of the science."—*Electrical Review*.

PRACTICAL ELECTRICAL MEASUREMENTS. An Introductory Course for Students and Engineers. By E. H. Crapper, Lecturer in Physics and Electrical Engineering, Sheffield Technical School. With 56 Illustrations. 2s. 6d.

INDUCTION COILS. A Practical Manual for Amateur Coil-Makers. By G. E. Bonney. With 101 Illustrations. 3s.

THE MODERN SAFETY BICYCLE. By H. A. Garratt, A.M.I.C.E., Head of the Engineering Department of the Northern Polytechnic Institute, Holloway. With 104 Illustrations and five Working Drawings. Crown 8vo. Cloth. 3s.

Catalogue of Works on Electricity, Engineering, &c., post free.

WHITTAKER & CO.,
White Hart Street, Paternoster Square, London, E.C.

Iron and Steel Structures, Twelvetrees, 7s. 6d.
Ironfounding, Horner, 4s.

Jack's Cooking, 2s.
—— Laundry Work, 2s.
—— Soups, Fish, and Vegetables, 1s. each.
Jacobi's Printer's Handbook, 5s.
—— Vocabulary, 3s. 6d.
Jukes-Browne's Geology, 2s. 6d.

Kapp's Electric Transmission of Energy, 10s. 6d.
—— Transformers, 6s.
Kemp's Screw Propeller, 2s. 6d.
Kennedy's Electric Lamps, 2s. 6d.
Kingdon's Applied Magnetism, 7s. 6d.

Lamps, Electric, Maycock, 6s.
—— Arc, Smithson, 1s.
Land Measuring Tables, 2s. 6d.
—— Surveying, Middleton, 4s. 6d.
—— Surveying and Levelling, Walmisley, 7s. 6d.
Landolt's Optical Activity and Chemical Composition, 4s. 6d.
Lathes, Horner, 21s. net.
Laundry Work, Jack, 2s.
Leather Work, Leland's, 5s.
Leland's Wood-carving, 5s.
—— Metal Work, 5s.
—— Leather Work, 5s.
—— Drawing and Designing, 2s.
—— Practical Education, 6s.
Lens Work for Amateurs, Orford, 3s.
Lenses, Photographic, Taylor, 3s. 6d.
Light, Sir H. T. Wood, 2s. 6d.
Lightning Conductors, Lodge, 15s.
Lloyd's Mine Manager, 1s. 6d.
Locomotives, Cooke, 7s. 6d.
Locomotive Engineer, McDonnell, 1s.
Lodge's Lightning Conductors. 15s.
Loppé and Bouquet's Alternate Currents, 10s. 6d.
Lukin's Turning Lathes, 3s.
—— Screws, 3s.
Lunge and Hurter's Alkali Makers' Handbook, 10s. 6d.

McDonnell, How to become a Loco. Engineer, 1s.
Maginnis' Atlantic Ferry, 7s. 6d.
Magnetism, Kingdon, 7s. 6d. [6d.
—— and Electricity, Ashworth, 2s.
—— —— Bottone, 2s. 6d.

Magnetism and Electricity, Houston, 3s. 6d.
—— —— Maycock, 2s. 6d.
Manchester Ship Canal, 3s. 6d.
Manual Instruction and Training.
Manures, Griffiths, 7s. 6d.
Marine Engineers, advice to, Roberts, 2s. 6d.
—— Drawing and Designing, 6s.
—— Electric Lighting, Walker, 5s.
—— Verbal Notes, Sothern, 3s. 6d. net.
Marshall's Cakes 1s.
—— Cookery, 1s.
Martin's Structures, 4s.
Massee's The Plant World, 2s. 6d.
Mathematical Tables, 12s.
Mathematics, Elementary, Hatton, 2s. 6d.
May's Ballooning, 2s. 6d.
Maycock's Electricity and Magnetism, 2s. 6d.
—— Electric Lighting, 6s.
—— Alternating Current Circuit, 2s. 6d.
—— Electric Wiring, Fittings, Switches, and Lamps, 6s.
—— —— Details Forms, 2s. 6d. net.
—— Electric Wiring Tables, 3s. 6d.
Mechanical Tables, Foden, 1s. 6d.
Mechanical Engineer's Pocket Book, 5s.
Medical Terms, Hoblyn, 10s. 6d.
Merrill's Electric Lighting Specifications, 6s. 6d.
—— Tables for Street Railway Engineers, 5s.
Metal Turning, 4s.
—— Work, Leland, 5s.
Metric System, Wagstaff, 1s. 6d.
—— Measures, Born, 3s.
Middleton's Surveying, 4s. 6d.
Mill Work, Sutcliffe, 21s.
Millinery, Ortner, 2s. 6d.
Mine, Coal, Boyd, 7s. 6d.
Mineralogy, Hatch, 2s. 6d.
Model Engine Making, 10s. 6d.
Modern Safety Bicycle, Garratt, 3s.
Moffett's Alternate Currents, 10s. 6d.
Motor Cars, Farman, 5s.
Motors, Electro, Bottone, 3s.
—— Houston, 5s.
—— Hydraulic, Bodmer.
Municipal Electricity Supply, Gibbings, 15s.
Nadiéine, Drainage, 1s.

CPSIA information can be obtained at www.ICGtesting.com
Printed in the USA
BVOW07s1045030314

346504BV00011B/393/P